Echoes of Armageddon, 1914-1918

An American's Search Into The Lives And Deaths Of Eight British Soldiers In World War One

By

B. Cory Kilvert Jr.

First published by AuthorHouse 08/18/04

ISBN: 1-4184-5659-4 (e-book)
ISBN: 1-4184-5658-6 (Paperback)

Library of Congress Control Number: 2004092423

Printed in the United States of America
Bloomington, IN

This book is printed on acid free paper.

ACKNOWLEDGMENTS

I owe many thanks to the following friends and family members whose encouragement and generous help made all my long days of research and nights of writing more worthwhile than could otherwise have been the case: Terry Rogers Kilvert, Janice Kilvert Murray, William Dunnell III, Rod Farnham, Laura Gingras and Charles Weston Phillips.

I dedicate this book to the memory of my father, Lieutenant B. Cory Kilvert, Canadian Expeditionary Force, 1917-1919

INTRODUCTION

In my home in New Hampshire may be seen the medals of eight British officers and men who served and died in World War One. Because these medals are named to each recipient and give his rank, battalion number and regiment, they have a distinct personality unknown to coins.

Over time, this scant information exerted a growing force on me to learn whatever might still be known about where and when these soldiers were born, where they fought and where and when they died.

This effort required writing over 700 letters and spending much time in four consecutive years driving through many areas of England and Wales as well as to battlefields plus military and municipal cemeteries in France, Belgium and the U.K. Adding extra research in both Canada and the Eastern United States, my travels by car exceeded 5,000 miles. The end result represents research and writing completed over the course of twenty-one years whenever business and family commitments allowed.

Tracing the lives of totally unknown World War One British army casualties is neither easy nor is it an activity for the faint of heart. It is rife with false leads, hearsay, misinformation often given in good faith and the temptation of wanting to believe something is true which may turn out to be only fantasy. More than once during my travels, I listened to a relative of a World War One British soldier say she thought he had won a Victoria Cross when I already knew he had not.

And because a few of these soldiers' next of kin were able to provide me with only minimal information, I sometimes had to rely on whatever might be available in other places that related to their war experiences in general. These included The Imperial War Museum in London, The Commonwealth War Graves Commission, battalion war diaries, the individual regiments of each man, municipal records, old newspapers available in larger libraries and many other resources.

Additional but brief specifics on officers and the many thousands of virtually anonymous, low-ranking British soldiers of World War One may also be available at the Public Record Office in London, but only to those who can prove a family relationship to each soldier concerned. So this requires locating someone related to the man who is willing to submit a request for his personal details. Complicating this process is the fact that less than forty percent of these records survived German bombs in 1940, and most of the ones that did were damaged by water required to extinguish the flames.

The several thousand British military books in my library were also most useful. In addition, unexpected information sometimes received from equally unexpected sources occasionally proved to be of considerable value.

I was well aware at the outset that, in a social sense, there was a vast gap between British officers and their men. The great majority of the former were products of good schools and universities, and not a few were members of the nobility. But many thousands of soldiers of humble birth whom they led to war were to achieve nobility of a different sort in the muck and perils of battle. I have tried to emphasize that quality throughout this book.

Having begun my research into these soldiers' lives in the early 1980s, I was late but not too late to try discovering as much as possible about them by finding elderly friends and members of their families with memories they would share with me. With help from a London researcher along with my own efforts, I finally managed to meet relatives of all of them, including a brother who was in his early eighties when I sat with him in his home on three occasions. I also was given photographs of all but one of these soldiers.

Sometimes I was able to locate the approximate site of several soldiers' deaths by relying on copies of old trench maps that reveal with great accuracy the front lines held by the many British Army battalions at specific times during the war. Too often, however, a battalion's location in the distant past has become nothing more photogenic than a field of sugar beets or potatoes.

I soon discovered, as have others before me, that occasionally the location of old trench lines might still be identified quite easily. Soil shoveled long ago from depths of five feet or more to form these excavations is often of a chalky shade that is much lighter in color than the topsoil that flanks them. Once this is seen, the eye is quick to identify other such lines.

Furthermore, old trench lines are sometimes on private property and—even worse—on land containing unexploded World War One ammunition. Many tons of these unstable explosives are still being removed each year from fields, and farmers stack them in piles on roadsides for removal and detonation under government supervision. Sometimes, young children who play with these dangerous objects are killed by them, a tragic reminder that this war of almost ninety years ago continues to add to its list of victims.

Bodies of British and Commonwealth soldiers from World War One are sometimes still located in France and Belgium, especially by construction workers but also by an amateur Dutch group known as 'The Diggers.' In cases where identity disks are found on their remains, these casualties are buried in nearby cemeteries maintained by the Commonwealth War Graves Commission. If no identity can be established, they are memorialized with other unknown soldiers at the same sites or at other ones nearby where well-kept lawns and flowers present a peaceful atmosphere of considerable beauty.

For more than 460 miles, the Western Front trenches of World War One ran like a septic wound from the North Sea to Switzerland, sometimes shifting east or west in irregular bulges created by attacks delivered from the west by British and French troops and by similar assaults launched by Germans from the east.

For more than four terrible years, these attacks hardly ever accomplished anything beyond the death and maiming of ever more soldiers from both sides. Yards of front line trenches captured one day would often be retaken almost at once, while both British, French and German military high commands stubbornly planned new assaults that would often be even more disastrous than those launched earlier.

Too regularly, eastward advances sometimes measured in mere yards were hailed as huge successes in the heavily censored British press, but any honest senior officer knew these High Command appraisals were a cover-up. So did the fighting men in the trenches who suffered in them. Unfortunately, heads of state and high ranking generals on both sides lacked the moral courage to condemn these costly and often meaningless attacks. So hundreds of exercises in sheer madness continued for over four years in one uninterrupted Armageddon of appalling proportions.

Total casualties inflicted on the British Army in World War One vary according to which source is examined. I have relied on a web site known as *The Long, Long Trail*, which may be accessed at www.1914-1918.net.

This site indicates that, in August 1914, there were 733,514 soldiers in the United Kingdom in the Regular Army and the Reserve and that 4,970,902 additional men joined later from England, Scotland, Monmouth and Ireland for a sum total of 5,704,416. Of these, 532,617 were killed in action or died of wounds on the Western Front and another 32,098 died of injuries or diseases.

I must state here that I am not a military historian. I am a freelance industrial public relations writer whose main avocational interest for more than forty years has been the history of the British Army, mainly in the 1914-1918 period.

I have lectured on the British Army at The United States Military Academy at West Point, New York, the Royal Canadian Military College in Kingston, Ontario, the Royal Canadian Military Institute in Toronto and also at numerous schools and societies in both the U.S. and Canada.

My family link to the British Army is through a Canadian cousin, the late Lieutenant-General Sir George Norton Cory, KCB, KBE, DSO. Having graduated from the Royal Military College of Canada in 1895, he joined the 2nd Battalion, the Royal Dublin Fusiliers, and served on the Northwest Frontier of India. He fought in the Boer War (1899-1902), was a member of the General Staff in France in World War One and also saw service at Salonika as well as in Iraq and India. He was knighted by King George V in 1926.

Having been recalled from retirement in World War Two, he was charged with overall responsibility for the training of Dutch, Czech, Norwegian and Polish troops who had escaped to Great Britain following the occupation of their countries by the Nazis. This fine old soldier lived to the age of almost ninety-four.

In researching the experiences of eight British Army fighting men who died during the grotesque catastrophe of World War One, I am indebted to numerous men and women whose generous help enabled me to recreate episodes in these soldiers' lives before as well as during the war. These generous people are mentioned throughout my text, but two of them deserve special recognition.

As my researcher in London, Mrs. Patricia Wolfston spent many hours tirelessly locating and photocopying innumerable documents, telephoning and writing to dozens of men and woman and traveling to several places in England to interview people on my behalf. At the start, I had no idea that Pat, like me, was an American.

In Warrington, Roy Thorniley provided me with many hours of his time spent finding several obscure sources of information relating to Acting Corporal Kirkham, which I would have had next to no chance of locating on my own. His advice was always sound, while his enthusiasm and encouragement were constant.

I have made no attempt to provide anything approaching a comprehensive outlook on World War One in Western Europe and in other parts of the world. Instead, I have limited myself to brief explanations of military, naval and political strategy and tactics in the context of how they affected many people both prominent and otherwise whose names are mentioned in my text. Wherever appropriate, I have also provided brief accounts of the war experiences of several Canadian relatives of mine who served in France and Flanders. These include the younger brother of General Cory, three members of a Winnipeg family and an officer from Hamilton.

I must note here that, to avoid misinforming the reader, I have relied on *The Times Diary & Index of the War 1914-1918* to provide me with correct dates for events mentioned in this book. I also must stress that I have made every effort to honor these eight British war casualties who were forced to fight under appalling conditions that ultimately offered them no chance for survival. Their steadfast endurance, pride in their regiments and great courage speak volumes for what have been hallmarks of the British soldier for centuries. But this is not only a military history of these few war casualties. It is also a social commentary on those who loved and lost them in a world that would never be the same again.

TABLE OF CONTENTS

CHAPTER 1

1891-1914

Private Arthur Small

1st Battalion, The Duke of Cornwall's Light Infantry

Mary Francis Boswill was born in Cornwall in 1873 but spent much of her youth in Europe with her parents. At the age of seventeen, she incurred their wrath when she met and began to travel in France with an itinerant cutler, a Channel Islander of Gypsy stock named Robert Small.

When it became known she was carrying Robert's child, the couple left for St. Helier on the island of Jersey where they were married in St. Andrew's Church on September 15th, 1891. They lived at 8 Pier Road. When the baby was born on December 12th, he had his father's dark complexion and brown eyes. Named after an uncle, he was also given the name Nehemiah, which came from his mother's family.

Almost ninety-one years after this event and knowing nothing of it at the time, I stood with my wife in Victoria Park in Redruth. Before us was a granite memorial inscribed with the names of men from the town and its vicinity who had given their lives in the Great War while serving with the Duke of Cornwall's Light Infantry.

1

I had recently acquired the medals of 10044 Private Arthur Small, whom I knew had been killed in action with the 1st Battalion of this regiment. Because the Commonwealth War Graves Commission had told me this soldier had enlisted in nearby Scorrier, I assumed the memorial would carry his name, but it did not. There was, however, an R. A. Small. A brother, perhaps, it seemed to me at the time, but it would be another year before I was to learn otherwise from an elderly man in Surrey whose memory was beyond dispute.

After returning home, I sent letters to three newspapers in Cornwall, seeking information on Arthur Small's family. It seemed possible that some of his relations would still be living there, and this proved to be so. In Redruth, a man named George Trethowan read one of my letters and sent it to his first cousin, who subsequently wrote to me from his home in Dorking, Surrey.

'I am the brother of the person you seek information about,' his letter began. It ended with an invitation to visit him on our next trip to England. The letter was signed 'S. Small.'

An active, alert and intelligent man of eighty-three when we met in 1983, Sam Small continued to respond to my requests for help as late as December 1986 without a trace of doubts and confusions that often afflict men and women ten or more years younger. When his oldest brother Arthur was killed, he was not yet fourteen years old.

He told me his parents left Jersey at some point prior to early June 1893 and that their second son, Jack, was born at that time in Redruth where five more sons and three daughters would also be brought into the world over the following twenty years. In their home, they spoke mostly French, but Arthur was their only fully bilingual child and, in Sam Small's opinion, their most intelligent one, as well.

Continuing their inbred Gypsy habit of frequently moving about, the Smalls settled next in St. Austell where Arthur received his education. There he spent hours reading the histories of great armies and of generals who had led them into battle. The close proximity of his county's own regiment added encouragement to his dreams of soldiering. Its story had an irresistible appeal to him, and its full-dress uniform was something he was determined to wear one day.

Originally raised[1] as Fox's Marines in 1702, it would be renamed thirteen years later as the 32nd Regiment of Foot. Present at Dettingen in 1743 and at Fontenoy two years later, it had fought for six years in Spain—at Vimiera, Salamanca and in other savage battles during the Peninsula War in the early 1800's. In 1809, the 32nd took part in the brutal 150-mile winter retreat to Corunna under the leadership of Sir John Moore, the recognized father of British light infantry. At Waterloo in 1815, the Cornwalls lost 685 men killed and wounded, the highest casualty rate of any British regiment on the field. But perhaps its most heroic tale was written in 1857 in the Indian Mutiny during the epic defense of the Residency at Lucknow against hordes of native Indian Army mutineers.

There the 32nd fought and died for eighty-seven dangerous days before reinforcements arrived and then held fast for another fifty-three days until the garrison, which included soldiers' wives and children, was finally relieved. At Lucknow, the regiment earned four Victoria Crosses.

In more recent times, it had formed part of the abortive Gordon Relief Expedition on the Nile in 1884 and 1885. Dispatched to the North West Frontier of India in 1897, the 1st Battalion soldiered in the tough Tirah campaign against the warlike Afridi hillmen and later along the Punjab Frontier. These and other

---

[1] British Army regiments were never 'begun,' or 'started' or 'organized.' The proper term was 'raised,' and this word will be seen again in this book.

accounts would all have fired young Arthur Small's imagination, but his family was not keen on his desire to be a soldier.

So, as an alternative, he took a job at the East Pool Mine between Redruth and Camborne. For centuries, the tin mines of Cornwall had been a source of employment for thousands of local men and boys. Dating back to the Bronze Age when explorers from the Mediterranean found this soft and lustrous metal in the rolling granite hills, the 'wheals' once numbered up to 600 during their peak production days, but now they have disappeared entirely.

The life of a 'tinner' soon proved to have no appeal for Arthur. So without telling his family, he enlisted in the Duke of Cornwall's Light Infantry (DCLI) on October 18th, 1912. At the age of almost twenty-one he would have been the pride of any recruiting sergeant. He had supplemented his schooling with self-education, and he was healthy and tall—five feet, eleven inches tall, to be exact.

In the same year, his brother Jack ran off to join the Royal Navy at the age of nineteen and served on several ships, including H.M.S. *Dreadnought*, a massive 15,000-ton battleship with ten 12-inch guns and new steam turbine engines that could drive it through the water at twenty-one knots. Christened in February 1906 by King Edward VII, it led immediately to a feverish arms race between Great Britain and Germany. More will be learned later about Jack Small's naval career.

Regimental documents show that Arthur was in G Company during his training at the depot in Bodmin. Having qualified in the rigors of 'square bashing.[2] and other strenuous military exercises, he was posted to the 1st Battalion on January 25th, 1913, and served with it in Ireland until the summer of the following year.

In August 1913, he came home on leave, and Sam Small recalled a conversation his brother had with their mother on that occasion. He spoke about how a fervent

---

[2] Drill with rifles on a square parade ground accustomed to the bashing of heavy leather boots.

militancy growing in Germany was causing grave concern in the British Army. "We're preparing for war," he said to her. Almost exactly one year later, Arthur was home once more, but after about one week his leave was canceled by a telegram ordering him to report back at once to his battalion in Ireland.

Few people in Cornwall would have concerned themselves with Sarajevo in Bosnia and fewer still would have believed that a pistol fired in its streets on June 28th, 1914, would be the first two shots in a conflict which was to bring sorrow and suffering into hundreds of thousands of British homes.[3]

While Arthur was on leave, his battalion had been on detached duty in Newry and Dundalk, guarding against an outbreak of disturbances stemming from the Ulster Crisis in March.[4] The Cornwalls' role was much the same as that played in more recent times by the British Army in that troubled land of timeless religious frictions. Having returned to the Curragh, the battalion received a telegram announcing a state of war with Germany as of August 4th, 1914.[5]

Ships carrying the British Expeditionary Force (BEF) to France represented the implementation of a master plan devised as early as 1906 when Lord Haldane, then Secretary of State for War, initiated and began to refine the complex procedures for mobilization which could put 150,000 British soldiers and 67,000 horses onto French soil within fifteen days and concentrate them at Maubeuge, about ten miles south of Mons in Belgium. But few who were destined to implement this plan could have anticipated the high level of efficiency with which it was carried out.

---

[3] These two shots killed Archduke Ferdinand of Austria-Hungary and his morganatic wife. This led directly to the Kaiser's promise to support Austria-Hungary against Serbia. Therein lay the seeds of World War One.

[4] In 1912, the British Government had started discussions on granting home rule to Ireland. A storm of dissent erupted, and Brigadier Hubert Gough plus fifty-seven officers in the 3rd Cavalry Brigade threatened to resign their commissions. This disturbance required several infantry battalions to help control trouble between Catholics and Protestants. Although Home Rule was passed in 1914, the outbreak of war and much civil unrest in Ireland prevented its implementation until the signing of the Anglo-Irish Treaty in 1921.

[5] King George V would soon change his German family name from Saxe-Coburg-Gotha to Windsor.

In the case of Arthur's battalion, it was brought up to war strength within only two days by the arrival of 650 Reservists from civilian life as far off as London. All had been fully equipped at Bodmin and would soon be rushed forward to Ireland.

On August 13th, s.s. *Lanfranc* stood lashed to her quay at Dublin Docks as the Cornwalls filed up the gangway and found what space they could on her crowded deck. Most of the 2nd Battalion, Suffolk Regiment, with whom they were joined in the 14th Brigade, 5th Division, also came on board, adding to the crush and confusion.

Each man carried a 1903 Pattern Short Magazine Lee-Enfield No.1 Mark III rifle with 150 rounds of .303-inch ammunition in a ten-round magazine. This weapon provided a flat trajectory for up to 600 yards, and its bullets were powerful enough to penetrate a 13-inch-thick brick wall. Every soldier was also burdened with a twenty-two-inch bayonet, entrenching tool, shoulder pack and other necessary items, all of which added sixty-one pounds to his own weight. In battle, however, he would carry only his rifle, bayonet, ammunition, water bottle and his pack for holding rations and personal items.

By 5:30 p.m., the vessel's lines were cast off. Slowly, she steamed into St. George's Channel as the cheers of well-wishers gradually faded away. The men began to sing quietly, their voices blending in a pleasant harmony as the ship set course down the western shores of England. The first few battalions in Britain's Regular Army of about 244,000 men were on their way to war. By year's end, about one million volunteers had joined up.

Arthur, however, was not with his enthusiastic chums who watched as the Cornish coast receded into a hazy outline. Although there would have been ample time for him to report to Bodmin, make good his kit deficiencies there and proceed to Ireland with the Reservists, Ministry of Defence records show he did not arrive in France until five days after the steamer carrying his battalion had reached Le Havre in a driving rain.

Why this was so remains a mystery, but this was not a time for soldiers to write a few explanatory lines to family members back home. Arthur would have been just as busy as any other member of his battalion while getting ready to go to war.

August 14th also saw fifty-six flimsy aircraft of the fledgling Royal Flying Corps take off from Dover, cross the Channel to Amiens and proceed to Maubeuge in order to fly reconnaissance missions which would help the BEF determine German intentions during their advance into France and Belgium. On the afternoon of that same day, Land's End became clearly visible to the Cornwalls from their ship, and spirits were high. As everyone knew, the war would not last past Christmas. After a few short battles, 'Kaiser Bill's' army would be whipped back to Germany. Then there would be medals for all, and things would return to normal. So here was an opportunity too good to miss! But what these men could not know was that on that same day, the Germans had completed their concentration on the Western Front with twenty-two corps. Twelve more were in reserve along with ten cavalry divisions for an estimated total of 1,600,000 men.

In command of the BEF was a man singularly unsuited to his forthcoming responsibilities. Irascible, insecure, vindictive and sometimes indecisive under pressure, General Sir John French was also quick to take offense. In his first meeting with General Charles Lanrezac, the senior French Army officer in the field, each developed an immediate antipathy toward the other which would not be resolved. Sir John especially disliked the Frenchman because he was neither a cavalryman nor a gentleman. Neither could speak the other's language, although there were enough obvious outward signs that they could never get along well. But Sir John need not have worried about many more meetings because Lanrezac was relieved of his command on September 3rd for being every bit as useless as Sir John would soon prove to be.

French had located his BEF command headquarters thirty-five miles away from where his army stood, and the lack of a single telephone made communicating with him far more difficult than should have been so. Soon after, he would be twice that distance from where the fighting took place, and he would also be facing major personal problems with officers within his own army. These included his I Corps commander, the wealthy and aristocratic Lieutenant-General Sir Douglas Haig, who had been his brigade major in the Boer War. The two men had been friendly then, but when Sir John—never able to manage his money—borrowed a considerable sum from Haig and neglected to repay it, the latter eventually recognized him for what he was and also developed increasing doubts about his superior's ability to command the BEF. Above all, Sir Douglas wanted French's job and would get it in time because he had influence in the right places.

French also held a grudge against Lieutenant-General Sir Horace Smith-Dorrien, his commander of II Corps. This dated from the time when the latter replaced him at Aldershot and expressed dissatisfaction with the cavalry's poor performance on the rifle range. But French also loathed him for being far superior to him in a social sense and in every aspect of soldiering except rank.[6]

Haig had his own animosities, especially in the case of Major-General Sir Henry Wilson, who for some years had cultivated a cordial relationship with Lanrezac and could speak his language. Wilson had expected to be Sir John's chief of staff, but the job had gone to General Sir Archibald Murray, who proved to be ill-suited in that role because of a sensitive nature and a nervous disposition not generally expected in a senior British officer.

[6] Both Smith-Dorrien and Haig were on friendly terms with the King, and Haig's wife was one of Queen Mary's ladies-in-waiting.

Wilson would make frequent visits to BEF headquarters where he did everything possible to undermine Sir Archibald's authority and ability to do his job. The latter suffered a nervous breakdown soon after the fighting started, but Wilson would not succeed him. The job went instead to Sir William Robertson, a clear-thinking and hard-working general who had risen from the ranks and, remarkably, would retire as a field-marshal.

Each of these personal dislikes in the BEF was hardly conducive to cohesion prior to Britain's first encounter with its German foe. Fortunately, the men in the ranks and their regimental officers were acting on far more sensible lines.

As infantry battalions and gun batteries of II Army Corps deployed along the south bank of the Mons-Condé Canal, their line looked much like a man stretched out on his back with his heels to the west near Condé and his head resting more than twenty miles east below Nimy and Obourg. Along the 'chin' were the 2nd Royal Irish, while the 4th Royal Fusiliers and 4th Middlesex were positioned at the 'nose.' Below the 2nd Royal Irish, a 'pigtail' running southeast on a refused right flank touched General Haig's I Corps line consisting of the 1st and 4th Guards Brigades, which connected with the left flank of the French *Fifth Army*.

To continue the analogy of the supine man, the 1st Cornwalls were situated at his mid-calf on August 22nd. To their east stood the 1st Royal West Kents and then the 1st Northumberland Fusiliers, whose right flank touched Mons. To the Cornwalls' left the 13th and 14th Infantry Brigades were due east of Condé but would be replaced by the 19th Infantry Brigade on the afternoon of the battle. A strong French force was supposed to protect the British left flank, but it failed to appear, creating a dangerous gap for von Kluck to exploit.

Soon after dawn on the 22nd, Major-General Sir Edmund Allenby's cavalry division began to make contact with enemy movements. In the village of Casteau, slightly northeast of Mons, Drummer Fred Thomas of C Squadron, 4th Royal Irish

Dragoon Guards, fired at a German cavalry officer, becoming the first member of the BEF to score a kill.[7]

From the Cornwall's position, three platoons from B Company had established an outpost slightly north of the canal and were facing Le Petit Crepin. The rest of the battalion stood ready to assist as needed and wondered like everyone else what might soon begin to happen. All present along the canal on that day were totally unaware that in front of them were 320,000 men of von Kluck's *German First Army*, who were equally ignorant of what lay ahead of them.

Well hidden in a deeply entrenched semicircle, the Cornwalls' small outpost north of the canal had an unobstructed view to their front. A single water-cooled Vickers machine gun pointed menacingly up the road to Ville Pommeroeul. Those who manned this weapon could only hope it would function properly because, at any moment, it was prone to cause one of more than nine different jammings.

A sentry post was thrown forward for an additional 200 yards and manned by three privates from 2nd Lieutenant F. C. B. Savile's Number 6 Platoon from B Company. This position was also artfully concealed, and the Cornwalls lay silently in the soil of Belgium, waiting. During the night, it rained.

August 23rd was a Sunday. At 6:00 a.m., a ground mist rose like a curtain to reveal a sunny day. Then, like actors coming onto a stage, a patrol of German dragoons jingled toward the three-man post, heedless of the tense faces eyeing them down the barrels of their rifles. Too late, an officer saw them and clawed at his holster.

Private Alfred Charles Sambrook squeezed the trigger of his rifle to become the first member of his battalion in the war to kill a German.[8] The bullet smacked

---

[7] Thomas served throughout the war and retired from the army in 1923.
[8] Sambrook, a Londoner, had enlisted at Limehouse in 1911. He was killed in action on the River Aisne a mere seventeen days after the Battle of Mons.

into the body of the dragoon officer, who fell forward in his saddle, mortally wounded, as one of his men reached for his reins to lead him off the field. By the time the other two British sentries loosed off a round, the horsemen were retiring. Prudently, the Cornwalls filtered back to the bridgehead. Unknown to them at the time, they had just made contact with von Kluck's *First Army* consisting of six divisions.

Returning within half an hour, the enemy this time rode within 100 yards of Lieutenant Savile's position, which then erupted in a storm of fire, causing several more casualties. By 7:00 a.m., an Uhlan patrol clattered south from Ville Pommeroeul and straight for the Cornwalls' well-concealed machine gun. To everyone's dismay, an overexcited rifleman let loose a round too soon at 700 yards. Had he awaited the order to fire, the results would have been deadly. As it was, only a single horse was killed and its rider captured.

As pressure mounted from the massive German right flank march, Royal Engineers prepared to blow the bridge at Le Petit Crepin, and one of the two Cornwalls' machine guns was withdrawn to safety south of the canal. Its place was taken by ten men behind a wall of pavé blocks removed from the road and built across it. Shortly before 5:00 p.m., a third German advance could be seen moving south from Ville Pommeroeul in tightly packed columns.

Factories and slag heaps from the many local mines around Mons hampered British visibility on both sides of the roadblock, and the only troops at Le Petit Crepin with a clear field of fire were the ten men posted behind their makeshift barrier. Phlegmatically and with full confidence in themselves and their training, they awaited developments. During the earlier lull, their young officer had determined the exact range of a railway crossing 750 yards to his front. With combined sights set at that distance and also 800 yards, his men were ordered to hold their fire until the Germans reached the crossing.

Here as elsewhere along the canal on that day, the time devoted earlier to 'mad minutes' on the ranges of Bisley and Hythe paid off in a rapid fire of deadly accuracy. Armed with the best rifle any combatant nation would carry in the war, many British soldiers of the old Regular Army could 'snap shoot' up to fifteen accurate rounds per minute with a weapon that required each spent cartridge to be ejected and a live round to be chambered before it could be fired again. This proved to be more than sufficiently fast for Savile's men to claim dozens of Germans at the crossing. The survivors spread out and went to ground as their advance melted into a maelstrom of death and confusion. A few German skirmishers fired ineffectively at extreme ranges but continued to lie low. By this time, the enemy was convinced that the storm of fire they had been facing could only have been administered by machine guns.

While German artillery shells searched for the bridge, the Cornwalls' spearhead retired across it and also over two barges, which their adjutant, Lieutenant A. N. Acland, had lashed together and then cut apart after the last man had reached relative safety on the south bank.[9]

Unknown to all present at that time, this retirement was the opening move of the BEF's epic retreat from Mons. The Cornwalls could not understand the initial order to fall back because they had held their own against considerable odds, and it wasn't until after dark that they learned they had taken part in a major battle along the entire canal.

August 23rd had also seen two members of the 4th Royal Fusiliers, Lieutenant Maurice Dease and Fusilier Sydney Godley, win the first Victoria Crosses of the war for defending a railway bridge with a machine gun for several hours to prevent

---

[9] Acland would win a Military Cross and Distinguished Service Order during the war and reach the rank of lieutenant-colonel.

a huge German force from crossing it. Dease was hit five times and killed, but Godley, though severely wounded, survived the war as a German prisoner.

All British forces along the canal had done especially well, but the unannounced retirement of the French *Fifth Army* had left the BEF's right flank in the air, making a retreat essential in order to avoid being outflanked and encircled by an estimated 160,000 Germans. So far, the Cornwalls had not sustained a single casualty, but before dawn on the 24th, five of their number were wounded, and Private William Thomas Gow was killed, the battalion's first fatality of the war.[10]

For the officers and men of this battalion, the thirteen-day retreat was much the same as it was for all others who took part in it. Long marches in hot sun, dust and rain, raging thirst and aching fatigue were interspersed with moments of terror and rapid firing during rear guard delaying actions.

The BEF withdrew to the southwest and away from its Channel bases, reinforcements and supplies. Its very survival was increasingly threatened by every backward step it took. Before dawn on the 26th, Smith-Dorrien, concerned about the huge force that was pressing him, took it upon himself to disobey John French's command to continue the retreat. He reasoned that fighting where he stood was the only way to prevent the BEF from being surrounded by von Kluck, but he risked his career with this courageous decision in order to make his stand outside Le Cateau.

Both French and Sir Henry Wilson approved of this decision, although the former asked Smith-Dorrien to continue the retreat as soon as possible. But in his memoirs published in 1919, he categorically denied he had done so.

---

[10] There were two Gows in the DCLI at this time. Because both were born in Shoreditch, London, and enlisted at Hackney, they probably were brothers. Private George John Gow would be killed in action on August 27th, 1914.

Among the other battalions on the field that day that were facing enormous odds, the 1st Cornwalls shot their foe to a standstill while the Royal Artillery's 228 guns gave far more than they received from almost 500 German artillery pieces. Discouraged by this unexpected repulse, the Germans rested on the field until 2:00 p.m. when the battle began again.

With the need to continue the retreat of paramount importance, the BEF managed to disengage and by 7:00 p.m. its forces were gone. Thus did Smith-Dorrien save the entire II Corps from almost certain disaster, but at the cost of many casualties, including almost 100 Cornwalls killed, wounded and listed as missing.

In the extremes of exhaustion, the men would have been in no mood for a history lesson, but they were then close to Crécy where 568 years earlier to the day, a woefully outnumbered force of Welsh longbowmen and spearmen had demonstrated their stubbornness under stress. There, led by King Edward III, they had stood fast against several French cavalry charges while archers fired twelve well-aimed arrows per minute to decimate their foe.

Arriving on August 27th at BEF headquarters in St. Quentin, Smith-Dorrien reported his decision to fight to his chief who flew into a rage and accused him of disobedience. Always one to hold grudges, this scheming military incompetent would hound his subordinate from his command with a stream of vicious lies, leaving Sir Horace no choice but to offer his resignation. This he did in a letter to Sir John on May 6th, 1915. Two days later, it was accepted in a curt letter of only sixty-one words. To add further insult, French refused to see Sir Horace, who was forced to return to England, never again to hold a command. But before long, Haig, Sir Henry Rawlinson and other senior officers would arrange for Sir John to make the same trip.

The retreat continued as the troops dragged themselves along in a daze. In a letter to his mother, Lieutenant Acland of the Cornwalls explained, 'For many miles [Lieutenant A. J. S.] Hammans and I marched arm-in arm to keep us from rolling too much like drunken men. We had no notion where we were going or what was behind us.'

On the night of August 29th, the battalion slept beside the road outside Bailly. By now the BEF stocks of rifle ammunition had fallen so low that, earlier that day, all ships of the Royal Navy's Grand Fleet had begun unloading half of their own supply to help ease the army's shortage. On the next morning, smoke and flames from farms and crops burned by pursuing German cavalry patrols were visible in the distance. These vindictive horsemen were never far behind their prey.

The Cornwalls still moved south through Peirrefond and past Morienval. Reaching Lagny-le-Sec, they were only twelve miles east of Paris but were then sent on September 5th to Tournan where they bivouacked at 8:00 a.m. Expecting a long rest at last, they received equally good news at midnight. The long retreat was over. They were to advance the following morning.

The massive German enveloping movement by men equally exhausted in their long pursuit had never managed to get behind the French and the BEF. The enemy had, in fact, swung east prematurely in front of Compiègne instead of striving to get behind Paris. Now, unwittingly, on the critical day of September 9th, the German *First, Second, Third* and *Fourth Armies* were facing the full might on a west-to-east line of the French *Sixth Army*, the BEF and the French *Fifth, Ninth,* and *Fourth Armies*. Unbelievably, the Schlieffen Plan, finalized in 1905 for the destruction of France, lay in shreds along the River Marne during this decisive five-day battle that ended on the 10th.

The hammer blow that followed is rightly considered one of the six most decisive battles of all time. With German forces reeling from defeat at the Marne, the final days of open warfare were acted out in the Allied advance to the River Aisne where both sides went into trenches and stayed in them for another four years. For Arthur Small, however, the journey was to end almost at the start of this advance.

Having crossed the Marne less than two miles northeast of la Ferté-sous-Jouarre on the 9th, the 1st Cornwalls encountered heavily wooded country broken by abrupt valleys and hills covered with vineyards. Known as the Pisseloup Ridge, this landscape with small, deep valleys was probably little changed from its appearance in 1914 when I saw it in 1982, and trees separated small pastures on which cows grazed contentedly.

Sixty-eight years earlier, this rugged terrain was a defender's dream, and with typical Teutonic thoroughness, it had been skillfully prepared with concealed machine guns and batteries of artillery. Having reached the top of a hill running north, the Cornwalls were within sight of Montreuil-aux-Lions. Vast stands of trees had hindered their communications, and B and C Companies were about to walk into a German ambush.

Short of some desultory firing, the trap was not sprung until after A Company, in support of C, had moved into view in two columns separated by a narrow wood. At that point, a devastating fire a mere seventy-five yards ahead and slightly to the right flailed A Company. To this was added heavy fire from the left flank aimed at the other two companies. High explosive shells dropping mostly on B Company caused mounting losses and forced the battalion to withdraw to less exposed positions.

Although 3rd Division gunners knocked out the German batteries causing these casualties and killed eighty enemy artillerymen, heavy German small arms fire continued from the left from which an abortive German attack was launched at 2:30 p.m. By nightfall of the 9th, A Company had pulled back to establish a defensive line covering the road connecting Caumont to the west with Bézu-le-Guéry to the east. The remainder of the battalion converged on that point.

One of those present on that day was Private Robert Rowe of the Cornwalls, a particular friend of Arthur's and a native of Redruth. According to Sam Small, Rowe had searched for Arthur and found him lying in the grass on the battlefield. High explosive shells, wreaking havoc on the landscape, had created many ugly craters in the rocky soil. Rowe found Arthur lying down on the grass. He was dead, killed by shell splinters.

This, of course, ends the story of Arthur Small. But there is a postscript worth recording which highlights the history of a single English family in the years of conflict which still lay ahead.

In 1986, I managed to contact Rowe's seventy-year-old son, Robert Leslie Rowe, through a newspaper serving Redruth. He told me in a letter that he remembered his father 'mentioning his friend Small and how he came across him shot up.'

Sam Small was fourteen when Private Rowe appeared in Cornwall after the events on the heights above the Aisne. He was the first soldier to return to Redruth from France, having been seriously injured in the back in a bad fall on the same day that Arthur was killed.[11]

Calling on the Smalls, he was invited into their home. Assuming they already knew of their son's death, he told them how sorry he was about what had happened.

---

[11] Rowe had enlisted in the DCLI ten months before Arthur did so. Discharged as medically unfit in February 1915, he managed to join the Forage Department of the Army Service Corps but was again invalided out in September 1916. A true warrior, he served with the Home Guard during World War Two in which he and others underwent training exercises, including some in which men were dressed in captured German uniforms. Thoroughly engrossed in his role as a defender of British soil, Rowe was sometimes rough with the 'enemy,' many of whom he knew well. He died in July 1975 at the age of eighty-five.

"Well, what do you mean?" asked Arthur's mother in considerable alarm.

"Haven't you heard?" replied Rowe.

No. They had not heard. Rowe, obviously distressed at having been the first to convey the dreadful news in such an abrupt fashion, gave Arthur's parents their son's buttons and badges.

" I cut them off his tunic when I passed him on the battlefield," he said.

After he had left, Arthur's mother wrote to the War Office, and it would be another terrible two weeks before the official notice arrived, confirming what Rowe had told her family.

Soon after the painful meeting with Rowe, Arthur's father made a terse announcement to his wife. "Now it's my turn," he declared. And on October 30th at the age of forty-five, he joined the 2/4th DCLI, a Territorial Force battalion, which had been raised in Truro in September. He had been in the wheals for a while, not as a professional tinner but because wartime demands for china repairs and his other manual talents had noticeably diminished.

Having learned the rudiments of soldiering on Salisbury Plain, the members of his battalion sailed from Southampton for India on December 12th. There they stayed for the duration of the war, but Arthur's father remained in England for reasons no longer known. In the same month, his daughter Cecilia died of dropsy (now called edema) at the age of only eight.

Near the close of 1914, an uneasy feeling had settled over Britain. The great adventure begun in August would not be over by Christmas, and long casualty lists had begun to dominate bulletin boards in every city and town. Strident calls continued to be made for more volunteers to fill the ranks of those slaughtered in October and November in the mud and misery of First Ypres where over 54,000 British soldiers had fallen in just three weeks.

By the end of December, more than 86,000 British officers and men had been killed or wounded, a statistic that would have caused their loved ones to wonder why they had seen them off to war in such a jolly manner.

'Good bye-ee, don't cry-ee, wipe the tear, baby dear, from your eye-ee,' ran the words to a silly popular song. 'Nam-poo, toodle-oo, good bye-ee,' is how it ended, and this would echo down through the years as the last goodbye of so many wives and parents throughout the land who would never see their loved ones again.

Although more than 1,860,000 British men had joined up by year's end, their enthusiasm for being trained to 'have a go' at the enemy was hampered by a serious shortage of uniforms, arms and munitions.

By 1916, the war was costing Great Britain £250,000 per *hour*! [12] Casualties in January of that year amounted to over 700 per day. It was now becoming painfully evident that the system of voluntary enrollment since the birth of British arms would no longer remain sufficient to replace the appalling losses already sustained on the Western Front, at Gallipoli and in Mesopotamia and the Dardanelles.

Championed since the autumn of 1915 by Lloyd George, created minister of Munitions in the wake of the artillery shell shortage made public that spring, the controversial Military Service Bill was passed overwhelmingly in the House of Commons on January 24th, 1916. Exemptions were granted to Quakers and others who could satisfy local panels of examiners that their moral aversion to war justified their objection to serving as combatants. Widely vilified by the press as 'pasty faces' and anarchists, 16,000 Britons became the world's first conscientious objectors, about 1,300 of whom were imprisoned.

Among those called up for war service was Arthur Small's twenty-one-year-old brother Robert. Employed at the time by the West of England Bacon factory,

---

[12] This figure is extrapolated from James Cameron's book *1916—Year of Decision.*

19

he appealed on the grounds of being a pacifist but was turned down by the tribunal hearing his plea.

Could this have been the R. A. Small whose name I had seen on the war memorial in Redruth? It seemed unlikely, but I put the question to Sam Small during one of my visits to his flat in Dorking.

'Oh, no," he answered. "It's just that Arthur didn't like the name Nehemiah. So on his own account he called himself Robert Arthur." And Redruth had remembered him as such.

During 1916, Arthur's father transferred to the Royal Defence Corps and was sent to a camp in Devonshire. His family followed him and settled for about two years in Plymouth where they sold new and used furniture from a shop at 41 Travel Street. Their son Jack was at sea with Jellicoe's Grand Fleet and fought that summer at Jutland.

Young Robert Small soon rethought his pacifist position and traveled from Cornwall to enlist in the Devonshire Regiment. Gassed in France in 1916, he was hospitalized and then granted leave in England.

"He was determined not to go back to the army," Sam Small declared. "So he deserted, and for a while there was a game of hide and seek between him and the Military Police. The next we heard of him, he had joined the Royal Irish Regiment under the name of O'Brian," he recalled. "This made my father very bitter against him."

Steadily incapacitated by exposure to poison gas and capable of only light, part-time agricultural work, he deteriorated steadily and finally died in 1921, a victim not only of war but of those who had flung so many of England's sons into it. His mother had died several months earlier at the age of only forty-eight.

Her husband was discharged in Kent, and his army character certificate described him as 'steady and well conducted.' He had been in uniform for over three years, and at the age of forty-nine his black hair was beginning to turn gray. He was eighty-two when he died in 1951 and was buried beside his wife in Brenchley, Kent. Their unmarked grave sites have long since vanished beneath the turf.

Jack Small, on board two ships which were torpedoed and sunk, survived the war unscathed and served on in the navy. He retired in 1934. Or so he thought. When war with Germany resumed in 1939, he reenlisted and returned to sea on one of the three cruisers that fought in the Battle of the River Plate in December. Outranged but undaunted, these ships attacked the German 'pocket battleship' *Graf Spee* off the coast of Uruguay and trapped her inside Montevideo harbor where she was scuttled by her captain who then committed suicide.[13]

Upon his return to England, Jack Small was told he was too old for further active service. So at forty-six, he lasted out the war at a training depot and lived until 1965.

And Arthur? What more is left of him?

At la Ferté-sous-Jouarre there has stood since 1928 the white marble British Memorial to the Missing who died at the battles of Mons, Le Cateau, the Marne and the Aisne. Impressive in its dignity, its panels—arranged by regiments and corps—are engraved with the names of 3,888 British soldiers whose bodies were never recovered after the Great War.

On an August afternoon in 1982, I located the panel for the Duke of Cornwall's Light Infantry and touched the name I had come so far to see.

Small, A.

Briefly, a little girl disturbed the quiet by roller-skating on the smooth base of the monument, and then suddenly she was gone. Nearby, the River Marne flowed

---

[13] As a ten-year-old in New York City, the author handled a greasy fragment of this German warship, which was passed around a meeting of boys he had camped with in the summer.

B. Cory Kilvert Jr.

gently through the farmland of France, its waters whispering of days long since lost to the fickle memory of mankind.

BIBLIOGRAPHY:

Ascoli, David, *The Mons Star, The British Expeditionary Force, 5th Aug- 22nd Nov., 1914* (Harrap, London, 1981)

Banks, Arthur, *A Military Atlas of the First World War* (Heineman, London, 1975)

Cameron, James, *1914* (Cassell, London, 1962)

Cameron, James, *1916—Year of Decision* (Oldbourne Book Company, Ltd., London, 1962)

Clines, Francis W., *Cornish Miners Now, Museum Pieces Tomorrow?* (The New York Times, July 2nd, 1986)

Coombs, Rose E. B., MBE, *Before Endeavours Fade, a Guide to the Battlefields of the First World War* (Battle of Britain Prints International, London, 1977)

Edmonds, Brigadier-General J. E (compiler), *History of the Great War, Military Operations, France and Belgium, 1914* (Macmillan and Co, Ltd., London, 1926)

French, Field-Marshal Viscount of Ypres, *1914* (Houghton Mifflin Company, Boston and New York, 1919)

Gordon, Major L. L., *British Battles and Medals* (Spink & Son, London, 1971)

Pound, Reginald, *The Lost Generation of 1914* (Coward -McCann, New York, 1964)

Simpson, Keith, *The Old Contemptibles, A Photographic History of the British Expeditionary Force, August to December 1914* (Allen & Unwin, London, 1981)

Smithers, A. J., *The Man Who Disobeyed, Sir Horace Smith-Dorrien and His Enemies* (Leo Cooper Limited, London, 1970)

Swinson, Arthur (editor), *A Register of the Regiments and Corps of the British Army, the Ancestry of the Regiments and Corps of the Regular Establishment* (Archive Press, London, 1972)

Terraine, John, Mons, *The Retreat to Victory* (Batsford, London, 1960)

War Diary of the 1st Battalion, Duke of Cornwall's Light Infantry, 4 August-12 September, 1914 (Public Record Office, Reference WO95/1564)

Wyrall, Everard, *The History of the Duke of Cornwall's Light Infantry 1914-1919* (Methuen, London, 1932)

This pre-war photograph shows Private Arthur Small (right) with Private Robert Rowe, his friend in the 1st Battalion, The Duke of Cornwall's Light Infantry.

CHAPTER 2

1881-1914

Captain The Honourable William Thomas Payne-Gallwey, MVO

1st Battalion, The Grenadier Guards

On Saturday, October 3rd, 1914, a twenty-one-mile line of thirty-one vessels left Quebec, sailed down to the mouth of the St. Lawrence River to the cheers of onlookers and set a course for England. These ships carried 25,000 enthusiastic, rough and ready Canadian soldiers going to the aid of the Mother Country.

Among the officers and men of this first contingent on board s.s. *Megantic* was twenty-seven-year-old Captain Robert Young Cory, B Company commander, 48th Highlanders of Canada, and a cousin of the author's. His experiences in Flanders will be recounted later in this book.

In England on that same October day, a more somber mood prevailed for two families in North Yorkshire. Under 'War Items' in the *Thirsk News*, the following notice appeared: 'Much sympathy is being felt in Thirsk with Major and Mrs. Bell, The Hall, whose son, Captain F. Bell (Gordon Highlanders) is still among the missing in the war. The same feeling is also extended towards Sir Ralph and Lady

Payne-Gallwey, of Thirkleby Park, who are suffering under similar suspense with regard to their son, Captain W. Payne-Gallwey (Grenadiers). It is hoped that the cloud of anxiety at present hanging over these families may speedily pass away. . .'

Although the first of these officers survived World War One, the second did not, and I set out to discover whatever might remain known about his life and the circumstances of his death.

William Thomas Payne-Gallwey was not a native of Thirsk but of a place about five miles to the south of this ancient market town, a place bearing a word of Danish origin, Thirkleby. It was there he spent much of his life.

While at Eton in 1900, he stood six feet tall, was fair and handsome with brown hair and blue eyes and had matured into a fine athlete. In that same year, he had represented his school against its archrival Harrow in a cricket match played at Lord's on July 13th and 14th. A seesaw contest of great excitement, it was considered at the time the best ever played between the two schools, whose rivalry extended back to 1805. Harrow had eventually won by one wicket.

Payne-Gallwey's main ambition from childhood had been to make a career of the army, but this desire had not been equaled by his scholastic record, which was undistinguished. Although his mother doted on him, she was at heart a stern Victorian who often chided him for his inabilities in French. Clearly, the most direct route to a commission, sitting for the examination for entrance to the Royal Military College (Sandhurst), was barred to him.

Obviously anticipating this roadblock to the Regular Army, his father, Sir Ralph Payne-Gallwey, who had long desired that his son should enter the Grenadier Guards, obtained for him a commission as second lieutenant in the 3rd (Militia) Battalion, York and Lancaster Regiment. This commission was dated January 25th, 1900, while the boy was still at Eton.

This approach through the 'back door' was a quite common procedure at the time, and in this young man's case it proved to be acceptable to the Guards on a number of counts. His years at Eton would have equipped him with the basic qualities of self-reliance and leadership, and his family background was sufficiently distinguished to prevent any embarrassment to either himself or his fellow officers in the Grenadiers. He was also acceptably tall to be a Guards officer.

Barring any unforeseen difficulties, he would fit in and do well, especially because he would already know many of the junior officers in his regiment and also in other Guards regiments.[14] So after only seven months with the York and Lancs, Payne-Gallwey was appointed second lieutenant to the 1st Battalion, Grenadier Guards, the British army's senior regiment. The date was August 29th, 1900, and he was nineteen years old.

At fifty-two, his father was third baronet of a lineage originating with one Ralph Payne, a supporter of Charles I and, after his beheading in 1649, of his son, Charles II, with whom he had fought at the Battle of Worcester in 1651.[15] The name Gallwey had been introduced much later and, later still, another member of Sir Ralph's family assumed the name and arms of Gallwey in 1762.

Also educated at Eton, Sir Ralph had seen ten years of military service, first as second lieutenant, 92nd Regiment (Gordon Highlanders), then as a full lieutenant with the 15th Foot (East Yorkshire Regiment) and finally as a captain, East York Militia. His wife was the former Edith Alice Usborne of Blackrock in Ireland's County Cork. Of their five children, the middle one was their only son, who was called Willie at home.

[14] At the time, Old Etonians constituted eleven percent of all officers in the Regular Army.
[15] In Bruges, Belgium, in 1656, Charles II was responsible for raising a Royal Lifeguard of Foot, which soon came to be called His Majesty's Royal Regiment of Guards, this being the forerunner of the Grenadier Guards.

27

Because his two older sisters had been born in 1886 and 1889, it seemed highly unlikely to me that either would still be alive when I started my research on this family in the early 1980s. So Pat Wolfston initially concentrated on discovering the nature of Sir Ralph's estate and learned it had been on wooded land of almost 265 acres, was well stocked with deer and offered delightful views of the Hambleton Hills. Throughout the area, farmers grew barley, oats and wheat and also tended pastureland.

Between 1780 and 1785, Sir Thomas Frankland, a forebear of Sir Ralph's, had built a huge stone classical Italianate hall on high ground, which was approached along a handsome avenue flanked by Scotch firs. This land had once supported an Elizabethan mansion, and prior to that, a dwelling was known to have existed there in 1308.

A true eccentric in a bygone age when odd preoccupations were accepted if not encouraged more so than today, Sir Ralph busied himself with his life's passions—duck hunting and fishing as well as medieval arms and armor. He also authored more than a dozen books, including what remains recognized as the definitive work on the crossbow. An avid builder of replica weaponry, he was known to have instructed some of his servants in their use because an album once kept at Thirkleby Park included a photograph of him supervising the arming of a ballista.[16]

While on the trail of Payne-Gallwey's relatives, Pat Wolfston read the will of Willie's mother, which was written in 1946 when she was ninety-one. It mentioned that only two of her five children, Dorothy and Geraldine, were then living. Digging further, she discovered that, surprisingly, Dorothy was still alive and a permanent

---

[16] As an example of another eccentric of the time, John Lord in his highly readable *Duty, Honour, Empire*, refers to the uncle and godfather of Colonel Richard Meinertzhagen, one of Payne-Gallwey's contemporaries in the army. On one occasion, he presented his infant godson with an elephant, and once at the dinner table he began to sob at the sudden realization that he had not enjoyed asparagus for an entire year.

resident of a nursing home in Hampshire. She was ninety-six, frail but mentally alert and quite willing to talk about her brother. Pat interviewed her in 1983.

By contemporary standards, life for the Payne-Gallwey children seems unduly harsh. Their mother did not believe in schools for girls, claiming they were a waste of money. As for Willie, he was sent away to a primary school in Yorkshire at the age of only four.

"He was just a tiny chap," declared Miss Payne-Gallwey. "I know people were always so shocked, but Mother was very tough. She brought us up hard. My brother was too much her favorite," she added, "but we girls were seldom allowed to move and could hardly say 'boo' to a goose!"

Relegated to the background, the two younger Payne-Gallwey girls were generally ignored by their aunts and uncles, several of whom were more or less in permanent residence at Thirkleby Park. Among them was Sir Ralph's younger brother Lionel, whose son Maurice grew up to idolize Willie, who was eight years his senior.

Sir Ralph instilled in his son a love of fishing and shooting, turning him into a first-class shot. His sister recollected that "he was a very clever man with a gun," a good qualification for a soldier. Clearly, young Willie's life style was as far removed from Private Arthur Small's as Thirkleby is from Redruth, but they would tread some of the same ground in the coming apocalypse that claimed them both.

Four months before Payne-Gallwey's appointment to the Grenadier Guards, the 3rd Battalion of his regiment had been among the first Imperial troops to sail for service in the Boer War. Leaving Gibraltar for South Africa aboard s.s. *Goorkha*, they were soon to clash with a stubborn foe armed with something not faced before by the British Army, modern German magazine rifles in the hands of resourceful men who could use them with deadly effect.

Although the battles of Belmont and the Modder River in late November 1899 were technically British victories, they had revealed serious shortcomings in military principles and planning. These were largely due to the fact that no senior general officers in 1899 had received any training as staff officers or could claim any experience in complex staff organization in the field. In past years, 'muddling through' had sufficed, but its days were now numbered.

At the Modder River, the 3rd Grenadiers, advancing with the rest of Lieutenant-General Lord Methuen's 1st Division against what were believed to be abandoned enemy positions, were suddenly assailed by a four-mile wall of dead accurate fire aimed by 3,000 Boers from concealed positions along the riverbed. Only the timely turning of the Boer right flank by the 9th Brigade prevented this ill-conceived action from becoming a rout.

Greater blunders would follow, although sheer force of arms was eventually to wear down the Boers, but at a high cost to their opponents. Like the conflict that would follow it, the Boer War in British minds could not last past Christmas of its first year. But it dragged on until the last day of May 1902, by which time its price had exceeded £200 million. In terms of human cost, the toll was more than 100,000 Imperial and Empire casualties, including 22,000 men who would remain forever beneath the veldt.

Lieutenant Payne-Gallwey was a late arrival on this scene. His Queen's South Africa Medal carries the two silver bars for 'Cape Colony' and 'South Africa 1902,' each of which provides an important clue regarding his service. The first bar indicates he had served with the 3rd Battalion of his regiment because the only other Grenadiers battalion to serve in the war—the 2nd—was not in Cape Colony in 1902. In addition, he was only attached to the 3rd Battalion and not actually a member of it because the Army List for the first month of 1902 shows him still with the 1st Battalion.

The second bar on his medal was awarded to those who served in South Africa from January 1st to May 31st, 1902. In Payne-Gallwey's case, his service was of short duration, a fact to be established shortly.

By the start of 1902, the army had already devoted some months to the tiresome task of attempting to round up Boers engaged in hit and run raids more often aimed at capturing much-needed supplies than killing their foe. These tactics had been forced on them two years earlier following the fall of their capital in Pretoria and the British annexation of the Transvaal.

In the wake of these successes, the British Commander-in-Chief, Lord Roberts, was sufficiently satisfied to proclaim that the war was over, and to prove this was so, he returned to England. But in reality, he was seeing shadow instead of substance. His successor, Lord Kitchener, famous for his reconquest of the Sudan in 1898, was left to counter a vicious guerrilla action masterfully conducted for another seventeen months by these farmer-sharpshooters whose capital came to be housed in an ox wagon on the endless landscape of the South Africa veldt. It is generally believed that at no time during this entire conflict did these tough Boers exceed 40,000 determined men.

To limit the movement of his enemy, Kitchener had ordered the construction of a vast chain of blockhouses built mainly along railway lines. These octagonal or round structures consisted of two layers of corrugated iron. Placed on the ground, roofed and loopholed, each contained an iron water tank, a telephone and a garrison of one non-commissioned officer, six privates and up to four natives used mainly for night sentry duty. Each blockhouse was also rendered bulletproof by four and a half inches of gravel and soil packed between each of its iron walls. Barbed wire entanglements further protected each garrison and impeded enemy surprise attacks.

Kitchener then organized a series of huge 'drives' involving thousands of troops marching almost shoulder-to-shoulder across the veldt to push back any Boers they encountered to the nearest blockhouse where, in theory, they would be captured. In practice, events often proved otherwise. But as the intervals between these iron structures in each new line were steadily decreased to 200 yards, this scheme eventually met with considerable success except in the western regions of Cape Colony ranging from the Atlantic Ocean to the Cape Town-De Aar Railway. There a vast, desolate area remained wide open to Boer incursions.

To close this gap, a 300-mile line of blockhouses had been begun in December 1901 to link Victoria Road with Lambert's Bay. It was never completed, but one has cause to wonder if this last barrier could have achieved its purpose. It was tested only once before the end of the war by British Intelligence personnel dressed like Boers who easily captured a number of these iron barriers in which black troops were unconcernedly playing cards.

The 3rd Grenadiers played only a supporting role in this perfunctory last act. Operating at its eastern end, they protected seventy miles of line from De Aar southeast to Naauwpoort and another forty-five miles running northeast from the latter town to Colesberg.

Boring at best and not the sort of work that Guards were often asked to do, at least this responsibility may have provided an officer the chance to shoot game for the mess, and in Payne-Gallwey's case, he was lucky because his tour lasted no longer than three months. This is known to be so because his sister recalled a grand party given at Thirkleby Park in honor of his twenty-first birthday. The date was March 25th, 1902, and his parents presented him with a silver cup on this festive occasion.

During the next twelve years, he remained in England, mainly involved with duties typical of a junior officer in the 1st Battalion, Grenadier Guards. He lived in a gilded age of ceremonies for visiting monarchs and state balls at which officers wore full dress, including swords. Although swords could be removed before dancing, an even greater hazard was posed to ladies' ankles by spurs fastened to the heels of officers' patent leather boots. As a precaution against injury, dancing backwards was understandably forbidden.

Other rules governed a Guards officer's behavior. When in uniform or mufti, he could never be seen in public carrying a parcel, suitcase or, especially, a baby. Cigarettes made of Turkish tobacco were allowed, but smoking a Virginia brand was not. Prior to World War One, his duties were minimal, and time allowed away from the regiment was generous, with captains given four months' leave and colonels six and sometimes more. A typical day while on duty in London began with Company Orders for which civilian dress was permitted. After a glass of port at noon, the remainder of the day could be spent in sports or relaxation, but each night the adjutant and recently-joined second lieutenants were required to sleep in barracks.

Duty at the Tower of London was always popular with younger officers because all they had to do was arrive there, after which hardly anything was required of them. However, exemplary conduct by all ranks and perfection on parade were matters of pride and habit throughout the Brigade of Guards, but it was war that all officers longed for because it was the path to awards and promotion. The brigade's first Victoria Cross had been won in the Crimean War by Captain and Adjutant Robert James Lindsay, 1st Battalion, Scots Guards, during the Battle of the Alma and later at Inkerman.

During Payne-Gallwey's service, the lighthearted Edwardian era radiated opulence and elegance that too easily blinded those who identified its sovereign almost exclusively with the pursuits of pleasure. But beneath a Falstaffian veneer, King Edward VII possessed the mind of a shrewd diplomatic negotiator, and in

1904, to the wrath of his German nephew, Kaiser Wilhelm II, his determination and skill had resulted in the signing of the *Entente Cordiale* with France.

In that same year, Payne-Gallwey was promoted lieutenant. Almost exactly four years later, he was appointed adjutant of the 2nd Battalion, succeeding Captain Bertram Norman Brooke, who had accepted a staff position with the Egyptian Army.

The life of an adjutant in the Guards was, and still is, the best training an officer could receive anywhere in terms of attention to detail. Responsibility for the appearance of every boot and button worn by the men was ultimately his, as was the proper discharge of all day-to-day duties of his battalion.

Ceremonial occasions can serve as a single example of this. An adjutant was required to see that every movement made by his battalion was carried out meticulously in accordance with the appropriate instructions regarding timings, dress, music and dozens of other considerations, both mighty and miniscule. But there were important compensations. Having successfully completed an average of two years as adjutant, a Guards officer would justifiably be considered fully trustworthy and well suited to hold higher rank.

Just two months after assuming these new responsibilities, Payne-Gallwey was immersed in his role in the state visit of President Fallières of France, an elaborate affair in which fifty-two Royal Navy vessels with more than 17,000 men on board lay off Dover to greet this dignitary. In London, members of the 2nd Grenadiers had been detailed to line various routes to St. James's Palace, the Guildhall and from Cheapside to Temple Station on the Embankment along which the visiting president and his entourage would pass.

On June 1st, a scant two days after M. Fallières' departure, the king presented new Colours to the 2nd Grenadier Guards, a ceremony then held in the garden at Buckingham Palace. *The Times* for the following day duly recounted this ceremony, which dated from the British Army's earliest days when each man was taught to identify his Colours for use as a rallying point in battle.

The old Colours having been trooped for the last time, the King was handed the New Colours by Majors Du Plat Taylor and Trotter. He then returned them to Lieutenants Dennistoun and Colston, who accepted them on bended knee. Captain the Honourable Robert Lygon was in command of the escort.[17]

Awards for service to the Crown followed. Because Lieutenant Dennistoun was already a Member of the Royal Victorian Order, the 5th Class of this decoration was presented to the battalion adjutant, Lieutenant Payne-Gallwey.

In the course of addressing the battalion, King Edward declared, "God forbid that we should have to call upon your services in the field, but I feel sure that, should the necessity arise, you will not fail to do your duty. . ."

On that same day, Kaiser Wilhelm II stood on the Tempelhoferfeld to review the annual spring parade of the Berlin garrison, while in Austria, the aged Emperor Franz Josef attended a similar display of might by troops garrisoned in Vienna. Who in 1908 could have known that the lines were already being drawn for a conflict of inconceivable horror? But it was now only six years to Armageddon.

Although Lord Haldane, the Secretary of State for War, continued to press his vital army reforms based on bitter lessons learned in the Boer War, there was still much to be done to prepare the British Army to face a major German power. It was not until around 1909 that each infantry battalion was provided with two machine guns for training purposes. Five years later, the German Army was believed to have 4,500 of these weapons in service. Once this imbalance had been realized soon after the war began, the War Office ordered 1,800 more of these guns and by

---

[17] During the Boer War, this officer was among those wounded at Belmont. Regimental adjutant from 1909 to 1911, he would win the Military Cross during World War One, and he lived until 1952. His medals have been in the author's collection since 1979.

the end of 1914, Vickers' output plus 2,000 ordered from the United States began to close the gap with Germany's production.

At first, few British officers understood these automatic devices or took much interest in their potential. Too often, battalion commanders assigned them to the care of subalterns who seemed less suited to what were deemed more important assignments. But this would not have been the case with Payne-Gallwey. After all, his father was fascinated by mechanical devices, and he himself was a "clever man with a gun." As a consequence, by 1914 he was well experienced with machine guns and the care they required. In pre-war years they were fixed onto a wooden frame with wagon-like wheels and a shaft that was drawn by a section including a sergeant, corporal and seven men. To fire this weapon, a man straddled the shaft and was fully exposed to enemy fire, a shortcoming which the designers had overlooked.

In the twilight of peace, army officers still had ample time for recreation. In early April 1913, the Inter-Regimental Tournament for the Army Cup took place on the Royal Cinque Ports Club course at Deal. In the second round in which the Seaforth Highlanders beat the Grenadier Guards eleven holes to five, Captain Kenneth Gray Buchanan trounced Payne-Gallwey seven to none.[18] Records show that the latter was by then with the 3rd Battalion of his regiment.

At Aldershot in July, the 1st and 3rd Grenadiers played in a cricket match against a composite team made up of officers of the Black Watch (Royal Highlanders), the Royal Munster Fusiliers and the Loyal North Lancashire Regiment. Payne-Gallwey bowled out seven batsmen and accounted for five more, but his performance as a batsman was only mediocre.

In two succeeding matches against other opponents in August and September, he ran up a total of forty runs in the first before being bowled out, while in the

---

[18] Of the eight officers from these two regiments who played in this match, five were to die in World War One.

second he met his match as a bowler when Lieutenant Furneaux of the 1st King's (Liverpool) Regiment made seventy-four runs before being caught out.[19]

Few would have suggested that this would be the last summer of peace, but the major powers were gathering momentum on a collision course toward a monstrous war that would engulf many nations across the globe and leave misery and ruin in its wake.

According to Willie's sister Dorothy, he was home on August 4th, 1914. His cousin Philip ('Pip') Francis Payne-Gallwey, whose father was rector of nearby Sessay, was also on leave from the 21st Lancers, who were at Rawalpindi in India. Pip was twenty years old and a graduate of the Royal Military College (Sandhurst). In the early evening, word was received at Thirkleby Park that the Grenadier Guards had been ordered by London District Headquarters to mobilize for war with Germany.

Centuries of hatreds which defined the Balkans while defying reason in more stable societies had caused the fuse lit at Sarajevo to sputter but not die. On July 23rd, twenty-five days after the assassinations, Austria-Hungary struck a bellicose pose by sending an especially harsh ultimatum to Serbia, which was rejected two days later. On the 30th, Russia began to mobilize, and Germany declared war on it when it refused to back down. By July 6th, a chain reaction had been set in motion following the Kaiser's promise to support Austria-Hungary against Serbia.

The Old World was rushing downhill to its doom, and no one could halt its momentum. Twenty-two days later, it gathered additional speed when Germany and Austria-Hungary committed their nations to war against Serbia, Great Britain, France, Belgium and Montenegro. Although Turkey and Bulgaria held back at first,

---

[19] Philip Templer Furneaux was killed in action at the age of twenty-five while serving as assistant adjutant of his battalion during an attack on the Belgian village of Molenaarelsthoek during the First Battle of Ypres.

they both came in later on Germany's side after millions of soldiers had already begun preparing for what was, by then, the inevitable.

In London, not everyone proved to be euphoric about the nation going to war. On August 2nd, prominent members of the Labour Party had spoken at an antiwar demonstration, and this was followed during the next few days by meetings organized by several diverse groups of citizens. These ranged from a distinguished Oxford historian to Cambridge Fellows and members of various branches of the National Union of the Women's Suffrage Society. More sinister feelings were shown by those who took to the streets with red banners and fought with those who supported the war.

But once Prime Minister Asquith had spoken on the 5th about the moral rationale for standing up against Germany, most dissenters quickly fell into line with him and loyally joined in the nation's determination to win the war at all costs. Little could they have imagined what the magnitude of those costs would be.

As a professional soldier, Lieutenant Payne-Gallwey would have had neither the time nor the inclination to concern himself with such matters. Having packed the things he needed most, he said his good-byes and left home at once. During his journey south, each Guards Reservist had already received a notice recalling him to active duty, and by August 6th, 3,000 of these men, armed and kitted out, were on duty with their battalions.

Payne-Gallwey, by this time a captain, had before the outbreak of war been appointed machine gun officer with the 1st (Guards) Brigade, 1st Division. Thus he was experiencing his first, and last, non-regimental appointment. His brigade consisted of the 1st Battalions of the Coldstream Guards, Scots Guards and the Black Watch plus the 2nd Battalion, Royal Munster Fusiliers.[20] Their comrades in

---

[20] If a brigade includes at least one Guards battalion, it is always called a Guards Brigade no matter how many battalions of line regiments may form a part of it.

Haig's I Corps included the four battalions of the 4th (Guards) Brigade consisting of the 2nd Grenadier Guards as well as the 2nd and 3rd Coldstream Guards plus the 1st Battalion, Irish Guards, who were going to war for the first time since being raised in 1900.

Payne-Gallwey most likely sailed on s.s *Cawdor Castle* with headquarters personnel of his brigade and the 2nd Coldstream, which landed at Le Havre on the afternoon of August 13th. Nine days later, the BEF marched into Belgium and occupied positions explained in the preceding chapter. Tactically, these dispositions left much to be desired, especially to the west around Condé where wide-open spaces were vulnerable to any German incursions that might be attempted in force.

This tenuous British line was never meant to be defended. It was considered only a stopping point on the forty-mile march east to Namur where Anglo-French forces would block further German advances. However, Lanrezac, having been attacked by the German *Second* and *Third Armies*, had fallen back, leaving Namur to its doom as huge sixteen-inch howitzers pounded its garrison into ruins. So the BEF would have to fight where it stood and would be doing so with its left flank wide open from about two miles south of Fresnes. Earlier, French forces had agreed to fill this gap but never did so.

Having lost his nerve completely by August 22nd, Lanrezac, bombastic prewar champion of offensive *élan*, ordered the *French Fifth Army* to abandon its position to the south of Haig's I Corps without telling his ally. This created another huge hole beyond the British 1st Division at the southern tip of the BEF's refused right flank extending southeast from Mons. This gap immediately presented von Kluck's *First Army* with another golden opportunity. But von Kluck, badly confused, had only a faint idea of what lay in front of him regarding the exact location of the British. So when he stumbled upon the BEF along the canal, he stopped to challenge it there. Had he driven further south of Grand Reng, he could have turned the newly exposed British refused right flank, driven beyond it to the west and trapped the entire BEF in Belgium.

As it turned out, fortune would favor the British.

Having successfully repelled wave upon wave of German assaults on August 23rd, the men, though vastly outnumbered, had given a good account of themselves on the canal and were fully prepared to hold onto their positions on the following day. But as German pressure from the north increased, they were forced to retire.

von Kluck remained a master of mistakes on that day. Incorrectly assuming his enemy would move northwest to reach ports on the Channel from which they could return to England, he sent off three of his divisions to cut them off. Next, based on another false assumption that the British would move south to the fortress at Maubeuge, he directed four infantry corps away to deal with them there. Instead, as indicated in the preceding chapter, the entire BEF escaped serious danger from its foe all the way to the southeast of Paris.

Nothing is known about Captain Payne-Gallwey during this period of stress and danger beyond the fact that the 1st Guards Brigade was in the vicinity of Mons on August 22nd and at Vieux Reng on the next day. However, Payne-Gallwey's sister recalled he had time to scribble a few letters to send home. After that, he emerged only briefly on September 1st in the course of a confusing battle in which he would vanish from sight.

At 6 a.m. on that day, the 1st Black Watch left their bivouac at Missy aux Bois, a village five miles south of Soissons. The brigade machine guns, which Payne-Gallwey commanded, are known to have been with the Black Watch on that day because their regimental history so states.

Acting as rear guard of the 1st (Guards) Brigade, the Highlanders moved south and entered the Forêt Dominiale de Retz, an especially somber expanse of beech trees sheltering thick stands of bracken, and marched on to Villers-Cottérêts where they halted for a hasty meal. By then, it was 1 p.m. Heavy firing could be heard from the northwest where von Kluck's German *First Army* was closing in on its foe.

The Black Watch took up positions at the north side of the village and remained in place while the rest of the 1st (Guards) Brigade passed through them, after which the Royal Highlanders themselves withdrew. They continued south for another eight miles to La Ferté Milon where they spent the night. During the day, they had made no contact with the Germans and had taken no casualties.

Further west, however, matters had been different for the 4th (Guards) Brigade, which was closer to von Kluck's hordes. There the 2nd Coldstream Guards and the 1st Irish Guards had entered the same forest as the 1st (Guards) Brigade had done earlier to shelter from German shellfire.[21]

Concealed along its northwestern fringe, they remained in place while the 2nd Grenadiers and 3rd Coldstream passed through their positions and proceeded south to hold a line along a grass road running east to west through the village of Ronde de la Reine. Early morning rain and mist had given way to blistering heat and humidity.

Upon reaching this wood in force, the Germans advanced into it, filtering through the gaps between the Guards' companies. A sharp firefight erupted almost at once in the dense undergrowth, which restricted visibility and literally swallowed up those who fell beneath it. At times, the two lines were no more than seventy yards apart.

Although machine gunners of the Grenadier and Irish Guards took a heavy toll, the enemy pressed on, briefly halted here and there by wild bayonet charges.

---

[21] This dense wood was no less gloomy and impenetrable when the author entered it seventy years later. One could easily become disoriented after walking into it for no more than fifty yards.

So confusing was the situation that when the order came to retire, it failed to reach two platoons of Grenadiers at Ronde de la Reine. Surrounded, they were attacked on all sides, and their regimental history pays them this brief tribute: 'True to the traditions of the Regiment, they stuck to their posts and fought on 'til all were killed or wounded.'

Elsewhere in this history appears another sentence: 'Captain W. T. Payne-Gallwey, MVO, who was in charge of the machine guns of the 1st Brigade, was reported missing,'

What had caused this to happen? Were he and his machine guns sent to support the further withdrawal of the 4th (Guards) brigade? Was he one of the killed and wounded who slipped out of sight beneath the forest's foliage? No one was ever to know, and all that remains clear is that he could not have spent the entire day with the 1st Battalion, Black Watch.

His sister Dorothy was among the first to hear the news. Early in the preceding year she had enrolled as a VAD and was serving with the York 2 Detachment.[22] Her parents, although alarmed to learn that their son was missing, assumed at once that nothing worse had happened to him. Soon after the Battle of the Marne, there seemed to be a slight justification for this belief when French forces, advancing to the River Aisne, retook Villers-Cottérêts on September 12th. Hastily retreating, the Germans had left behind four wounded British officers whom they had captured on the 1st. Three of them proved to be from the Irish Guards. The fourth was not Payne-Gallwey but Lieutenant Hugh John Sladen Shields of the Royal Army Medical Corps.

This selfless, twenty-seven-year-old doctor had been commissioned in 1912. When war was declared and he went to France with the 1st Battalion, Irish Guards,

---

[22] In 1910, Voluntary Aid Detachments were organized by the British Red Cross to provide assistance in emergencies to professional military nurses of the Territorial Force.

he soon became an inspiration to both officers and men who were in awe of his courage.

Sir Harold Alexander, then an Irish Guards lieutenant,[23] stated, "He was with us all the time up to Villers-Cottérêts, where he stayed behind with the wounded and was taken by the Germans. . . He rejoined us again at Soupir. . . where Hugh did such frightfully good work by carrying the wounded, both English and German, out of a burning farm which was being very heavily shelled."

With Shields' dangerous habit of casually walking across the battlefield, unconcerned with his own safety, it was inevitable that he would pay for his courage, and this happened near Ypres when he was shot in the neck and killed on October 26th while helping a wounded man only 200 yards from the enemy lines. He was recommended for a Victoria Cross but received nothing.[24] He was one of many officers and men in his corps who, without hesitation, would sacrifice themselves for their comrades throughout the war.

In 1983, while visiting Thirsk, I passed the small local historical museum, which was closed. Stopping at a nearby office, which proved to be where James Herriot, the author of so many endearing books about animals, conducted his veterinary practice, I asked for a piece of paper on which I scribbled a few words about my interest in Captain Payne-Gallwey. Sticking this note in the museum door, I went on my way. Upon my return home, there was a letter awaiting me from a Dr. Peter Wyon, who gave me some details on the early owners of Thirkleby Park and later put me in touch with another resident of Thirsk, Colonel Peter Consett, whose family had known the Payne-Gallweys.

---

[23] Utterly fearless, an inspiring leader, and a perfect gentleman, Alexander won a French Legion of Honor, a Military Cross and a Distinguished Service Order in World War One. For services rendered in World War Two, he was created First Earl Alexander of Tunis. He lived until 1969.
[24] See *The Roll of Honour*, Vol. 1, Part 2, page 274.

Responding to a letter I sent to the colonel, he wrote, 'I was always led to believe from my parents that Sir Ralph and Lady Payne-Gallwey for many years refused to accept that their only son had been killed. I also understand that his body was never found and that there were no eyewitnesses to his death in action.'

The official date of his death is an equal mystery. Assuming that the two days from September 12th to the 14th were spent on searches and queries regarding those still missing from the fighting on the 1st, a more accurate official date of Payne-Gallwey's death would have been the 1st, the last day on which he was seen alive.

Continuing to grasp at straws, his parents lived on in the slim hope that their son was a German prisoner suffering from amnesia. Theirs would be a lonely vigil through the years of bloodshed that would take a mounting toll of their family.

On the last day of October 1914, Willie's cousin 'Pip' Payne-Gallwey was shot through the head and died near Messines in Flanders while attached to the 9th (Queen's Royal) Lancers. During a German attack on their trenches, they were fired on from both flanks, driven back but regained them, only to lose them again. Under the circumstances, the young lieutenant's body had to be left behind.[25] Equally sad news would follow.

On September 26th, 1916, Willie's other cousin, Lieutenant Frankland Hylton Maurice Payne-Gallwey, serving as a subaltern with No. 3 Company, 4th Grenadier Guards, was killed near Lesboeufs on the Somme at the age of twenty-seven.[26]

On the date of the latter's death, his company had taken part in an attack which moved the British front line forward for less than three-quarters of a mile while suffering losses of seven officers killed, four wounded and one who died of wounds on the 29th. In the ranks there were 445 casualties. The Grenadier Guards'

---

[25] He had served with his regiment since 1912 when he was nineteen. His regimental journal for December 31st, 1914, referred to him as 'a bold and fearless horseman' who showed great promise of becoming a first class polo player.

[26] Having returned from the Malay State when the war began, he enlisted in King Edward's Horse and fought in France before receiving his commission in September 1915 after a brief spell of training.

regimental history rated this attack as 'one of the most successful operations in which the Guards Division was engaged in the war.' Daily casualty rates as high as these—and much higher—had become commonplace in all combatant nations, and no one could assume they would not continue wherever the war was being fought.

On the home front, this dreadful war proclaimed its presence in thousands of cities, towns and villages throughout Great Britain. In Thirsk, Bamlett's Foundry, having suspended its line of horse-drawn grass cutters for the duration, hired many young women to manufacture munitions and iron screw posts to support barbed wire. In 1915, the town hall had been converted into a military convalescent hospital staffed by a local ladies' VAD, and Willie's father wrote a short work entitled 'The War, a Criticism' in which he supported the argument for compulsory military service.

In November 1916, Sir Ralph died at the age of sixty-eight. Thirkleby Park passed to his nephew, Major Sir John Frankland Payne-Gallwey, Royal Engineers, whose wife disliked the estate with the result that it was sold almost immediately.

As the last British prisoners held by the Germans returned in 1919, Lady Payne-Gallwey, finally faced with conclusive proof that her son had not survived the war, reacted initially with anger, an emotion not as uncommon as might be expected, especially for a woman who had always sought to control events in her life. According to her daughter, she willfully destroyed all her photographs of her son, and Colonel Consett's parents remembered her as a sad, retiring figure for the rest of her days.

On November 12th, 1953, she died in her ninety-eighth year when a cerebral hemorrhage struck her down at The Grange, her home in Bedale, North Yorkshire. She had survived by twenty-six years the demolition of the great hall at Thirkleby Park by a syndicate locally disparaged as 'The Forty Thieves' who provided many of its interior appointments to buyers in the United States and sold the timber and stone locally. Dr. Wyon told me of a house in Thirsk which now contains some of its intricately carved mantel shelves.

There was little to be seen on the grounds of the old estate on which a caravan park had been established when I drove onto it in the 1980s. The stable walls still existed, and the old decoy cottage was serving as a private residence, as were two lodges that flanked a graceful 1792 pedimented stone archway. During my visit there, the current landowner accosted me and refused to allow me to take photographs until I told him how many miles I had traveled to do so. He then relented but told me to be quick about it.

Somber reminders of Captain the Honourable William Thomas Payne-Gallwey, MVO, of the Grenadier Guards and Private Arthur Small of the Cornwalls live on at the British war memorial on the banks of the River Marne in France. There, social status and rank count for nought, and British soldiers from long ago are honored equally for their endurance, courage and final sacrifice.

BIBLIOGRAPHY:

Beckett, Ian F. W. and Simpson, Keith, *A Nation in Arms, a Social Study of the British Army in the First World War* (Manchester University Press, Manchester, 1985)

Belfield, Eversley, *The Boer War* (Leo Cooper Ltd., London, 1975)

The Bond of Sacrifice, a Biographical Record of All British Officers Who Fell in the Great War, Volume I, Aug-Dec 1914 (Anglo-African Publishing Contractors, London, 1916)

The Chronicle of the Royal Highland Regiment, The Black Watch, 1913 (Printed for regimental circulation by T. and A. Constable, Edinburgh, 1913)

The Chronicle of the Royal Highland Regiment, The Black Watch, 1914 (Printed for regimental circulation by T. and A. Constable, Edinburgh, 1914)

de Ruvigny, The Marquis, *The Roll of Honour, A Biography of Members of His Majesty's Naval and Military Forces Who Fell in the Great War 1914-1918,* volume I, parts I and II (Facsimile edition, The London Stamp Exchange, Ltd., London, 1987)

de St. Jorre, John, *The Guards* (Crown Publishers, Inc., New York, 1981)

Dunlop, Colonel John K., OBE, MC, TD, Ph.D, *The Development of the British Army 1899-1914* (Methuen, London, 1938)

Kipling, Rudyard, *the Irish Guards in the Great War*, volume 1 (Doubleday, Page & Co., Garden City, NY, 1923)

Marwick, Arthur, *The Deluge, British Society in the First World War* (Little, Brown and Company, Boston, Massachusetts, 1965)

Official History, Military Operations, France and Belgium, 1914, vol. II (Macmillan and Co., Ltd., London, 1925)

Paget, Julian, *The Story of the Guards* (Osprey Publishing Ltd., London, 1976)

Ponsonby, Lieut-Colonel the Right Hon. Sir Frederick, *The Grenadier Guards in the Great War of 1914-1918,* vols. I and II (Macmillan and Co., London 1920)

*The Roll of Honour of the Empire's Heroes (*published for private circulation, no date)

Ross-of-Bladensburg, Lieutenant-Colonel Sir John, KCB, KCVO, *The Coldstream Guards in 1914-1918* (Oxford University Press, London, 1928)

Terraine, John, *Mons, The Retreat to Victory* (B. T. Batsford Ltd., London, 1960)

Thirkleby Park, Yorkshire (Country Life, February 17th, 1972)

The Times, May 25th-27th; June 1st and 2nd, 1908

The Times History of the War in South Africa 1899-1902, volume V 1907

The Times History of the War in South Africa 1899-1902, volume VI (Sampson Low, Marston and Co., Ltd., London, 1909

Towns and Villages, Thirkleby (supplement of the Yorkshire Herald, January 28th, 1928)

War Diary of the 1st Battalion, Royal Highlanders, 27 August-14 September, 1914 (Public Record Office, reference WO95/1263)

Wauchope, Major-General A. G., CB, *A History of the Black Watch, 1914-1918,* volume 1 (The Medici Society, London, 1925)

Whitworth, Major-General R. H., *The Grenadier Guards* (*The First or Grenadier Regiment of Foot Guards*) (Leo Cooper, Ltd., London, 1974)

Captain William Thomas Payne-Gallwey seen wearing a frock coat of a second lieutenant in the Grenadier Guards. This photo was taken prior to 1904 when he was serving with the 1st Battalion.

Lodges on both sides of this 1792 stone archway are among the few features that remain today of the grandeur that was once Thirkleby Park.

CHAPTER 3

1885-1914

Private Albert Armitage

2nd Battalion, The East Yorkshire Regiment

Britain's military adventures in the East, as elsewhere, often owed their origins to commercial avarice, which in the case of Burma was exemplified by the Bombay-Burma Trading Corporation's lust for teak.

As early as 1823, war over this issue had erupted along the Burma-India border, and sharp fighting on both sides of it culminated in 1826 with the surrender of large tracts of Burmese land to British Indian control. And this was only the beginning.

In 1852, the two sides went at it again with the inevitable result that the entire province of Pegu in South Burma was annexed by the British in December of the same year. An approximation of peace then prevailed for the next twenty-six years while King Mindon busied himself by building a palace of spectacular vulgarity protected by a wall enclosing one square mile. This wall, in turn, was surrounded by a warren of shops, dwellings and bazaars divided by thoroughfares with surfaces ranging from dust to mud, depending upon the weather.

Although this new capital 'city' might not have measured up to its innocuous creator's claim as the Center of the Universe, it was unquestionably a major center for flies, malaria and typhoid fever. Situated on the banks of the Irrawaddy River, its name was Mandalay.

Upon the death of Mindon in 1878, one of his many sons, Thebaw, ascended to the throne. Within seven years, this avaricious and murderous simpleton created a furor by attempting to develop trade with the French. Horrified at the thought of losing the teak monopoly, British commercial interests with connections at Whitehall promptly arranged for a military expedition to be sent up the Irrawaddy towards Ava where Thebaw surrendered in 1885 before events got entirely out of hand.

Seizing this opportunity to further solidify her hold on the country, Great Britain greedily annexed 160,000 square miles of Upper Burma in 1886. Over the next nine years, depredations by murderous packs of roving native 'dacoits' were stamped out, and the country was pacified by 1895. After that, it was simply a matter of garrisoning key areas with British troops who maintained order, thereby keeping the trade routes open.

On the last day of January 1906, a 20-year-old soldier from Brightside, Sheffield, arrived in Rangoon to begin the twisting journey upriver to Mandalay.

Albert Armitage had left Southampton Docks for Bombay thirty-three days earlier with the 2nd Battalion, East Yorkshire Regiment, and now he and his chums were about to transship from RIMS *Hardinge* to one of the many 'flats' which were a common sight along the Irrawaddy.

Lashed to the sides of large paddle steamers built in Glasgow and captained by Scots, these shallow-draft barges could carry over 1,000 soldiers as well as their weapons and baggage. Once aboard, they sweated and swore and ate and slept each night during the long journey north.

There was plenty for them to see. Animated groups of smiling Burmese, who had paid for sitting room on these steamers' decks, presented a microcosmic pageant of an indolent Buddhist society in which moral precepts and meditation played a dominant role. It was now more than miles that separated Albert from his home for here he was worlds away from Brightside.

The oldest of seven children of William Henry Armitage and his wife, the former Ellen Surgey, Albert had been born on April 5th, 1885, at Dane Street in a poor, working class neighborhood where run-down brick buildings surrounded courtyards in which chickens, pigs and donkeys roamed at will on filthy, unpaved surfaces. Inside these squalid dwellings, living conditions were appalling, and raw sewage seeped from them to run into the River Don.

In 1882, cholera killed 300 Sheffield residents and in the year of Albert's birth, one in every six children died before its first birthday. Before Albert was three, there was a smallpox epidemic. And when he was nine, his family moved a short distance to 514 Brightside Lane where their life would have been no better and might easily have been worse.

His father was a steel mill iron roller, most likely at Vickers where his brother was a lathe operator. The hours were long and the work exhausting and sometimes dangerous, increasing the risk of injury, disease and premature death. Trapped in this wretched environment, it was no wonder that drunkenness was widespread among a populace which drank largely undistilled gin which was readily available, inexpensive and often deadly.

I came upon many of these facts in a circuitous manner. Early on, Mr. H. Warburton, responding to a letter I had mailed to the postmaster in Sheffield, wrote to inform me that my request for information on Albert Armitage had been forwarded to the local press, as I had requested.

This letter, published in *The Star*, encouraged six Sheffield residents to write to me, one of whom, Mrs. Edith Burton, had this to relate: I think my mother Nelly Surgey must have been a cousin to Ellen Surgey. I was born in Brightside Lane, but we moved when I was a few months old. I remember my mother talking about an Albert Armitage and also I believe a Jack who was badly shell-shocked in the 1914-18 War.[27]

In the meantime, my researcher had telephoned the two Surgeys whose names she found listed in the Sheffield telephone directory. Her second call was answered by Mr. Wilfred Surgey, who told her that Albert had been his cousin. Mr. Surgey was seventy and a former steel worker, and his father had been Albert's uncle.

Mr. Surgey mentioned no brothers of Albert's, but he did recall the names of his three sisters—Elsie, Clara and Ada. He then added that Ada's three daughters were still alive and that one of them lived not far from him. He was unclear about her married name, but he thought it might be Goodwin.

In an effort to spark his memory further, Pat sent him a brief questionnaire I had prepared, which he completed and returned to her. On this he did much better by recording the names of Albert's three brothers—George, John Willie and Ernest. He was also able to recall that Ada's daughter lived in Guildford Rise and that her name was Grace Goodwin. He even sent a photograph of Albert in uniform, which later proved to have been taken between 1904 and 1905 when he was stationed at Aldershot.

Having consulted the Sheffield directory once more, Pat sent me Grace Goodwin's address, and I wrote to her at once. I never got a reply, but exactly twenty days later I received something even better—a telephone call from Albert's grandson, Barry Armitage, whom Miss Goodwin had contacted.

---

[27] Remarkably, especially from an American's standpoint, a Mr. Jack Burton, of whom I had no prior knowledge, kindly wrote out and sent to me the first initials and addresses of 181 people named Armitage in the Sheffield and District telephone directory!

We spoke briefly, and he told me he would lend me a photograph of Albert taken in Burma and also send me a photocopy of his pay book, which went up to 1912. Albert had recorded a brief account of his duties in Burma and India in this small book and added a few details about his two brothers who were serving elsewhere in different regiments.

At sixteen, Albert's brother George Henry became the first in his family to enlist in the army. Around 1902, he joined the 4th West Yorkshire Volunteer Artillery and soon after in Sheffield transferred to the Royal Field Artillery. Having been posted to the 65th Battery at Woolwich and later to Ballinrobe in the west of Ireland, he completed his required six years of service with the Regular Army and then passed into the Reserve around 1908.

For Albert, his younger brother's experiences must have had a strong influence on him because one week after his nineteenth birthday, he enlisted in Bewsley, Sheffield, in the 3rd (Militia) Battalion, East Yorkshire Regiment.

Following eleven weeks of training at the depot in Beverley, he transferred to the Regular Army and three months after that was posted to B Company of his battalion on September 24th, 1904. For the next fifteen months he would serve at Tournay Barracks, North Camp, Aldershot, with only brief training operations conducted nearby.

'The Snappers' were being hardened for service in the East.[28] On December 29th, 1905, they left the Empress Docks at Southampton on the first leg of their journey to Burma by way of Bombay and Rangoon. Along the way, they lined the rails of their vessel to watch the 1st Battalion of their regiment bound west for

---

[28] On September 11th, 1777, at Brandywine Creek, the old 15th Regiment of Foot formed part of Lord Cornwallis' force charged with the task of turning the right flank of the Continental Army. Short of ball ammunition, the Yorkshiremen heard their colonel roar, "Snap and be damned!" Hastily, they passed their remaining bullets to the best shots while the rest 'snapped' by firing small powder charges to make their musketry look more formidable. Having deceived their foe, the British marched on and captured Philadelphia.

England on a similar vessel. Perhaps they taunted these returning soldiers if only because a competitive spirit between battalions of the same regiment was common throughout the army and occasionally led to unpleasantness the way it sometimes could between brothers.

After a 485-mile trip up the Irrawaddy River for fifty-six days, Albert's battalion reached Mandalay on February 13th, 1906. At an average of thirty-eight miles per day with halts each night because of shifting sandbars, the steamer had carried them past many strange sights—pagodas rising above lush tropical foliage, rice paddies and elephants loaded with teak. The lads looked in wonder at monks in saffron robes and at the endless passage of Chinese and native Burmese, who relied on the river for their very existence. During stops for wood fuel, these men of Yorkshire would stare at everyone passing before them, who in their turn, stared back at these foreigners who now controlled their destiny. Without a trace of rancor, the Burmese called their new rulers *kalas*, which meant 'beasts.'

This river valley was a land of scorpions and centipedes where pythons up to twenty feet long sought prey among the unwary. Swarms of adjutant birds with vile, regurgitant calls descended upon dead animals to rip their bones bare of flesh. Disease in many forms was rampant, and soldiers fresh from England soon had *dhobi*[29] itch from clothing washed in the river by Burmese.

At Mandalay, the 2nd Battalion entrained for its Upper Burma hill station. Rattling east for twenty-five miles along their iron rails, the rickety cars rose from sea level to heights of over 5,000 feet. Puffing to a halt, the engine gave a steamy sigh as soldiers jumped down to line up on the platform. They had reached Maymyo, so named for Lieutenant-Colonel James May, commanding officer of

---

[29] A Hindustani word meaning 'washerman,' British soldiers in the East usually learned enough of this language to make themselves understood by natives.

the 72nd Bengal Native Infantry, which had formed its garrison during wartime in 1887. This would be Albert's home for the next three years.

Here Indian fakirs would mystify the lads by performing tricks which defied reason by often relying on mass hypnosis. Vendors clamored to sell them pineapples and mangoes, eggs and ducks to supplement their army rations. In the wet canteen, beer was sold at a penny a pint, and temptation was everywhere. At the battalion brothel, Japanese girls, deemed cleaner than their Burmese sisters in sin, catered to a steady clientele, while down in Mandalay, native whores danced naked at Lulu's Bar for soldiers just arriving in Burma and time-expired men waiting for passage home.

Whenever heads were heavy the morning after, a corporal or sergeant striding down the ranks was certain to tear a strip from any 'swaddy' who dropped his rifle during inspection. Discipline prevailed, as usual, and it paid off when the 2nd East Yorks won several competitions in field service marching order, skirmishing and physical drill.

Albert was a model soldier. In June 1906 he was granted Class I service pay of sixpence per day, which meant he was a first-class marksman and the holder of at least a third-class education certificate. On the same day, he was given the first of the two good conduct badges he would earn. Well pleased, he had his photograph taken in white tropical kit, complete with topee and swagger stick. On his lower left sleeve rested his inverted good conduct chevron—still too new to have been sewn onto his tunic. Four months later, he extended his service to eight years and received a bounty for doing so.

By 1907, his brother John Willie had joined the 3rd Battalion, The King's Own Yorkshire Light Infantry, and he too quickly extended his enlistment to seven years with the Regular Army and five with the Reserve. A year later, he sent Albert a postcard photo of himself with some of his chums after being appointed a paid lance corporal.

In early 1909, Albert's battalion made ready to leave for India, embarking at Rangoon on February 8th on RIMS *Dufferin* bound for Calcutta where two British Army battalions served at all times. Fetid and filthy, its climate could sap a man's energy quickly, and for soldiers in the ranks it was undoubtedly the most hated military station in all of India. But, fortunately, the East Yorks left the city almost at once by troop train bound upcountry to Fyzabad. This was a military station on the Gogra River about eighty miles east of Lucknow, renowned for its epic fifty-two-day defense against 60,000 natives during the Indian Mutiny in 1857.

Few specifics survive of Albert's days at Fyzabad, but after fifteen months at Kandahar Barracks, his health began to fail him. Most likely suffering from enteric fever (now known as typhoid), which was a common malady then and one that would kill nineteen of his comrades in 1910, he was sent as a sick transfer to Darjeeling where huge tea plantations covered the slopes overlooking Nepal.

Having escaped the murderous heat of the Indian plain where barrack rooms often reached temperatures of up to 120 degrees Fahrenheit in June, he remained there until mid-November 1910 when he was posted back to his battalion. But the fever was still not finished with him, and he was hospitalized once more in the spring of 1911. This time, he would recover at two different hill stations among the many maintained for all British regiments during the hot season.

As one of several convalescents on April 3rd, 1911, he joined six officers and 236 men of his battalion who were on their way to Kailana. Together they would travel by train to Dehra Dun, itself a so-called second-class hill station, which had long been used by Gurkhas. From there, healthy soldiers would march, while two-pony *tongas* big enough to carry four sick men would take the rising, twisting road to the coolness of Kailana or Chakrata at altitudes of up to 8,000 feet.

60

Separated by about one mile, these two military cantonments were topographically similar. Mountainous and virtually devoid of flat land, their surfaces had been hacked at for half a century by British military work parties and civilian laborers. Grudgingly, the rock had yielded small shelves on which bungalows were precariously perched and connected by serpentine roads. The surrounding hillsides, crowned by masses of somber pines, harbored black bears and thousands of monkeys, while overhead, huge eagles with silver bellies soared and screeched and searched for food.

The air, though crisp and clean, was extremely thin, and recent arrivals gasped at the least exertion until their lungs became accustomed to it. At the time when Arthur was helped from the pony cart, good weather could still be counted on for a spell, broken only by occasional thunderstorms. But these were followed by the rain-laden seasonal monsoons of southern Asia and the Indian Ocean, which each year blew hard from the southwest at some point in April and continued until October.

Following this period, the scene by autumn would turn to one of stunning beauty with views of countless mountains, including Nanda Devi, British India's highest peak, rising to 25,600 feet and clearly visible at more than 120 miles to the east. Beyond it by another 200 miles, the dim outline of Mount Everest would sometimes appear through a cloud bank. Here was a climate in which a man could shake a fever quickly.

Soon well enough to take on light work, Albert on June 14th, 1911, was on night guard duty in the bazaar at Kailana to prevent disturbances and watch for furtive native'loosewallahs' bent on breaking into shops which were closed until morning. Meanwhile, loosewallahs of a different breed were breaking into a box by Albert's bed and helping themselves to twenty-nine rupees of his savings.

Returning to his bungalow shortly after ten o'clock, he found the stub of a candle on the floor where hobnail military boot marks were visible. Beds had also been torn apart in search of other men's concealed possessions. Although Albert never collected any hard evidence, he suspected 7118 Private A. Ryan of his own company and Gunner Williams of the 74th Battery, Royal Field Artillery.[30]

Albert was a sensible man, careful with how he spent his money. But he knew that the fine silk sold in many of the native bazaar stalls would make wonderful gifts to send home. Of course, to pay the initial asking price was unthinkable, but at least half an hour was needed to work down the dealers with a spate of Hindustani swear words. In British Army parlance in India, this strategy was known as 'slinging the crab bat,' and any experienced soldier could sufficiently awe a dealer with a wealth of scorn and obscenities into discounting anything in the shop by seventy-five percent. Albert selected several cashmere shawls and mufflers, nine silk handkerchiefs and two blouses worked with silk.

Physically fit once more, he returned to Fyzabad on November 1st and there he would remain until his enlistment was almost up. On February 13th, 1912, Major Sweetman, formerly Albert's company commander and now temporarily in command of the 2nd Battalion, rated him as being of 'exemplary character, sober, reliable and trustworthy.' Six days later, he was on his way to Bombay, and on the 23rd he sailed for England on the transport *Dongola*, arriving at Southampton in the early afternoon of March 14th.

At Fort Brockhurst in Gosport, Albert was given the customary inexpensive suit and ten shillings. He also was granted furlough until May 13th, pending his discharge to the Reserve in June. Still penciling in his experiences, he noted his

---

[30] Theft within the early 20th Century British Army was rare prior to World War One, and it was rarer still for a soldier to steal from a man in his own company.

arrival by rail at Sheaf Station in Sheffield. It was 7:40 p.m. on March 16th, and he had been away from home for six years.

In July, a doctor at the local recruiting office passed him as fit for service with Section A of the 1st Class Army Reserve from which he and others who were in it could be called back to the army immediately, if necessary. He would be paid one shilling per day for the next ten months before beginning his time with Section B.

Albert would have looked for work, and his friends and family members in the steel mills most likely helped him find a job. Having been prudent with his money, he was financially well off from a former private soldier's standpoint. Prior to leaving India, he had transferred his savings account to the Brightside Lane post office where his 1,141 rupees were exchanged for more than £77. But on an April day in 1914, he suddenly withdrew £60 of his funds from that account.

Earlier, he had met a young woman, an unusually beautiful one who lived across the railroad tracks from Brightside Lane and beyond the Grimesthorpe Steel Mills. Edith May Cooper was only eighteen, but on the first of June in 1914, she and Albert were married at All Saints Church in their neighborhood. They would have two months together before their world and the life they looked forward to was shattered by news from Europe.

Recalled to the army at once, Albert joined the 1st Battalion of his regiment at York. He and other men from the Reserve formed sixty percent of the BEF's strength, the rest consisting heavily of untried boys who had seen only limited service with the Regular Army. Collectively, in courage and endurance, they were soon to justify Colonel-General Hellmuth von Moltke's prewar evaluation of Britain's small standing army as 'a perfect thing apart.'

But German senior officers tempered this evaluation with the belief that Britain's standing army was too small to make an appreciable difference in the war. So, instead of denying it access to French and Belgian ports on the Channel, the German navy was assigned to different tasks.

This was one of several significant miscalculations made in the war by the Kaiser's most high-ranking army and navy staff officers. Having spent years of meticulous planning and calculating the responses their enemies might make to their aggressions, they too easily assumed they had overlooked nothing. So they often seemed to be stunned whenever a finalized plan failed to develop along the expected lines. Although they had a talent for adjusting rapidly to such misconceptions, this ongoing characteristic would play a significant role in Germany's ultimate defeat in 1918.

At the start of hostilities, a great spy scare swept through Great Britain, and both the army and police were deluged with reports of suspicious-looking characters who almost always turned out to be innocent citizens walking along a beach or cycling from one village to another. Infrequently, when strangers with foreign accents were apprehended with maps and sketches, their presence only increased this national hysteria, which at the time was seen as a very serious threat to national security.

Once the Defence of the Realm Act passed in Parliament on August 8th, what had long been a largely hands-off state was now granted emergency powers to impose censorship, requisition property and even control labor. The government also authorized police to interrogate suspicious persons and to imprison those who would not answer their questions. In addition, assistance to the enemy became a capital offense.

Sent north from Northern Command Headquarters in York on August 8th to participate in this search for spies, the men of the 1st Battalion, East Yorks, remained in Edinburgh for the next six days on coastal defense duties. While peering toward the Firth of Forth, they watched for invaders who never came. They then moved down to Cambridge where the entire 18th Infantry Brigade of the 6th Division would assemble before marching to Newmarket on September 7th. In command of the division was Major-General J. L. Keir, CB, and the 18th Brigade commander was Brigadier Sir Walter Norris Congreve, VC, CB, MVO.[31]

From Newmarket, a train carried Albert's battalion to Southampton for embarkation to France at 6:15 on the morning of September 8th on board s.s. *Cawdor Castle*, on which Captain Payne-Gallwey of the Grenadier Guards had most likely made the same crossing one month earlier. Disembarking at St. Nazaire, the East Yorks numbered twenty-seven officers and 958 rank and file.

Chantier Rest Camp outside St. Nazaire proved to be less than its name suggested because the battalion left it only a few hours after arriving there. Boarding a train, they reached Coulommiers at 5:00 a.m. on the 12th and were billeted in Doué. The men could hear artillery fire resounding along the River Aisne where the Germans had dug in after their retreat from the Marne and were showing no signs of being driven out.

On September 14th, the East Yorks managed to cross the Aisne to relieve the 2nd Battalion, Royal Sussex Regiment, then in trenches in front of Fort Troyon. A mere toehold, this British occupation of the north bank was being restricted by a stubborn foe who held higher ground in force, which would become commonplace as the war progressed. With their heavy artillery sited to dominate the valley and its approaches from the south, the German lines were practically impenetrable, and dozens of guns blew hails of steel both day and night. Albert's 1st Battalion, shelled on its way up to the front line along the Chemin des Dames, sustained its first casualty when a member of A Company was killed by a steel splinter. Pressing on, the men took up a position with their left on a factory. To their right was the

---

[31] Congreve had won the Victoria Cross during the Boer War in 1899 in a gallant but futile attempt under enormous fire to help recover several British artillery pieces stranded in the open at Colenso.

2nd Battalion, Durham Light Infantry, whose right touched a formation of French Moroccans.

Early on the 20th, the Germans attacked these Colonial 'Turcos,' who in the mêlée that ensued lost all of their officers and briefly fell back in some confusion and fear. Exploiting their gain, the enemy rushed on in an effort to fill a gap in the British line. Observing this breach, the Durhams counterattacked immediately, and Lieutenant-Colonel Benson of Albert's battalion personally took command of his A and B Companies and led them forward to within fifty yards of the German positions. Caught in the open by an enormous crossfire from shrapnel and machine gun fire, the British were forced to retire after almost one hour, but during the attack two East Yorks officers were killed, four were wounded, including Colonel Benson, and one was later listed as missing.[32] Casualties among the other ranks totaled seventy-three killed and wounded.

Having been repulsed on that perilous September day, the battalion was back at its starting point by 4:30 p.m., the men spending the next four days learning to keep their heads down during almost constant shelling of their trenches. On the 24th, they suffered another twenty-one casualties while being relieved by the 2nd Battalion, Sherwood Foresters (Nottingham and Derbyshire Regiment). Outgunned and outranged, British artillery could make only token replies while the infantry held on grimly.

As it became increasingly evident that neither side would be able to achieve any significant gains, operations along the Aisne gave way to stalemate, resulting in the 'Race to the Sea' which accomplished nothing but more deadlock and mounting casualties. Huge battles were fought at La Bassé and fourteen miles north of it

---

[32] Evacuated to St. Nazaire Base Hospital, Benson died on the 27th. In 1884 at the age of twenty-one, he had joined the East Yorks when it was still known as the 15th Regiment. A Boer War veteran, he served in Cape Colony in 1902 as adjutant with the 4th Battalion, East Surrey Regiment.

at Armentières, and the Belgian city of Ypres would forever after be known as 'Wipers' but would also be remembered as the graveyard of Britain's old Regular Army. It is the second of these struggles which concerns us.

Reaching Compiégne by a series of marches, the East Yorks entrained at 8:00 p.m. on October 9th for the 125-mile trip north past Péronne, Arras and Béthune to St. Omer. Having been reinforced twice since their first engagement on the Aisne, the battalion's strength was identical to what it had been when it first landed in France, but now its officers numbered only seventeen instead of twenty-two. This shortage of experienced Regular Army officers would soon grow even worse throughout the army as their casualty rates continued to climb. The East Yorks' acting commanding officer was now Major W. H. Young, who had assumed temporary command as soon as Colonel Benson was mortally wounded.

By October 12th, Albert's battalion was southeast of Hazebrouck on outpost duty, watching for signs of German movement and waiting for the BEF offensive to begin. From the steep grades along the Aisne, the men of Yorkshire had come to flat, monotonous farmland interspersed by heavy woods and hop fields bisected by narrow, slow-moving brooks and drainage ditches. On that same day, the Allied withdrawal from Ostend and Zeebrugge would enable the Germans to establish submarine bases at both of these ports with dire consequences for British and French shipping.[33]

For the East Yorks and other British battalions, visibility in Flanders was limited to the next hedge, which might be sheltering enemy riflemen in force, and efforts to form defensive systems were invariably frustrated by a water table so near to the surface that trenches flooded even while being dug. So what would be

---

[33] October 12th also marked the death of Edith Louisa Cavell, a British nurse serving with a Red Cross hospital in Brussels. She was arrested, tried and shot by the Germans for having harbored about 200 British soldiers and helping them escape to the Dutch frontier. This retaliation and later German excesses against civilians throughout areas its army controlled in Belgium and France caused a worldwide storm of revulsion and rage.

known as the First Battle of Ypres that raged in the closing months of 1914 was often fought behind raised, sandbagged barricades that made perfect targets for artillery fire that blew them and their occupants away with gruesome regularity.

On the morning of October 13th, the entire 18th Brigade left Hazebrouck, forming part of the 6th Division's right wing. Steadily, this force headed east in III Corps' advance in the direction of a line extending from Armentières in the south to Wytschaete in the north.[34]

By early afternoon on the 13th while northeast of La Couronne and Pont Rondin, the 18th Brigade closed with its foe, who retreated slowly behind a rearguard of machine gunners and cavalry, conforming to a German decision to avoid major engagements until its new *Fourth* Army had begun its attack north of Ypres.

But the speed of the British advance upset this timetable by appearing to pose a threat to Lille, which the Germans had held for only two days and could not afford to lose. As a result, enemy resistance had hardened considerably by October 18th when the East Yorks, enfiladed on their left by machine gun fire, struggled forward to a point half a mile west of Capinghem. Their last objective for the day, it remained in German hands as the battalion dug in for the night only four and a half miles west of Lille. One mile to their southwest, the 2nd Durhams had taken Ennetières.

Although what remained of three companies of Albert's battalion were relieved and moved west to billets at La Fleur d'Ecosse, C Company remained in place, guarding what proved to be part of a highly vulnerable salient which invited dangerous flanking attacks. The 18th Brigade line, perilously strung out over three miles, was manned by only a small group of men with huge gaps between them. Their losses had already been enormous and were soon to grow even heavier.

---

[34] Wytschaete, like Ypres, was beyond the ability of anyone who wasn't Flemish to pronounce correctly. So the Tommies called it 'White Sheet' and let it go at that.

On October 20th, three-quarters of the *13th German Army Corps* struck this salient and gave it everything they had in an effort to collapse it. Three times their attacks were repulsed, but in the late afternoon, three entire German battalions rapidly burst through the weakening British line. Ennetières fell at 5:00 p.m. despite a stubborn defense by the 2nd Sherwood Foresters who, assaulted on all sides, fought on until most of them had been killed, wounded or captured. Withdrawing slowly, the survivors were once again surrounded and their numbers depleted further.

C Company of the East Yorkshires, also pushed back, was reinforced by three companies of the 2nd Durhams, who rushed up from Brigade Reserve to plug a hole between the 'Snappers' and the 1st North Staffordshires. In the face of enormous odds, rapid shifting of men performed by elements of three brigades prevented a collapse of the 6th Division's line. Here was further proof of the indomitable courage and discipline of the BEF while face-to-face with a far stronger foe.

By nightfall of the 20th, severe German losses from shellfire took much of the momentum out of their attack. Peering into the gloom at muddy beet fields strewn with enemy dead, the 1st East Yorkshires stood firm as their wounded began the long and painful journey back to the advanced dressing station at La Chapelle d'Armentierès. At midnight, the rest of the battalion retired slowly through Rue du Bois and on for another mile or so to divisional reserve at Bois Grenier.

After stragglers had returned on the 21st, the 2nd Sherwood Foresters' strength was tallied at only two officers and 253 other ranks, this being only twenty-six percent of the battalion's normal manpower complement. East Yorks' casualties had also reached alarming proportions—especially among its officers. Lieutenants Peter Clutterbuck and Mark Robinson Pease, initially listed as missing, were later reported as having been killed. Captain Frank Hind, wounded, was taken prisoner and died nine days later. Lieutenant James Hugh Coles and Second Lieutenant T.

M. Robson were wounded. Casualties among the other ranks totaled forty-nine missing and eighty-one wounded. Three men had been killed.

Elsewhere, the war continued to widen. On October 23rd in far off Mesopotamia (now Iraq), British Indian Army forces already garrisoned in Bahrain moved up the Tigris Valley and captured Basra in what would prove to be the first war fought for control of the Middle East oil fields. Their fate will be outlined in a later chapter.

At sunset on Sunday, October 25th, the East Yorks took over front line positions from the 1st Leicestershires of the 16th Brigade and settled down to three days of intensive shellfire. Before the smoke had cleared after one of these bombardments, figures in field gray—hastily estimated to be in battalion strength—were seen working their way forward. Squinting down their rifle sights, the Yorkshiremen shot these attackers to pieces, although several of the enemy reached within fifty yards of the British position.

Again, German shells fell with precision along the shallow, muddy trench, their bursts sometimes overlapping as they swept back and forth for the remainder of the day. Miraculously, only eight more men were killed, but thirty-nine were wounded, and one man was missing. Fountains of mud hurled up by each shell burst had begun to jam British rifle mechanisms, drastically reducing their rate of fire and enabling the enemy tides to surge even closer. Earlier, men had been seen hammering feverishly on their Enfield bolts with entrenching tools in efforts to eject spent cartridges.

As German pressure continued unabated, enemy riflemen managed to get behind the Durhams, who were forced to abandon their position. Anticipating this turning movement, the East Yorks' Major Young posted one of his platoons in a drainage ditch 100 yards behind the beleaguered Durhams. Upon reaching this thin defensive screen, the German attack melted away in a crash of accurate fire unleashed by determined marksmen. Without hesitation, two platoons from the East Yorks' A Company then rose from the mire, raced toward their foe and recaptured the Durham's position. What these men could not know was that all German attempts to break the British lines at Arras, La Bassée, Dixmude and Ypres had failed in the face of a remarkable defense along the entire line fought by soldiers at the limits of exhaustion.

Less than three months earlier, most of these men and boys had been home in England. Now, from October 26th through the 28th, another 145 officers and men were listed as killed, wounded and missing, and Albert Armitage was identified as one of the missing.

Shelled for the rest of the 28th, the 1st East Yorks' survivors held on grimly, and as daylight began to fail, 100 dead Germans could still be seen within yards of their position. After dark, what was left of the battalion was relieved at last, and the men made their weary way back to billets at L'Armée. These accommodations would have been little else beyond damaged barns and other buildings with leaking roofs and blown out doors and window. Though seriously weakened, the battalion remained unvanquished.

In Sheffield on that same day, the war was becoming an increasing focal point. British wounded continued to arrive at the local base hospital with most of them wearing the same uniforms they had left England in, although they were torn and stained with blood and filth. Several wounds would be showing signs of gas gangrene contracted on farmland fertilized with livestock wastes. Healing would sometimes proceed, but then the wound would get worse, often leading to death.[35]

Starved for current news of the fighting, civilians throughout Great Britain

---

[35] The Royal Army Medical Corps discovered later that fly maggots introduced into these wounds would consume the infected tissue and greatly reduce the number of deaths from this cause.

often relied on these wounded men for information because a strict press censorship prevented newspapers from publishing any specifics on the war.

Secretary of State for War Kitchener's aversion to members of the press was already in full flower during his march up the Nile to Omdurman in 1898. There Winston Churchill had encountered his displeasure by turning up in the dual capacity of a lieutenant attached to the 21st Lancers and war correspondent for the *Morning Post*. By 1914, Kitchener barely tolerated newspapermen, refused them permission to visit the front lines, and threatened those who did with arrest.

Initially, the general public in Britain had to make do with a range of news reports which sang of forbearance and courage and glossed over setbacks but made no mention of high casualty rates caused by front line realities. Numerous books with flowery prose and illustrations published during the early days of fighting showed lots of glory but none of the gore.

Douglas Haig would also develop a distrust of the press, which would further impact on reporters' access to news. Although many of these men were gifted writers, their profession was regarded by many as a haven for drunkards and wastrels, and yet in time they were to gain wide respect among their readers.

By May 1915, reporters could travel to France and Belgium but were not allowed to go wherever they wished within the war zones until 1917. By then, it was finally realized that men like Philip Gibbs, Beach Thomas and Colonel Charles Repington represented real value as propagandists and helped the public to stay focused on the war. But Britons would have next to no accurate conception of the immense losses taken by their army until the 1920s!

In France and Flanders in 1914, the BEF would suffer 90,000 casualties, including 50,000 killed or missing. Albert's sister Clara had lost her husband, Walter Buckley, in August, and her family would grieve for more of its members in the days ahead.

It seems unlikely that Albert would have received any mail from home during the chaos of battle. So he would not have learned that his wife Edith was expecting a child. The baby was born at her parents' home at 603 Carlisle Street East on February 24th, 1915. A boy, she named him after his father. Sixty-eight years later, he would tell me about his mother as we sat in his own son's home in the town of Wales, just east of Sheffield.

Only brief glimpses of her life remain, including a damaged photograph of an especially pretty young woman with an infant on her lap. She is seen staring plaintively at the camera as if still wondering how so much sadness could have happened so soon.

As the war progressed, many women began applying for jobs once held exclusively by men who had gone off to war. They worked as chauffeurs, farm laborers, taxi drivers, bus conductors and in many other ways. At some point after mid-1915, Edith took a job in Sheffield as a munitions worker—at Vickers, Firths or Hadfields. Emancipated by high wages, 825,000 women by 1918 were helping to manufacture a wartime total of more than 200 million filled artillery shells. This work in the 'danger buildings' required them to wear fireproof overalls, and their hair had be drawn into caps because hair pins were not allowed. Wooden clogs were also required because steel nails on the bottom of their shoes could, and sometimes did, cause sparks to ignite gunpowder on the concrete or brick floors. Almost 240 of their number were killed in explosions and other accidents.

In addition to its obvious hazards, this occupation frequently caused jaundice from exposure to chemicals, which turned skin yellow, and women so affected became known as 'canaries.' Having brought little with them beyond enthusiasm and good humor, they were initially resented by their male co-workers but eventually won their esteem through sheer determination, ability and wonderful courage.

In the early 1920s, Edith was married again, this time to a miner, and she went to live with her new husband near the colliery at Petton Park. She died in 1967.

Of Albert's brother, George Henry, little more is known, although it seems almost a certainty that in 1914 he was recalled from the Reserve by the Royal Artillery.

John Willie served as a sergeant in France and Flanders until severely shell-shocked. To hundreds of hopeless neurasthenia cases, sudden noises could set them off. Sweating and sobbing, trembling, hallucinating or stammering, they might lapse into stupors or scream uncontrollably. His mind haunted forever by the horror of pounding artillery barrages, gas attacks and hideous sights on the battlefield, John Willie was eventually committed to Middlewood Hospital in Sheffield where he died in 1972 at the age of eighty-three.

Ernest Armitage, twenty in 1914, went into the army, but no one in his family could recall which regiment he served with. Captured by the Germans, he was ill treated as a prisoner of war and in later years was able to work only occasionally. He lived until 1973.

Little remains of Albert's world. The district of Sheffield he knew as a child was destroyed by German bombs in World War Two, and the church in which he was married was demolished in the early 1980s. His notes from the East remain, of course, as do a few photographs and a curved Burmese sheath knife. A bronze memorial plaque with his name on it and three service medals he never lived to wear survive, as well.

Private Albert Armitage is commemorated on panel four of the Ploegsteert Memorial to the Missing in Belgium at the Yorks Corner Extension. There two stone lions guard the honor of 11,447 British soldiers who, like Albert, disappeared without a trace.

BIBLIOGRAPHY:

Crosthwaite, Sir Charles, *The Pacification of Burma* (Frank Cass and Company Limited, London, 1968)

Edmonds, Brigadier-General J. E. (compiler), *History of the Great War, Military Operations, France and Belgium, 1914* (Macmillan and Co., Limited, London, 1926)

Farrar, Martin J., *News from the Front, War Correspondents on the Western Front 1914-1918* (Sutton Publishing Limited, Stroud, Gloucestershire, 1998)

Jones, Robert J. A., *History of the 15th East Yorkshire Regiment (The Duke of York's Own, 1685 to 1914)* (published by the Regiment in 1958)

Kelly, John, *'The Bad Old Good Old Days,'* (The Star, August 20th, 1983)

Rawson, Geoffrey, *Road to Mandalay* (Harcourt, Brace & World, Inc., New York, 1967)

Sheffield Daily Telegraph, April 6th, 1885; October 28th, 1914

The Sheffield Weekly News, November 28th, 1914.

War Diary of the 2nd Battalion, the Durham Light Infantry, October 27th-31st, 1914 (Public Record Office, Reference WO95/1617)

B. Cory Kilvert Jr.

War Diary of the 1st Battalion, The East Yorkshire Regiment, October 27th-31st, 1914 (Public Record Office, Reference WO95/1618)

Wyrall, Everard, *The East Yorkshire Regiment in the Great War 1914-1918* (Harrison & Sons, Ltd., 1928)

Private Albert Armitage, 2nd Battalion, The East Yorkshire Regiment. This photograph was taken in Burma in June 1906. He is shown in tropical kit with his pith helmet and swagger stick. The good conduct badge he was granted earlier that rests on his sleeve still needed to be sewn on.

This damaged photograph taken in 1914 shows Edith Armitage holding her son
whom Albert would not live to see.

CHAPTER 4

1879-1915

Acting Corporal William Kirkham
1st Battalion, The King's (Liverpool) Regiment

It was August 9th, 1879. Residents of Shrewsbury were reading newspaper accounts of the final moves in the Zulu War. A special despatch telegraphed from Madeira told of the fugitive Zulu king as 'practically a dethroned outcast' as his chiefs gathered to hear Queen Victoria's orders, which would be read to them by Major-General Sir Garnet Wolseley.

Twelve miles to the northwest, more mundane matters were underway in Cockshutt. The 'lengthman' responsible for the roads there cleaned up the village as he did every Saturday, while its residents swept the steps and brickwork of their homes to reclaim them from dust which drifted in clouds from the wheels of passing wagons and carriages.

During that day, a woman named Sarah Kirkham gave birth to a boy whom she and her husband named William. Sarah had been born in Wales, but her husband, Thomas, was a Cockshutt native and an agricultural laborer who in 1874 had found work at nearby Petton Estate, then owned by William Sparling.

A census report for May 1881 shows the Kirkhams were living in School House. Dating from 1856, the New School, as it was called, was a fine brick building and remains one to this day. Presiding over it was Emma Graty, who served as schoolmistress and also postmistress. But because she was a spinster of only twenty-two, she and Thomas Kirkham were both listed as family heads, even though the Kirkhams were actually lodgers.

When I first saw this building, a post office sign hung from it. So I assumed it had no significance to me, but three years later when I discovered I was mistaken, the last piece of a difficult puzzle would almost be ready to be put into place.

By 1884 at the age of five, young Will Kirkham would have begun his schooling. His sister Ann, born in 1881, would remain at home but maybe venture a peek down Shrewsbury Road on school days. There the village children could be seen filing past Saints Simon and Jude Church, its two bells said to sound out 'Tom Townsend, Bill Watkins.' The oldest headstone in the churchyard dated from the 1660s, but Cockshutt had far more ancient origins as part of a manor in Saxon times.

The children, of course, would have more immediate matters in mind, such as raising their caps or curtsying if they encountered the Reverend Wilcox or any members of the local gentry as they hurried along. It would never do to be late because this was an age when education was meted out in a harsh environment in which girls as well as boys were caned for the slightest transgressions.

Attendance at school had been mandated by law in 1870, but it often varied according to the need for labor because this was and still remains a farm community. So even at the age of five, Will Kirkham would have had chores to perform, such as pulling weeds from cobblestone yards and 'sticking' after high winds to collect kindling for the winter coal fires at home.

At best, Will's days as a student would almost certainly have ended by the time he was thirteen, an age when the children of working men became laborers themselves to help support their families and toiled for long hours at hard and often menial tasks.

Mrs. Peggy Husbands, a lifelong resident of the village and author of a charming history of it between 1910 and 1980, had Kirkham family connections. However, she could tell me nothing about the man whose life I was tracing when we met during a brief visit I made to her home. Some months later, she asked the oldest native person still living there if she had heard of William Kirkham, but she had not.

In 1892, masons, bricklayers and carpenters assembled in nearby Petton to build a mansion on Sparling's 200-acre estate, which had passed to his daughter, Mrs. Ellis Brooke Cunliffe. Three years later, Thomas Kirkham is shown in Kelly's Directory as a gardener on this estate, and by 1909, he is listed again as parish clerk and electrical engineer to Captain Cunliffe, who had served with the 6th Dragoon Guards at the siege of Sebastopol in the Crimean War. Thomas Kirkham was also known to have been living with his family in Church House in Petton from 1900 and probably earlier, and he would remain there until his death at the age of seventy-one.

Nothing is remembered about his son's days in Petton, but near to the village stands a simple brownstone memorial close to a small 1727 church. This shows the names of two members of the parish who gave their lives in the Great War. One of them reads:

Corpl. William Kirkham

1st King's Liverpool Reg.

Richebourg

May 16th, 1915

Oddly, I have never seen that memorial and only learned of its existence from a total stranger in Warrington, Cheshire, who was to play a major role in my search for facts concerning this soldier's life.

Earlier, I had found William Kirkham's name among the list of casualties in the World War One history of the King's (Liverpool) Regiment. This source gave what would prove to be the correct date of his death—May 18th, 1915. I also discovered in *Soldiers Died in the Great War* that Kirkham had enlisted in Warrington, then part of Lancashire.

Reasoning that he might have lived there and that letter carriers might still deliver mail to persons of that surname, I sent a letter to Warrington's postmaster, outlining what little I knew about Kirkham and asking for assistance. Although I never received an answer, someone else was about to act on my request.

On a winter evening, a technical illustrator sat down in his home in Warrington and wrote me a few lines, enclosing a newspaper clipping of my letter. He stated, 'On Warrington war memorial I looked to see if his name was recorded. Sad to say, it was not there. . . I checked through the old local papers for the period May to July, 1915, for any mention, without success.' The letter was signed 'R. Thorniley.'

One month after I had responded to this letter, another one arrived. Obviously, Mr. Thorniley had been thinking in the interim, and this time the message was more positive. 'I have good news for you,' he wrote. 'Corporal William Kirkham has been found.' He explained that he had used my few facts on Kirkham to reconstruct the probable thinking of a man in or near Shrewsbury searching for a job seventy years earlier.

'Because most people didn't have cars and did their traveling by rail and with Shrewsbury being on the main line of two railways to the north, he may have relocated to a town on those routes.'

The average correspondent would have left matters there and wished me luck. Not Roy Thorniley! Soon after, while returning home from a business trip, he encountered a two-hour wait between trains at Crewe and decided to 'have a look' in Crewe Library on my behalf. There he found the World War One *Roll of Honour for the London and Northwestern Railway Employees 1914-18*. In that volume was the name W. Kirkham of Warrington who had worked at the Earlestown station as a laborer.

This seemed like a wonderful find, but was this the W. Kirkham I was seeking? Several days later, Roy searched through the old Earlestown newspapers and struck gold in the *Newton and Earlestown Guardian* for Friday, July 9th, 1915.

'Killed at the front,' read the small headline. 'News has been received that Corpl. W. Kirkham, King's Liverpool Regiment, brother to Mrs. Tomlinson, has died of wounds received at Richebourg on May 16th. He was employed at the Viaduct [this being the name of the local railway wagon works] before the war and was a Reservist, joining his regiment and proceeding to the front at once on the outbreak of hostilities.'

I reasoned that Mrs. Tomlinson was Kirkham's younger sister, Ann, who might have had other relatives living in Earlestown then and, possibly, descendants living there now. And this is where I began to be led astray by assuming something was true which turned out to be otherwise.

Equally unaware of this blind trail, Roy sent me extracts from the Newton-le-Willows and Earlestown Electors Lists for 1914, which included the names and addresses of three Tomlinsons.

I sent letters to 'Resident' at each of these addresses, outlining the nature of my search and asking for whatever information might still be known about those who had occupied these premises sixty-nine years earlier.

To guard against the possibility that these homes no longer existed, I typed on each envelope: 'Postmaster; if undeliverable, please open and read.' At the end of each letter, I asked him to forward it to his local radio station. These procedures had worked well for me in finding other World War One soldiers' families whose medals I had, but this time I received no answers.

In the meantime, Roy had not been idle. One month after my first meeting with him in his home, he sent me the names of two Tomlinsons living in Newton, which he had found in a current telephone directory. I wrote to both of them, and within a month I received an answer from one B. Tomlinson.

'After making inquiries with an elder cousin in Powys, Wales,' he wrote, 'a strong possibility exists that we are in fact related to Mrs. Ann Kirkham Tomlinson.'

Mr. Tomlinson went on to say he would try to give me more positive information later and added that one of the Tomlinsons I had written to earlier was his mother. Mrs. Tomlinson was living at 62 King Street, one of the three addresses to which I had sent my unanswered letters addressed to 'Resident'.

What I didn't realize at the time was that I was now in touch with the grand nephew of William Kirkham's sister. But it would be another six months before I would learn that her first name had not been spelled as I had assumed.

When my researcher Pat Wolfston sent me a list of Ann (and Anne) Kirkhams throughout the United Kingdom who had been married between March 1897 and June 1916, there were sixty-three names on it. Where to begin? It seemed more than likely that one of the women on that list was William Kirkham's sister. But which one?

Soon after, Pat found Kirkham's birth certificate, which stated his mother's maiden name had been Hall and that she had been married in the village of Stockett in 1861 to a man named Daniel Edwards. Stockett no longer exists but was once situated to the north of Cross Mere and is known to have been in existence from the late 12th century. One of the last mentions of it appears in an 1885 marriage register for Cockshutt which shows that Price Tomlinson, twenty-five, a carpenter of Preston Gubbals, wed Sarah Edwards, a spinster of Stockett, also twenty-five, the daughter of Daniel Edwards, gardener. So here was Corporal Kirkham's stepsister, a woman nineteen years his senior.

Roy Thorniley took up the chase from where he had found the three Tomlinsons named in the Electors Lists for 1914. In Newton Library, he located published accounts of Sarah Edwards Tomlinson's death in 1935 and also her obituary, which stated that 'Mother, Tom and Anne' (sic) were among those to send floral tributes to her funeral.

Somehow, somewhere, I had to find a member of the Kirkham family who could identify 'Tom and Anne'. In the meantime, I began to research William Kirkham's experiences in World War One based on his obituary, which Roy had found in an Oswestry newspaper, the *Border Counties Advertiser* for July 21st, 1915:

'. . . Corporal Kirkham went out with the Expeditionary Force at the beginning of the war, was in the retreat from Mons and fought in many actions. He was only absent from the front for a very short time, owing to sickness. He had several hairbreadth escapes. Corporal Kirkham was wounded on May 16th and died on May 18th . . .'

This obituary proved he was an 'old sweat' who had completed a minimum of seven years' service with the Regular Army before passing into the Reserve at some point prior to the start of the war in 1914. He had also been an 'Old Contemptible,' a member of that élite among Britain's comparatively small army of professionals who had served within range of German guns in France and Belgium between

August 5th and the stroke of midnight on November 22nd, 1914.[36] As such, he was entitled to the bronze bar bearing those dates on the ribbon of his 1914 Star, which he never lived to wear.

It was Kaiser Wilhelm II who caused the British Expeditionary Force in 1914 to embrace an intended insult when he sent a pompous order to his *First Army* commander, General Alexander von Kluck. That order read: 'It is my Royal and Imperial Command that you concentrate your energy for the immediate present upon one single purpose, and that is to address all your skill and all the valor of my soldiers to exterminate the treacherous English and walk over General French's contemptible little Army.'[37]

This was an especially bellicose message, considering its author was King George V's first cousin, but with British soldiers' famous wry response to such challenges, they accepted this affront as a badge of honor and wore it with pride for the rest of their days. The King's (Liverpool) Regiment had long before been called by many names. Raised in 1685 as Princess Anne of Denmark's Regiment of Foot, it was renamed The Queen's Regiment in 1702 when Princess Anne became Queen of England. Two different names followed, and in 1881 it was given the name it took into World War One. Its officers and men had long been known as 'The Leather Hats.'

The regiment's 1st Battalion left Southampton on August 12th with twenty-seven officers and 991 other ranks.[38] Having landed at Le Havre, their first serious confrontation with the enemy took place on the afternoon of September 1st, shortly after they had marched about two miles beyond Villers-Cottérêts. They and the rest

---

[36] This latter date marked the end of major German penetrations of British positions around Ypres. One week later, the front line was stabilized in a way that would not be significantly altered until the final German and Allied offensives in 1918.

[37] In recent years, a few historians have come to believe this statement may have been fabricated at the War Office by Sir Frederick Maurice and publicized as having been made by the Kaiser.

[38] Between October 14th, 1914, and February 19th, 1919, eleven of these officers were killed in action or died of wounds.

of the 6th Brigade were called back there suddenly to cover a fighting withdrawal by the 4th (Guards) Brigade through the Forêt Dominiale de Retz, the same thick stand of trees in which Captain Payne-Gallwey of the Grenadier Guards had vanished.

During this action, they also saved the 70th Battery, Royal Field Artillery, from being cut off by putting down a storm of accurate rapid fire. This cost them about seventy casualties from German shellfire that replied to them, but the gunners galloped their teams onto the field near the edge of the wood and into a hurricane of steel. Quickly and expertly, they hooked in their 18-pounders and dashed off to safety to the echo of ringing cheers which rippled down the British line from all those who could see them. The gunners had left only one ammunition limber on the ground, which had been destroyed by a German shell burst.

According to Lieutenant W. A. T. Synge of the 1st King's, the battalion '. . . had [also] halted at the edge of the wood facing Pisseleux, and the Guards began coming through us.[39]

'At this moment, a terrific shrapnel fire began: the shells were bursting over the railway line . . . We got orders to. . . hold on until the guns could get away. . . Just as my platoon arrived at the railway, we appeared to get hung up in front.

'For about twenty minutes we lay behind a small bank about two feet high under a perfect hailstorm of bullets. . . After some time, we managed to re-form on the road. . . and having been told that we had accomplished our object—namely to cover the withdrawal of the guns—we proceeded on our march through Boursonne to Thury en Valois where we arrived about 10 p.m. and bivouacked for the night.'

As a Reservist only recently recalled to the Colours, Kirkham would most likely have found his new army boots a torture to his feet as they carried him along

---

[39] This information on the retreat and what followed it was serialized anonymously in *Blackwood's Magazine* in 1915. Its author later proved to be Lieutenant Synge,

the irregularly surfaced pavé roads during the more than 200-mile stressful retreat from Mons. All those who survived that epic retirement remembered it as a time of enormous strain in which exhaustion blended events into a macabre, dreamlike fantasy, just as it had for Private Small of the 1st Cornwalls and Captain Payne-Gallwey of the Grenadiers.

At 3:45 on the morning of September 2nd, the battalion began a twenty-four-mile march, and by noon, the heat was intense. The strong shouldered two rifles to help their mates, while the walking wounded hobbled on as best they could past villages and farms along the seemingly endless roads. Not until 8 p.m. did the column reach Trilbardou where the bone-tired men slept at a farm, only to resume the march at 2:45 the next morning, passing through Meaux, Trilport and Marceaux on 'another intensely hot day,' according to Synge.

By September 5th, the battalion had finally ended its withdrawal, which Captain P. Hudson estimated had required marching for 236 miles in fifteen days. Now the 1st King's would begin to move forward in the BEF's advance to the heights above the Aisne, which Albert Armitage's battalion had already reached on the same day.

Synge described the devastating effect of a large caliber German howitzer's shells, which fell almost vertically before exploding. The men dismissed its perils by ridiculing it as 'Silent Susan' and at month's end were referring to a pom-pom which shelled them rapidly as 'Little Demon.'

On that same day, Captain Ralph Tanner was badly wounded while advancing with his men through a heavily wooded area. Two stretcher-bearers who managed to reach him were killed by a shell burst which wounded Tanner again, but more of his men ran forward at once and carried him back for four miles to a dressing station where he was treated by Dr. Arthur Martin-Leake, RAMC, VC, whom he had known at Westminster School.[40] Sadly, Tanner died at No. 4 Hospital in Versailles on September 23rd.

While above the Aisne in a densely wooded area, Captain John Batten of the King's distinguished himself by steadying his men so successfully during a savage firefight that his colonel claimed 'he saved the whole line on 20 September just by his grit. Nothing could move him from the line he had to take up in that awful wood. . . He was killed outright crossing a small gap in a hedge by some men hidden in a house about 500 yards away.'

The 1st King's remained along the Aisne until October 15th when French troops took over their positions, and that night the battalion entrained at Fismes with the rest of the regiment. Its destination was Ypres where the men remained totally unaware that huge German forces lay in front of them on a collision course.

Like Verdun for the French, Ypres would become a martyred city with almost religious significance to the British. Every inch of it was under observation by German artillery spotters on the surrounding heights, and to walk in it during daylight was too often a ticket to Eternity. The enemy had soon recognized Ypres as the gateway to the only worthwhile route that could be taken to capture the Channel harbors from which their submarines could challenge the Royal Navy's blockade of German ports. Hundreds of thousands of lives on both sides would be spent savagely fighting over this medieval city with its magnificent Cloth Hall, which was begun in 1260 and completed forty-four years later, but the Allies would hold it for the entire war.

It was in this vicinity in 1914 that the war resumed for Kirkham's battalion, and young Lieutenant Synge had several close calls from snipers and shelling.

---

[40] Martin-Leake had won a Victoria Cross in the Boer War as a surgeon captain with the South African Constabulary. He would earn another one for deeds performed during October and November, 1914, and would become one of only two soldiers so honored since the inception of this award in 1856, the other recipient also being an army doctor.

He wrote that, while sleeping in the cellar of a destroyed farmhouse, 'there was a terrific bang. . . We found that a shell had burst about three yards away. Three men who had been boiling some tea inside had been blown clean over the wall. . . Two were dead and the other. . . died in a few minutes.' Losses like these would soon become commonplace, not only in Flanders but later when the battalion returned to France and the horrors that awaited them at Festubert.

In Petton, the Kirkhams, like all other parents of soldiers in battle, would have been concerned about their son. Casualty lists of local soldiers were being posted regularly in cities and towns, and families throughout the land were just beginning to dread the sight of telegraph boys careering down the streets on red bicycles in hundreds of communities, bearing messages to those who, tightlipped, received them in silence.

Sarah Kirkham was about seventy-three at this time, and I wondered how much longer she had lived. Roy Thorniley managed to find out, but the answer simply posed new questions. Although Sarah died at the age of ninety-six on January 31st, 1937, her place of death was given as Lincoln, which on a straight line is about 100 miles northeast of Petton. I wondered: What would have caused her to move to Lincoln? To live with a relative, most likely, but Roy and I had no evidence to substantiate that belief.

While in the Midlands one day, Roy stopped in at Lincoln Library where he was shown the newspapers from 1937. They offered no clues, but the voters' lists for the years 1933 through 1937 revealed that Sarah Kirkham had been living at King's Arms Yard since 1934. Also in residence were Florence and James Williams, both of whom seemed irrelevant to our search, and it would be another year before Roy and I would learn otherwise.

I turned again to events in France. On November 14th, Field Marshal Earl Roberts, VC, had died at the age of eighty-two at British Army Headquarters while on a visit to Indian troops then in France and Flanders. He had spent almost his entire life in the British Indian Army and was perhaps best known for his epic twenty-two-day forced march from Kabul to Kandahar during the Second Afghan War in 1880. A national icon, he had long been revered by the British public as 'Our Bobs.'

By the end of 1914, 90,000 officers and men of the British Expeditionary Force in France and Flanders had been listed as killed, missing and wounded—swept away at Mons, the stubborn retreat to the Marne, the advance to the Aisne and in the fury of First Ypres. Like all other British battalions, the 1st King's had been reinforced, but even so, thirty-three officers and 814 other ranks had been listed as casualties by the latter date on that narrow bronze bar on the 1914 Star.

The remaining men of the 1st Battalion could be proud of themselves, and they were. On November 11th, with little to sustain them beyond biscuits and rum, they and the men of other battalions in the Gheluvelt salient had helped bar the way to Ypres, less than five miles to their west. Facing them was the finest force their enemy could hurl at them, an entire division of the Prussian Guard, selected for the sole purpose of destroying them.

Rushing forward, this élite enemy formation almost reached the Royal Field Artillery's gun line but was systematically decimated by a blizzard of shrapnel fired over open sights. Soaked to the skin, some of the King's men would have been suffering from trench foot, and by the end of that winter, 20,000 British soldiers would be invalided because of it.

Late that night of the 11th along the southern fringes of Polygon Wood, the 1st King's remained exactly where they had stood at dawn. In a turnip field not more than seventy-five yards ahead of them lay a serpentine wall of dead and wounded from the shattered German *3rd Foot Guard Regiment*. Exhausted, shivering and caked with mud when relieved in the rain and cold, the battalion's survivors were still facing front, unvanquished. They had been in battle for three straight weeks.

Ypres would become not only a symbol of Britain's stubbornness in denying this ancient city to the Germans. It would also be remembered as a shrine to the many thousands of her men and boys who had fought so gallantly to hold it at such high cost to themselves. Their misery in Flanders was intensified when King Albert of the Belgians ordered the flooding of his country from the sluice gates at Nieuport south to Dixmude even though he knew the salt water was certain to poison farmland soil for a long time. By spreading for about fifteen miles above Ypres, this vast swamp's main benefits were to reduce the Allied front line by twenty miles while denying this saturated land to the Germans.

Elsewhere on the Western Front, General Sir Douglas Haig's offensive at Neuve Chapelle on March 10th, 1915, cost the BEF 13,000 casualties within just three days in return for occupying only 1,000 yards of putrid soil extending over a width of the same distance. The Germans lost no time in responding to this modest advance by launching the Second Battle of Ypres on April 22nd and introducing to the Western Front a new tool of terror. This would have a serious effect on two members of the author's family whose experiences highlight the devastation it could cause to those with no protection from it.

On the morning of that warm and clear April day in Canadian Expeditionary Force (CEF) trenches slightly northeast of the Flemish town of St. Julien, members of four battalions reported seeing hundreds of pipes being pushed through enemy parapets. Not until 5 p.m. would their purpose be revealed when a high, pale greenish-yellow fog began to drift south to engulf a division of French Territorials and Algerians. This fog was asphyxiating chlorine gas, and the Germans had released it earlier in Poland with moderate success even though its use had been discouraged but not banned by Hague Conventions in 1899 and again in 1907. The effects of this caustic gas interfered with the bolt action on many rifles, especially the Canadians' Ross, which had a disturbing habit of often dropping its bayonet after being fired a few times. But far worse, gas prevented lungs from absorbing oxygen, causing many seriously affected men to drown in their own sputum.

Retching, gasping and panicking, these French Colonials fled south, but none of the four Canadian battalions or the British 28th Division to their southeast were seriously affected and held onto their positions. However, all present soon realized that hordes of Germans were pouring through a wide gap in the line vacated by the Algerian French 'Turcos' and were heading for St. Julien less than two miles to the south. If this enemy mass could not be stopped, the Allied front line would be separated from its supplies and allow the Germans to continue south, capture Ypres and then head for the Channel ports to cut off the British from their lifeline.

Essentially, the Canadians were still Saturday night soldiers with next to no experience in modern warfare, although some of them were Boer War veterans. So their remarkable stand during the next few terrifying days was one of the war's great achievements, and the story of the 15th Battalion (48th Highlanders of Canada) is typical of their stubborn defense. The regimental history notes, 'Here the Battalion, still green, but gallantly willing, was blooded. Here, with the rest of those great 1st Canadian Contingent battalions, the 48th Highlanders wrote a mighty story into the annals of British arms. Here, at St. Julien. . . the Regiment found its soul. . . Three times they were to spend periods before her [Ypres] and always she was unutterably vicious.'

On April 24th during another gas release, heavy enemy artillery fire also landed squarely on the 48th Highlanders, and this time Captain (later Lieutenant-Colonel, OBE, VD) Robert Young Cory, second in command of No. 2 Company, was gassed and wounded. Losses in his battalion alone came to seventeen officers and 674 men from the 912 effectives prior to the gas attack. Two days earlier, their numbers had stood at 1,034 rank and file.

Two nights later, Billy Congreve, a British staff officer and the son of General Sir Walter Congreve, VC, walked up at night from Ypres toward the 15th Battalion's trenches northeast of St. Jean. With him went his Canadian friend from the staff, Brevet Major George Cory, who was anxious to discover what had happened to his brother. Along the way, they both inhaled some of the gas, which by then was dissipating. When they found the 15th Battalion's acting commanding officer, he could tell them little about Bob's fate.

Congreve noted in his diary entry for that day, 'From all accounts, he [Bob Cory] made a gallant fight, for after the rest of the [15th] Battalion had retired, he was heard to be going on fighting with his machine gun and the remnants of his company. So that was all they knew about him, and he may be dead or wounded, and anyhow, a prisoner.'[41]

Having been wounded, gassed and captured, Cory was incarcerated in five different officers' prison camps in Germany, during which time he was promoted to major for his part in the battle at St. Julien. Suffering from weakness and bleeding gums seriously affected by gas, he and his fellow Canadians were often denied sufficient food, blankets and also warm clothing beyond what got through from their families. Eventually paroled to Holland in April 1918 with other Canadian officers, he and his friends occasionally amused themselves by throwing their German counterparts into the canals at night. And regardless of his physical infirmities, this tough old soldier lived to the age of eighty-five.[42]

---

[41] Major William Congreve, DSO, MC, of the Rifle Brigade, who held Bob Cory in high esteem, was killed on the Somme on July 20th, 1916. Like his father in an earlier war, he was awarded a Victoria Cross, this being the second of only two father and son winners in the history of this decoration since its inception in 1856.

[42] Late in his life, Bob Cory told the author that following his capture, the Germans had the effrontery to try him as a war criminal for having shot with his revolver several 'Turcos', who were coming through his lines and spreading panic. He was exonerated for lack of evidence.

Also on that dreadful day on April 24th, another cousin, Private (later Captain) Thomas Dennie Harris, 8th Battalion, CEF, was badly affected by gas at St. Julien while he and his mates were to the immediate left of Cory's battalion. Declared medically unfit, he was sent back to Canada but somehow arranged to return to England for a non-combat assignment to train troops at Shorncliffe Camp in England. Two days later, his brother in the same battalion, Lieutenant (later Major) Guy Mewburn Harris, was wounded by shrapnel in the right shoulder and right leg. He was also too badly injured to serve in combat again, although he would eventually be able to lead a normal life. Readers will learn in a later chapter that the Germans were still not through with the Harris family.

Not until May 3rd would the Canadian public learn that these gas and artillery attacks had caused at least 6,000 casualties, including more than 2,500 who had been listed as missing.

Following these events came major Allied setbacks at Vimy Ridge, Aubers Ridge and elsewhere. At Loos, a huge casualty rate had been the price for advancing across 8,000 yards of poisoned ground. This costly battle and too many others to follow it would prove the fallacy that heavily laden men moving slowly under tremendous fire could be expected to prevail over the fearsome weapons of industrialized nations.

General Erich Ludendorff was correct in his assumption that members of the British High Command were concentrating on all of their strategic goals without giving enough serious thought to realistic tactics. But this stubborn 19th century British military mindset would continue largely unchanged for another three years.

On April 25th, five officers and sixty-three men under Lieutenant A. D. Jones arrived at Béthune in France as a reinforcement for the 1st Kings, who were in billets in Rue d'Aire. A private diary kept by their commanding officer shows that

9070 Corporal William Kirkham was one of those men. Earlier in the month, he had been hospitalized for fever—enteric, most likely—caused by contaminated water which gathered in shell holes and endangered all those who might drink it whenever a pure water source was unavailable.

Punctually at 11 a.m. on that same day in Béthune, red-tabbed staff officers gathered in far more comfortable surroundings to attend a First Army conference called to plan a new offensive at Festubert.[43] This offensive should never have been fought, but one of its purposes was to take pressure off an already faltering Russia by drawing some of Germany's might away to the Western Front.

Even at this early stage of the conflict, neither British nor French military minds with an insight into Russia expected much from the Czar's forces. How could they think otherwise? In 1902, Czar Nicholas II had been led to believe that his empire could be considerably expanded through a quick and easy war against Japan in Korea, but this dream turned into a nightmare in 1904 soon after his first cousin, Kaiser Wilhelm, talked him into provoking the Japanese.

Wasting no time, ten undersized Japanese destroyers carrying torpedoes surprised and sank many unsuspecting ships of Russia's Far East Fleet at Port Arthur in Manchuria. This was followed in 1905 by destruction of the Czar's Baltic Fleet, which had sailed around the world to its doom at the Tsushima Strait. Numerous savage and costly land battles were also fought, but Japan proved to be the ultimate victor. For Russia, turmoil was waiting in the wings.

Consisting heavily of serfs whom the St. Petersburg élite had long referred to as 'the Dark People,' Russia's army would achieve some early successes in

---

[43] April 25th would also be marked by another hopelessly misconceived offensive launched with the landing of British and French troops on Turkey's Gallipoli peninsula. With nothing to show for it except about 252,000 British, Australian, New Zealand and French dead and wounded, the High Command ordered an evacuation, which lasted from December 10th, 1915, to January 9th, 1916. Ironically and mercifully, masterful planning for a change enabled it to be completed with the loss of only one man.

1914 but eventually would be badly beaten by the Germans at Tannenburg and the Masurian Lakes. Underfed and treated like cattle, its ranks would be decimated by deaths and wounds in which medical aid ranged from rudimentary to nonexistent.

Resentment over harsh treatment in the army and the rising rate of starvation at home caused malcontent to explode into revolution throughout Russia. This led to the abdication of Czar Nicholas on March 15th, 1917, a violent overthrow of the Romanov regime, and the murder of the Czar and his entire family in July 1918. By war's end, Russian casualty rates had reached 9,500,000 out of a total of 12,000,000 men mobilized.

On May 13th, two days before the British offensive was scheduled to begin at Festubert, *The Times* of London revealed a serious shortage of artillery shells, but this did nothing to deter the planners who, by then, had finalized an assault designed to draw attention away from a much grander scheme to be launched by the French in Artois. As a result, shells for British 18-pounder guns had to be rationed to only ten rounds per day—a disastrous reduction for trained gunners who could fire ten rounds per *minute*.

Given this disability, the High Command's concept was too ambitious and failed to factor in the enemy's customary capacity for resistance. Throughout the preliminary moves at Aubers Ridge on May 9th, the 1st Kings remained in Corps reserve at Le Touret and later among the blackened beams and shattered bricks of what had once been Richebourg St. Vaast. With little to do in this latter place, the men watched the lugubrious procession of stretcher-bearers carrying the killed away for burial, a portent of things to come for themselves.

Festubert would be the second phase of the offensive and the British Army's first large-scale night attack of the war, which the British had estimated would be a great tactical success. In preparation for it, the Royal Artillery bombarded German strong points and their trenches on May 15th, and kept up their fire for the whole day as artillery shell stocks continued to plummet. German guns retaliated by saturating the British first and second lines with high explosive bursts, which reached a crescendo of violence at 4:30 p.m.

Half an hour before the attack was to begin, troops of the first wave crept unnoticed over their parapets, crawled through their own wire and hugged the earth, waiting. At 11:30 p.m., the men of the 5th and 6th Brigades rose silently like specters and advanced with fixed bayonets over open ground toward the enemy front line about 300 yards away.

For almost half that distance, not a shot was fired, but then a torrent of flame and steel engulfed them. The survivors dashed through the broken German wire and jumped into short sections of damaged trenches, in one of which the enemy had been caught during a relief of one unit by another. While some of the attackers threw hand grenades to prevent losing the space they had just occupied, others called for reinforcements and tried to consolidate their position.

The lads in the 6th Brigade were still in comparative safety at this time, waiting to be called up as needed. But heavy German shelling had fallen on them, wounding several men. As the fighting intensified, C and D Companies of the 1st King's were ordered forward on May 16th to support the first wave, which was now being held up by stubborn resistance. At 3:30 a.m., B Company also tried to cross no man's land by platoons, the first of which was shot to pieces by enfilading machine gun fire from the right flank. At once, a second platoon attempted the dangerous crossing before it could be stopped by Lieutenant-Colonel C. J. Steavenson, the 1st King's commanding officer, who could see the hopelessness of the situation.

It was during this time that an extraordinary scene was about to unfold on a battlefield already littered with the crumpled shapes of British dead and resounding with the cries of wounded men. As dawn began to increase visibility, German snipers began to pick off anyone who moved amidst the wreckage on no man's land.

The survivors of B Company's advance had begun to slip back to the British lines. One of these men, Lance Corporal Joseph Harcourt Tombs, came upon a badly wounded man and slowly helped him to safety, their journey through the battlefield wreckage taking almost one hour to complete under heavy fire. What followed is worth recounting in greater detail.[44]

Tombs had only been in France with the 1st King's since March 25th, having transferred from the 3rd Battalion, which he had joined in 1911. A 31-year-old resident of Warrington, he had already seen a lifetime of adventure—in Australia, on the Panama Canal, in Cuba and the United States.[45] A man of wide experience, he was about to show himself as a soldier of immense courage.

Leaving the relative safety of a trench, he jumped onto the parapet, stood erect and made a dash to a second wounded man whom he brought in. He then rescued a third, whom he had to support while both men crawled on hands and knees, briefly taking cover in a shell hole. Finally a fourth crossing was made, this time to a man so badly injured that Tombs had to use two rifle slings to bring him in. Connecting these around his neck and under his comrade's arms, he slowly edged them along the muddy ground while both men lay flat on their backs until they reached their own lines. Each journey had been of 100 yards or more under increasingly severe enemy rifle, machine gun and artillery fire. Tombs was awarded the Victoria Cross,

---

[44] This account is adapted from an article published in the Warrington *Examiner* for July 31st, 1915, which quotes Tombs during a discussion of his exploit. It is interesting because it differs somewhat from eyewitness versions in other published sources, which have come to be accepted as fact by most military historians.

[45] At the Imperial War Museum, a folder on Great War VC winners indicates that Tombs was born in Australia, but this seems to be incorrect because no record of his birth is on file in Canberra. He claimed to have been born in England but was curiously reluctant to identify his place of birth.

and it is fair to suggest that any one of these four rescues would have qualified him for this award,

By 3 p.m. on the day of this remarkable exploit, leading elements of the 6th Brigade were still clinging to sections of German trenches. Substantially reduced in numbers, they were now cut off from their supports and were sending back urgent calls for ammunition. Lieutenant William Murray Hutchison promptly led a carrying party from the 1st King's A Company across 300 yards of fire-swept ground on which one-third of his men fell. The rest, racing on and then crawling along as best they could, arrived with each man carrying four bandoliers of bullets. The carnage continued.

It became even worse when the enemy began to drop a number of new 200-pound explosive devices into the British trenches. Each of these cigar-shaped projectiles was known as a *minenwerfer* and could be seen slowly turning end over end in the air, giving the King's men time to seek shelter before hearing a huge explosion. Retaliation was possible with a new trench mortar battery, but this countermeasure would soon become unpopular with all British troops because of the retaliatory fire it always attracted.

At 6 p.m. on the 16th, the 1st King's and 2nd South Staffordshires were ordered to relieve elements of three other battalions in the old German lines. By 11:30 on that night, the King's men held 150 yards of what had been the enemy second line. It was raining, and the trenches were thick with mud. Eventually, water and food arrived, but Germans still clung to a salient on the right flank, keeping up a murderous fire as another day died.

At some point during the 16th, William Kirkham's luck ran out. Badly wounded, he was evacuated to No. 1 Casualty Clearing Station, which had been set up four months earlier in the village of Chocques, about eight miles west of the Festubert battlefield. There was little anyone could do for him there although he lingered on briefly. On the 18th he died, and ten days later, his father was dead.

The 1st King's losses at Festubert between May 15th and 20th totaled fourteen officers and 639 other ranks killed, wounded and missing. These figures would never be exceeded in any of the battalion's subsequent battles up to the Armistice in 1918. One measure of the chaos at Festubert may be seen by the fact that the war diaries of both the 1st King's and the 6th Brigade were lost and never seen again, which suggests that the bodies of the officers responsible for keeping these records were not found. All that the High Command could claim from this catastrophe was the capture of ten machine guns plus a few thousand yards of devastated ground. However, the British attack had prevented the Germans from transferring troops to the left where a French assault at Arras had succeeded.

By the end of 1915, William Kirkham would be one of 285,000 British casualties in that year, including 92,000 killed and missing in a war that would continue with unabated ferocity. However, Germany had actually experienced a higher casualty rate than the British. The Kaiser's army had suffered losses of 612,000 men, and the British would list over 270,000 of their own. But in that year alone, French killed and wounded had reached a total of 1,292,000 soldiers.

During a visit I made to Roy Thorniley's home in Warrington, he knew I was on my way to Lincoln and suggested I visit the registrar's office on the chance I might discover something about Florence Williams living at King's Arms Yard with James Williams in 1934. I had always assumed they had no bearing on my research and were therefore irrelevant.

How wrong I was!

Earlier, I had tried to determine the fate of Kirkham's sister Anne but had made no progress whatever. But later in that year, Roy Thorniley began searching for Kirkham wills at Somerset House in London, and it was there that he finally found the last piece for our puzzle. In a volume for 1948 appeared an unexpected and electrifying entry: 'Kirkham, Thomas, of King's Arms Yard, Lincoln. . . Probate granted to Florence Kirkham, widow.'

This prompted me to send a letter addressed to: Resident, 1856 New School, Cockshutt, Shropshire. This was the building I had seen three years earlier with its post office sign. In my letter, I explained my interest in Kirkhams who had once lived there.

I received a reply signed by David Davies, headmaster of the Cockshutt Church of England Primary School. 'The only Kirkham I have any records of is a Thomas Kirkham born to Thomas and Sarah in 1884,' he wrote. 'He was admitted to school in 1889.' But strangely, Mr. Davies had no such records for William and Ann, perhaps because they may have been educated in Petton.

During a conversation with a complete stranger in the Lincoln hotel where I was staying, he gave me the name of the deputy assistant registrar and told me he was *the* authority on the city's people and places. On the following morning, I found A. J. Gadd in his office, and he put before me Thomas Kirkham's death certificate. This document showed he had died of acute hepatitis at Jimmy's Club where he was the proprietor and that his daughter, M. A. Kirkham, had been present at his death.

Now, finally, here was something to go on!

In Lincoln Library, I found a newspaper obituary for Thomas Kirkham which read: 'Well known in the Midlands in his younger days as a boxer in the lightweight class, Mr. Thomas Kirkham, known professionally as Jimmy Williams. . . died suddenly on Sunday at the age of 64 . . . Jimmy was a fighter of considerable prowess and won many bouts in Lincoln. . .'

Later, Tony Gadd suggested in a letter that I try a notice in the *Lincolnshire Echo* in an attempt to trace Thomas Kirkham's daughter. 'If you wish to use my home address for replies, that will be okay,' he offered, providing me with his telephone number, as well. A few weeks after that, I had a second letter from Tony. 'Bingo!' he exulted. 'I think we have hit the jackpot.'

Anne Williams Kirkham, whose married name was Good, had telephoned him after reading the newspaper notice, and here was the Anne of 'Mother, Tom and Anne' who had sent the wreath to Sarah Tomlinson's funeral in 1935. We corresponded several times by mail and met at last when she visited my home in New England.

Far from Lincoln, there is a road in France on which I was driving one afternoon. Reaching an intersection, I turned right onto Route D171, proceeded slowly for about half a mile, then stopped and walked across the road to gaze ahead of me. Two men in work clothes eyed me, a stranger, with suspicion. And why not?, I reasoned. They expect no good from strangers.

For centuries the farmers of France, dour and uncommunicative, have seen their land fought over and destroyed the way this very spot I was on had been destroyed in 1915 at the Battle of Festubert. Fields of blood red poppies that surrounded me bobbed their heads in the breeze as if blushing at the age-old stupidity of mankind's wars. Returning to my car, I headed west.

Three miles beyond Béthune stands Chocques Military Cemetery, its white marble headstones arranged in straight ranks befitting those who lie beneath them. To the left of the entrance in Plot 1, Row C, stands Grave 34. Looking down at it, I read its simple inscription:

9070 Corporal

W. Kirkham

The King's Liverpool Regt.

18th May 1915

B. Cory Kilvert Jr.

BIBLIOGRAPHY:

Ascoli, David, *The Mons Star, The British Expeditionary Force, 5th Aug-22nd Nov 1914* (Harrap, London, 1981)

Beattie, Kim, *48th Highlanders of Canada 1891-1928* (Published by the Regiment, 1932)

Blackwood's Magazine, No. MCWCI, Vol. CXCVII, January-April 1915: 'Diary of a Subaltern'

Buchan, John, *Nelson's History of the War*, vol. VII (Nelson, London, no date)

Burke-Gaffney, Lt.-Col. J. J., MC, *The Story of the King's Regiment 1914-18* (Sharpe & Kellet, Liverpool, 1954)

Currie, Colonel J. A., *The Red Watch. With the First Canadian Division in Flanders* (McClelland, Goodchild & Stewart, Limited, Toronto, 1916)

de Ruvigny, The Marquis, *The Roll of Honour, a Biographical Record of Members of His Majesty's Naval and Military Forces Who Fell in the Great War 1914-1918, Volume I, Part I* (facsimile edition published by The London Stamp Exchange Ltd., London, 1987)

Free Press and Shropshire Telegraph (9 August 1879)

McWilliams, James L. and R. James Steel, *Gas! The Battle for Ypres, 1915* (Vanwell Publishing Limited, St. Catherines, Ontario, 1985)

Norman, Terry (editor), *Armageddon Road, A VC's Diary 1914-1916* (William Kimber & Co., Limited, London, 1982)

Steavenson, Lt.-Col. C. J., *War Diary, 1st Battn., The King's (Liverpool) Regiment, 1st to 31st May, 1915* (Public Record Office, Reference W095/1359)

Sulzberger, C. L., *The Fall of Eagles* (Crown Publishers, Inc., New York, 1917)

War Diary of the 1st King's (Liverpool) Regiment, April 24-30, 1915 (Public Record Office, Reference WO95/1359)

War Diary of the 2nd Division, April 26-30 and May 1-18, 1915 (Public Record Office, Reference WO95/1285)

Warrington *Examiner* (31 July 1915)

Wyrall, Everard, *The History of the King's Regiment (Liverpool) 1914-1919*, vol. 1: 1914-1915 (Arnold, London, 1928)

CHAPTER 5

1892-1916

Captain Bleddyn Williams

17th Battalion, The Royal Welsh Fusiliers

Well into 1915, politicians and high-ranking generals in all Allied countries, although still hopeful for a decisive victory on the Western Front, had no realistic plan for achieving that goal. Too many lives had been sacrificed in savage battles, which continued to drain treasuries to the brink of national insolvency, but the egos and ambitions maintained by each nation's civil and military leadership demanded ever-greater efforts to continue the fight. To seek ways out of this dilemma, Great Britain and France began to explore opportunities in other regions of Europe that might offer them an advantage.

On May 23rd, 1915, five days after William Kirkham's death, they were encouraged when Italy came into the war on the Allies' side and immediately launched a series of attacks on their Austro-Hungarian foes along a 275-mile front located mostly in the rugged mountains to the north. This appeared to be little more than a sideshow, but readers will learn more about this war zone in a later chapter.

Back in 1914, military bands had played in the streets while battalions marched off behind them to their destiny. "On to Berlin!" had been Britain's battle cry then. "Nach Paris!" shouted Germany to the beating of drums and the staccato sounds of their marching music.

On August 10th of that first year, The Royal Welsh Fusiliers had left for war when A and B Companies of the 2nd Battalion left Southampton for France and were followed three days later by the rest of the battalion. By war's end, the regiment would consist of forty-three battalions of which twenty-one had served overseas, including the 17th. In that one battalion alone, twenty-one officers and 582 other ranks were killed in action or died of wounds. The cheering had long since faded away.

In the case of Bleddyn Williams, the Commonwealth War Graves Commission notified me that, on January 22nd, 1916, he had 'died,' which seemed to indicate he had not been killed in action. But he has no known grave, and his name is among 20,712 inscriptions to be found on the Loos Memorial in France. The Commission's letter to me also stated he was 'the son of Robert Williams, JP, of Fron, Abererch, Pwllheli, Caernarfornshire, and the late Louisa Williams.

On April 17th, 1892, Bleddyn had been born in his parents' home over the Metropolitan Bank on Bangor Street in Caernarfon, where his father was the manager. The baby's Welsh first name meant 'wolf' and dated from the 5th century.

There already were three children in the Williams home—a girl, Mary Catherine, and two boys, Caradog and Goronwy. Two other children were yet to arrive—a second daughter, Buddug, and a third son, Meredydd.[46]

---

[46] For those unfamiliar with the Welsh language, these names are pronounced as follows: Bleth-IN (Bleddyn), Car-AY-Doc (Caradog), Gor-ON-oy (Goronwy), Bith-IG (Buddug) and Mare-ED-ith (Maredyd).

In seeking information that might lead to a living relative, Pat Wolfston found the will of Bleddyn's father. Written in 1932, it showed that Buddug had married a man named Charles Lane, then of 'Cartref,' 29 Croindene Road, Norbury, London. Lane was shown as an executor as was Colonel Hesketh Hughes of 'Claremont,' Caernarfon. Pat then turned to Buddug Lane's will, which dated from 1934 and was proved twenty years later. Among others, this named Mary Catherine Hughes, also of 'Claremont.'

It seemed certain we were dealing with members of the same family. But what appeared to be the major prize in this second will was the name of Buddug's daughter, Margaret Louisa, who at the time was under twenty-five and unmarried. So now it became a matter of trying to find this woman, which might not be easy, especially if she had married after 1934 because her married name would not be known to us. So Pat suggested I first try to determine if Colonel Hughes had sired any children.

I mailed a letter to 'Resident' at the address for 'Clarement.' Apparently, however, this was undeliverable, a possibility I had covered during my research for Corporal Kirkham's kin by typing on my envelope a request to the postmaster to read my letter and pass it along to his local newspaper.

Within two months, I received a response from a woman named Catherine Griffiths of Pwllheli who wrote: 'Your letter published in the Caernarfon and Denbigh Herald dated 22 April 1983 was of much interest to my sister and myself. Bleddyn Williams was our first cousin, his father, Robert, being our mother's eldest brother.' She added that Robert Williams' father had been a tailor in Pwllheli and was a good friend of David Lloyd George to whom he was related.[47]

---

[47] Lloyd George would become prime minister in 1916.

Soon after, I received further word from Miss Griffiths, who told me that Buddug Lane's daughter, Margaret Louisa, was now Mrs. E. R. J. Primmer of North Walsham in Norfolk. I exchanged letters with Mrs. Primmer and later met her in her home, but she could tell me nothing about Captain Williams.

Surprisingly, I also received a letter from a Mr. Humphrey Jones, a ninety-one-year-old resident of Mansfield, Ohio, who had seen my letter in the Welsh newspaper. He told me that he and Bleddyn had been classmates at Caernarfon County School from 1906 to 1909. Pat located copies of his school magazine, *The Arvonian*, which showed that Bleddyn had played forward in the soccer final in February 1908 and in the same year had won a prize in Chemistry. So here was a scholar as well as an athlete.

Soon after receiving this information, another sudden and unexpected avenue of information was about to open for me, which would lead to an enigma surrounding this young officer who died in France.

Pat had contacted Clive Hughes, then a staff member at the Imperial War Museum in London, who had been helpful to me with some other cases. She showed him everything we had to date on Williams and, fortuitously, he recalled at once that, in 1978, while preparing his MA thesis, he had cited the case of Bleddyn Williams as an example of political influence used to secure commissions in Lloyd George's so-called Welsh Army of 1914-1915.

Standards of the times frowned upon such activity, but to place it in its proper perspective, one must first go back to late September 1914 when Lloyd George bullied Lord Kitchener, the Secretary of State for War, into sanctioning the Welsh Army Corps (WAC).

From the start, this Corps laid great stress on its desire for Welsh officers, and on the 29th of that month its creator met a man whom he saw at once as being ideal for assuming two roles—spokesman for recruiting in Gwynedd and also as commander of the 1st (North Wales) Brigade.

At fifty-six, Lieutenant-Colonel Owen Thomas was five years older than his mentor. During the Boer War in 1899-1902, he had served with Brabant's Horse and later raised and commanded the Prince of Wales's Light Horse. But of far greater significance, his views on the type of officer who would be acceptable to the WAC coincided with those of Lloyd George.

Thomas believed that if a prototype combined a prominent social position with an ability to speak or at least understand the Welsh language, recruiting would be substantially increased. To date, it had been nothing short of dismal. In fact, during the first five days of hostilities with Germany, exactly seventeen men had come forth to enlist throughout the whole of Wales.

This was hardly surprising because soldiering had always been disparaged there, but other factors were responsible as well, one of which was overcrowded slums in many towns where diseases proliferated. Furthermore, substandard housing for workers on the land had further weakened the health of much of the manpower pool which otherwise might have been drawn to the army if only as an alternative to unemployment.

Well aware that something had to be done to break this deadlock, Lloyd George once more confronted Kitchener, stating his dissatisfaction with the current candidate for command of the 1st Brigade. When asked to suggest an alternative, he slipped in Owen Thomas' name and was both surprised and delighted when Kitchener appointed Thomas a brigadier within minutes. This did little to endear 'LG' to the War Office or the Regular Army, both of which viewed with extreme reservations the entire concept on a 'national' army raised by a political figure.

But once again, Lloyd George had gotten his way, and in a style that was typical of his nature, he lost no time boasting in a letter sent to his home that his two sons' chances for promotion were never better because Thomas was reputed to appoint his own officers. Furthermore 'LG' knew he could manipulate Thomas at will.[48]

Conveniently, the new brigadier proved this was so in December 1914 by accepting both of Lloyd George's sons in his brigade and seeing to it that all three of his own sons were commissioned in it as well. But these two venal characters were not the only players in this game of influence. Certain private citizens were hard at it as well, one of whom was a bank manager in Caernarfon.

Prior to these appointments, Robert Williams had written a letter on October 26th to O. W. Owen, secretary of the Welsh National Executive Committee, stating that three of his four sons wished to join either Kitchener's New Armies or a Territorial Force battalion. Obviously aware of the then-current requirements for commissions, he added that all three of these young men held responsible positions—two with banks and one with an insurance company. He concluded his letter with the bland observation that he was related to Lloyd George.

Owen duly replied, suggesting that perhaps only two of Williams' sons should apply for commissions. So for a start, Bleddyn's name was put forward on November 5th as an officer candidate. The desperate need for officers in France and Flanders was highlighted on that day in a *Times* article about the Grenadier Guards which reported that its 1st Battalion had been brought out of the 7th Division's front line position at Ypres with only one officer and less that ninety men still on their feet. But typical of its high standards, the battalion immediately began to reform the King's Company and went through a full hour's drill.

On November 10th, Bleddyn was described in his father's second letter to O. W. Owen as 'a six-footer, an all-round athlete, and he knows Welsh thoroughly. . . He

---

[48] When obliged to deal directly with Lloyd George after the latter had become prime minister, Sir Douglas Haig curtly labeled him 'a cad' in letters to his wife.

will be in a position financially to keep his position as an officer with respect and dignity.' At the time, Bleddyn was employed at his father's bank.

All 1st Brigade prerequisites had been met. But Robert Williams could not resist adding in his letter that Mrs. Lloyd George had now taken an interest in the matter by forwarding to her husband not only Bleddyn's name but also that of his brother, Caradog. Goronwy was not sponsored because, as an asthmatic, he had recently been rejected as medically unfit to serve in the war and would die young of tuberculosis.[49]

This time, Owen's response suggested that Bleddyn should enlist in the North Wales 'Pals' Battalion, which was later to be designated the 13th Battalion, Royal Welsh Fusiliers.[50] This Bleddyn did, a fact substantiated in one of his obituaries.

Raised at Rhyl on September 3rd, 1914, this battalion had attracted well-educated and socially acceptable recruits, but because its numbers had increased slowly, its 300 members were merged at the end of the month with 350 men of the same background who had joined the University of Wales Battalion. Although many of these men would later receive commissions, it was believed that a few months in the ranks would be useful to all concerned until places could be found for them as officers.

Bleddyn's star began to rise on January 30th, 1915, when O. W. Owen of the Welsh National Executive Committee wrote to Brigadier Owen Thomas of the 128th Brigade (formerly the 1st and soon to be retitled the 113th). Thomas was at

---

[49] Maredydd was not sponsored, either. Always an independent spirit, according to Miss Griffiths, he had emigrated to Australia before the war but would come back to Great Britain with the Australian Army.

[50] Early in the war, certain Service Battalions of numerous regiments were raised as a means of encouraging friends from specific neighborhoods and members of the same vocation or social class to enlist as a group. A cynical and exploitive concept at best, it appeared to offer not only plaudits of a grateful nation but also excitement as an alternative to the servilities of many civilian jobs. In far too many cases, it would prove to be a mass death sentence.

Llandudno at the time, having set up his headquarters in a hotel there in early November.

Owen's letter began: 'I am sending you the papers of Bleddyn Williams, son of Robert Williams. . .of Caernarfon. Is it possible to do anything for the young fellow? He is deserving of something, if only for his father's sake.'

Bleddyn's name subsequently appeared on the 7th Supplementary List of applicants for Welsh Army Corps commissions, his date of seniority as a second lieutenant being given as February 18th, 1915.

Preceding this listing, Owen Thomas's influence in Gwynedd had led to much patriotic tub-thumping by prominent members of the Caernarfonshire community, and a series of marches through those areas where few eligible young men had come forth to enlist began to bear fruit. By the first day of February 1915, the 1st Brigade totaled over 5,000 men, a sufficient number to justify raising an additional battalion, the 17th, at Llandudno and in the depressed slate-quarrying area of Blaenau Ffestiniog twenty miles to the south. Second Lieutenant Bleddyn Williams would serve with that new battalion.

Elsewhere, favors had also been in full swing. Back on December 13th, 1915, Lord Plymouth, chairman of the Welsh Army Corps Executive Committee, announced in a letter to Lloyd George that he had put forward the name of Major Victor Paget to be appointed commander of field artillery in the 1st Division (later redesignated the 38th [Welsh] Division). To lend weight to his endorsement, Plymouth added, 'Major Paget is my brother-in-law.' In the meantime, Brigadier Ivor Phillips, a Liberal MP since 1906, was seeking command of the 1st Division, which ultimately would encompass five battalions of the Welsh Regiment and five of the Royal Welsh Fusiliers, including the 13th and 17th.

While clearly lacking the military qualifications for this appointment, this former Indian Army major carried unassailable political credentials, having been occupied for six months with responsibilities at the Ministry of Munitions, which was then presided over by none other than Lloyd George. His boss was more than willing to help, largely because Phillips' brother had once offered to lend £500 to 'LG' in his earlier years of political and personal need. Although he had declined this kindness, he remained grateful—but at a price: if Phillips got the division, he would get with it Lloyd George's son, Gwilym, as an aide-de-camp.[51]

In January 1915, Phillips got both, as well as a promotion to major-general. For the time being, he was effectively immunized from the wrath and resentment of passed-over Regular Army officers who were senior to him in rank. To many onlookers, being Welsh was grossly overemphasized for all levels of leadership in the 1st Division—from major-general down to subaltern—while ability in soldiering counted for nought. But Phillips' inexperience would catch up with him when he was sacked on July 9th, 1916, in the aftermath of his division's failure to take Mametz Wood in the opening moves of the British offensive on the Somme.

To further emphasize this over-reliance on Welsh officers, by August 1915, Brigadier Owen Thomas could boast that almost sixty-seven percent of those in his brigade were of Welsh nationality. Unfortunately, however, only ten of them could claim prior military experience, a shortcoming shared more or less equally by the rest of the 38th Division's 326 officers who included only six who had ever heard a shot fired in anger. Others were too old for active service and would have to be replaced before their battalions left for France.

This WAC predisposition toward Welsh-speaking officers with political connections cost it many able-bodied and intelligent men who would prove to be outstanding soldiers, one of whom, Hugh Rowlands, is mentioned in Clive Hughes' thesis as follows:

[51] Lloyd George had accepted a loan from Robert Williams at about the same time but never repaid it, according to the latter's granddaughter, Mrs. Primmer.

115

'A headmaster from Lleyn, he enlisted as a private in the North Wales Pals Battalion and unsuccessfully applied. . . for a commission. Early in 1916 he was granted a T[erritorial] F[orce] commission in the 7th Battalion, R.W. F. and at the end of the year was attached to the 2nd London Regiment. By the end of the war he had become a captain and company commander and won three awards for gallantry.'

Well into August 1915, battalion training was accelerating. Billeted in Llandudno, the 17th Royal Welsh Fusiliers had become a familiar sight in town, and on Saturday mornings crowds lined Trinity Street to watch the men being put through their paces. Before the end of the month, they were ready to move to Winchester where their division had begun to assemble.

By this stage of the war, all British officers in service dress had begun to wear rank badge 'stars' on their shoulders instead of on their cuffs because German snipers could easily see who were officers and who were not. It was jokingly suggested that these shoulder 'wind up' stars denoted fear among those who wore them, which was not even remotely true. They were ordered to wear them because their purpose was to make officers less conspicuous in battle than before.

Prior to leaving Llandudno, the 17th Battalion was presented with a goat named Billy by the wife of its commanding officer, Lieutenant-Colonel the Honourable Henry R. H. Mostyn.[52] Recently recalled from retirement, this officer had begun his service with the regiment's 2nd Battalion in 1876. Well over fifty and thus too old for the rigors of active service, he was replaced in November 1915 by Lieutenant-Colonel John Arthur Ballard of the Oxfordshire and Buckinghamshire Light Infantry. At forty-seven, Ballard had served with this regiment in the Boer

---

[52] By ancient tradition, a goat was carried on the establishment of every Royal Welsh Fusiliers battalion. Decorated with a silver head plate and gilded horns, it marched at the head of the battalion with a drummer known as the goat major.

War and in 1914 was adjutant of its 4th Battalion. But because of his lack of Welsh interests or connections, these shortcomings would soon earn him the sobriquet 'Colonel Bastard.'

Replaced on November 25th by Brigadier Price-Davies, VC, DSO, an officer nineteen years his junior, an embittered Owen Thomas would retire from the army in 1916 to observe from the sidelines with mounting horror a war that would claim all three of his sons.[53]

At this time, Captain Llewellyn Griffith, the battalion's adjutant, was also replaced. An officer of the Welsh Regiment who had served with the British Indian Army since 1906, he was probably home on leave when the war began. Being Welsh as well as available, he had been offered a job with Owen Thomas' brigade and shared with Thomas only modest military qualifications for his responsibilities. His place would by taken in December 1914 by Captain P. Welton, a Regular Army soldier of the 2nd Royal Welsh Fusiliers who had served in France from the start of the war as regimental quartermaster-sergeant. Here, at last, was a soldier with some firsthand experience of modern war.

In the ranks, Welsh nationals predominated in Bleddyn's battalion, but it had been brought up to strength only by bringing in recruits from Lancashire and Staffordshire. Many of these new men were familiar with the North Wales summer resorts and were attracted to the thought of training in such surroundings. They would soon settle in with their new Welsh comrades who accepted these Englishmen with far less fuss than had been made over this issue by many of their officers.

---

[53] A substantive major, Brigadier Llewellyn Alberic Emilius Price-Davies served in the Boer War with the King's Royal Rifle Corps. As a 23-year-old lieutenant in April 1901, he was awarded the DSO, and on September 17th of the same year, he won the Victoria Cross during an attempt to prevent the capture of British guns by several hundred burghers at Blood River Poort in Natal.

From tents on Flowerdown outside Winchester to the muddy parade ground in a half-completed camp at Hazeley Down, the 17th Battalion moved on in November to Larkhill on Salisbury Plain. Once a sufficient number of rifles had arrived and been issued, the men shot their musketry course and were inspected in a driving rain by Her Majesty Queen Mary on November 29th. Little time was now left to them in England, and beginning in December, batches of men had been sent home on seven-day embarkation leaves.

Miss Griffiths told me that Bleddyn had come to her parents' home to say farewell before leaving for France. Just a young child at the time, she searched back in her memory for almost seventy years for the sake of an American who was paying her a visit in Pwllheli.

"He gave me a shilling," she was able to recall. And then he was gone, never to be seen by her family again.

Bleddyn would soon be a temporary captain with date of rank from November 27th. Tall, athletic and aloof, his presence in front of the men was most likely the deciding factor in his promotion because no military qualifications existed, another indication of the dire shortage of experienced officers. With this promotion came added responsibilities as second in command of B Company.

At 7:15 on the morning of December 4th, 1915, the 17th Battalion left Winchester and marched in the rain for more than thirteen miles to Southampton where they spent the night in a large, cold building on the docks. By then, British soldiers were no longer wearing soft caps, which provided no protection from head injuries. *The Times* for October 31st, 1915, had noted that leather-lined steel helmets had begun to be introduced on the Western Front.

Early on December 5th, the battalion filed aboard three transports, one of which was a paddle steamer, which many men recognized as *La Marguerite*, an erstwhile commercial pleasure vessel which in summer days of peace had carried carefree crowds on holiday from Liverpool to North Wales. Cast now in a more serious role, this ship was about to take 380 men under Captain C. H. Jones to France.

Once there, the pace of training quickened. Generally in pouring rain, route marching and musketry practice occupied most of the men's time while the rest were trained as bombers, machine gunners and signalers as everyone prepared for the inevitable move to the fighting lines.

On Christmas Day, troops from their 115th Brigade, 38th Division, met briefly in No Man's Land with their foe, exchanging food, tobacco and sign language seasonal pleasantries until angrily recalled by their officers. Similar impromptu fraternizing had occurred in December 1914 along the Western Front but on a much broader scale.

On the following day, the 17th Battalion marched to Laventie where they were met by members of the 3rd Guards Brigade to which they would be attached for instruction in a quiet sector of the front line. Bleddyn and his men in B Company were assigned to the 4th Grenadier Guards.

In the distance, enemy machine guns tapped out their threatening message and nearby artillery ranged on distant German targets. Before the afternoon was over, A and D Companies began working their way through a communication trench, sliding on slippery duckboards which squelched in the mud from the weight of this heavily laden column.

Enemy counter-battery fire lit up the night sky as daylight slipped away like a lantern left behind them, limiting their vision to the shapes that moved directly ahead of them. Every sound both near and far seemed magnified and fraught with malice as these untried men and boys plodded forward to the front, still known to them only in the abstract as some fearsome and voracious monster.

This time, their imaginations would outdo reality. After two uneventful days, they were relieved by C Company and also by the men of Bleddyn's B

Company, who occupied positions around Picantin, while C extended southwest to Fauquissart. These deployments remained in effect until January 6th when the battalion filed back through Laventie and moved into billets at Hamet Billet, about two miles from Robecq. At this stage of the war, battalions were rotated in and out of the front line, support trenches and the reserve line further to the rear. Ideally, these moves were completed in the course of twelve days, but necessity often dictated otherwise.

In Bleddyn's case, this initial exposure to the perils of warfare—though brief— had been thorough in true Guards fashion, and no losses had been sustained.[54] His battalion had been lucky, but in large part its good fortune had been due to an enemy master plan.

In the opening months of 1916, German grand strategy called for an overwhelming assault on the French at Verdun in February. Elsewhere on the Western Front, the Kaiser's troops would remain on the defensive, further strengthening their already formidable positions, which included thick belts of barbed wire and deep frontline dugouts which were virtually immune to shellfire short of a direct hit. As a result, monotony quickly set in on the British side as one day followed another with boring predictability.

During daylight, men slept beneath whatever cover they could find, emptying the trenches of all but a few men picked for duty. While in the front lines, men lived with incessant foul odors that hung over the battlefields and rose from unburied bodies of men and animals, while the stench of cordite, rotting food, poison gas and sweat combined to increase everyone's misery.

Snipers searched patiently for victims, while sentries alternated resting first one foot and then the other to fight fatigue and carelessness that could lead to

---

[54] Officers and men of all line regiments, while covered with filth and mud in the trenches, never failed to be amazed at the sight of Guardsmen of all ranks who were renowned for their immaculate appearance whenever they went beyond their own front line perimeters.

death. Only after dark would a troglodyte community emerge from the earth like giant ants to run on vital errands.

Some men pumped water from their trench. Others filled sandbags. Wiring parties were told off to repair breaks made by high explosive enemy artillery fire. Dead bodies were buried. Other men revetted trench walls with timbers brought up from the rear with rations, mail from home and water that reeked of chlorine and sometimes even tasted slightly of petrol. Limited free time was spent 'chatting,' a name the men gave to holding the seams of their uniforms over candle flames to destroy the eggs of lice which infested their bodies.

One needed to be careful at all times. The Germans were known to have established pre-aimed rifles flanked by sandbags to steady them on their parapet. Their triggers could be pulled without exposing the men who fired them, and the bullets were aimed at known places in the Welsh trenches, such as ration points and cook houses. Officers were a prime target, of course, and many divisions ordered them to wear rankers' uniforms and webbing and carry rifles in order to look less noticeable.

Generally, however, a somnolent atmosphere prevailed along the front line. Although this was agreeable to the French, it soon became anathema to the British High Command, which considered it corrosive to the offensive sprit and thus a threat to discipline. As a result, orders for raids and reconnaisances began to filter down to battalion commanders who were charged with keeping the Germans on their toes.

The Royal Welsh Fusiliers' regimental history dismisses this period with a total of ten words: 'There is no special activity to record during the winter.' But the human costs of war continued to be paid. During their first tour in the line without instructors, the 17th Battalion lost one man killed and two wounded. On January 19th, the men added rapid fire to a night artillery bombardment of enemy positions. Retaliatory fire wounded one officer and nine men, and three other men were killed.

Following two days of rest in billets at Riez Bailleul, the 17th Battalion plodded east in the gloom to relieve the 16th Battalion of the Welsh Regiment in the front line. Having settled in, the men were warned that a sergeant and private would soon be going out with an officer from B Company on a patrol from the 'Duck's Bill,' a name given to a complex of former German communication trenches.

Perpendicular to these positions was a sap dug to a point just short of a crater, which had been created earlier in No Man's Land by the explosion of a German mine. This crater was to be reconnoitered for signs of enemy activity. If found vacant, it might be occupied later as part of the endless game of inches along the Western Front which sacrificed the lives of so many young men.

There was time for the tall officer and his sergeant to synchronize their watches and coordinate their plan in low tones. And then all three men were on their bellies, moving cautiously over their parapet and slipping through their own wire in which narrow passages had earlier been cut. Hugging the damp, sour-smelling earth, they crept silently along, freezing whenever gun flashes or a flare illuminated shapes ahead of them. Reaching the lip of the crater, they separated, the two men going in one direction, while their officer went in the other.

Captain Bleddyn Williams never returned.

The war diary of the 17th Battalion gave this laconic account of his disappearance: 'Captain Bleddyn Williams, 2nd in command of B Coy, went out with a patrol of 1 sgt and 1 pte during the night. He lost touch with his patrol and did not return. Search was made by patrols throughout the night but nothing was discovered of the missing officer. Casualties, one sergeant killed, 1 man wounded.'

Were these two men the other members of Bleddyn's patrol?

According to Emlyn Davies, who was there, they were not. Years after this episode, it was briefly described in a book by this man, who had been one of the 17th Battalion's signalers on that night in 1916. He wrote: 'An officer leading a patrol failed to return after losing contact with his men.' He then added this unsettling note: 'He was suspected of having gone over to the enemy. . .'

Some months before I finally met Clive Hughes at the Imperial War Museum, he attempted to help me learn more about the present holder of the draft data for Davies' book, whose name we agreed should not be made known to me. In reply to his request, he received a long latter, which quoted Davies' explanation for leaving Bleddyn's name out of his final version:

'I well remember Bleddyn Williams. . .but did not mention his name because he had friends in Colwyn Bay, some of whom were also my friends, He was well liked in the battalion, though he seemed a loner, rarely seen with any companions.

'I was in A Company. . .in the front line behind the spot where his patrol went out. . . .The story was he told his [two men] to start from the left, he went in the opposite direction and was never seen again. . . After a time, the patrol returned through the barbed wire and regained their trench and reported. . .'

As in all such cases, a court of inquiry was held as soon as possible at which witnesses were questioned and all stated facts pieced together in an attempt to reach a decision in the matter. In the case of Bleddyn Williams, however, Davies declared in his book that the decision was not published in orders. As a signaler, he would have had reason to know this was so. Why it *was* so will never be established.

There were two newspaper notices. The first one, published on January 28th, 1916, explained that Bleddyn being listed as missing 'does not necessarily mean that Captain Williams has been killed or wounded . . .' The second notice, which appeared on February 2nd, stated: 'It is almost certain that Captain Bleddyn Williams has been taken prisoner.'

The latter notice added to the confusion by including a letter, which had been sent home on January 26th by Lieutenant G. G. Roberts of the 17th Battalion.

'We have had a terrible time,' he wrote. 'Bleddyn Williams and I led two bombing attacks. His lot was captured. I managed to get back by a very narrow squeak. I was out for several hours looking for him but he had gone, poor chap. Two others were wounded and several of my men have gone. . .'

This is where the mystery begins to deepen. No mention at all is made in the 17th Battalion's war diary of bombing attacks led by Lieutenant Roberts, Captain Williams or any other officer on the date of the latter's disappearance, but Roberts was emphatic in his letter about what had transpired on that night.

'Since Griff Jones [The Reverend G. W. Jones, who was a subaltern] left us, Bleddyn was my best pal. . .I can hardly realize he has gone. I am confident he has been taken prisoner, for had he been killed I would have found his body. I made a thorough search both nights till daybreak.'

One might speculate forever on what actually happened out in No Man's Land to this young officer from Caernarfon. But when *Officers Died in the Great War 1914-1919* was published in 1919 and the regimental history appeared in 1928, the matter was honorably laid to rest as follows:

'Williams, Bleddyn, Capt., k. in a. 22-1-16.'

The utter insanity of the war was perhaps best reflected six days after his death. A notice in the same edition of one of the newspapers which had announced he was missing invited more young men in Gwynedd to enlist.

'The newly-formed "Gwynedd" Battalion (22nd Welsh Fusiliers), commanded by Colonel Lloyd Evans, himself a Welsh-speaking Welshman, and the officers and men of which will be almost entirely Welsh-speaking, affords a suitable opportunity for young Welshmen to join a unit where they will find themselves in congenial company.'

A funereal leitmotiv, even today it can make a man shudder.

BIBLIOGRAPHY:

Davies, Emlyn, *Taffy Went to War* (privately circulated, 1973)

Griffith, Wyn, *Up to Mametz* (Severn House Publishers, Ltd., London, 1981)

The Herald, Caernarfon (January 28th, 1916)

Hughes, Clive, *Army Recruitment in Gwynedd, 1914-1916*, Chapter III (University of Wales, MA, 1983)

Hughes, Clive, *A Nation in Arms, A social history of the British army in the First World War*, Chapter 4 (Manchester University Press, Manchester, 1985)

Hughes, Colin, *Mametz, Lloyd George's 'Welsh Army' at the Battle of the Somme* (Orion Press, Gerrards Cross, Bucks, November 1982)

Kirby, Major, E. L., MC, TD, DL, *The Royal Welsh Fusiliers 23rd Foot* (Pitkin Pictorials Ltd., London, 1974)

Official History, Military Operations, France and Belgium, 1916 (Macmillan and Co., Ltd., London, 1932)

War Diary of the 17th Battalion, Royal Welsh Fusiliers, December 4th, 1915-January 25th, 1916 (Public Records Office, Reference WO95/2561)

B. Cory Kilvert Jr.

Ward, Major C. H., DSO, MC, *Regimental Records of the Royal Welsh Fusiliers (23rd Foot}, vol. III, 1914-1918, France and Flanders* (Forster Groom & Co., Ltd., London, 1928)

Welsh Army Corps Papers 'File W,'(National Library of Wales, Aberystwyth. Dyfed)

Yr Udgorn (2 February, 1916)

Second Lieutenant Bleddyn Williams (center, standing) shown with fellow officers in his battalion prior to their departure for France in 1915. To his left is his best friend, the Reverend Griff Jones.

CHAPTER 6

1886-1916

Second Lieutenant Jeffery Bradley Penfold

7th Battalion, The King's Own Scottish Borderers

Long before this officer arrived in France, his battalion of the King's Own Scottish Borderers (KOSB) had been raised on September 12th, 1914 at Bordon, but its members were to wait for almost one year before being sent overseas to Allouagne, southwest of Béthune in France. With them went their history and traditions, which have always been cherished by every British Army regiment and handed down through the ages.

The KOSB dated from March 19th 1689, in Edinburgh when 1,000 recruits joined it in a mere two hours, which not only reflected Scotland's martial spirit but most likely some bad economic times as well. Originally named Leven's Regiment after the nobleman who had raised it, its reputation for toughness was forever after firmly established on August 1st, 1759, at Minden in Germany. There it fought alongside five other British Army regiments, which repelled numerous charges by 10,000 French cavalrymen and broke the enemy center while being subjected to heavy flanking artillery fire. With another one of its early names, The Edinburgh

Regiment, it was granted the unique honor for all time of having the right to march through its streets with its Colours flying, bayonets fixed and drums beating.

In the 19th century, its men soldiered in Afghanistan, the Sudan and the Boer War, and during World War One, 6,859 officers and other ranks of 'The Kosbies' Regular Army, Territorial Force and Service Battalions would give their lives. Our story tells of one of these casualties.

Having arrived in France in early July 1915, the 7th Battalion's men began being fed into the front lines in batches to become accustomed to combat conditions, and they sustained their first loss on August 21st when Major G. S. D. Forbes, CMG, DSO, was mortally wounded by a German artillery shellburst. Many more men were to suffer similar fates in an attack which erupted at Loos on September 25th, 1915.

Meticulously planned in great detail, this assault was aimed at reaching the coal mines around that town as well as Lens, and it was hoped that it might even recapture Lille. The French agreed to cooperate by launching an offensive in Champagne that would force the enemy to allocate forces to resist two assaults instead of only one.

The 15th (Scottish) and the 47th (London), the first two of Kitchener's New Army divisions, were chosen to form part of the British attacking force. When all was ready, a massive four-day British artillery bombardment helped to drive a salient into the German lines, but a counterattack recovered all of the ground lost earlier. But south of the Hohenzollern Redoubt in the western outskirts of Hulluch, the British pushed forward for 3,500 yards, took Loos village by 8:00 a.m. and Hill 70 also fell.

Named for its height in meters, Hill 70 bisected the Lens-La Bassé road, and both sides recognized its importance for the purpose of observing enemy activity for a considerable distance over mostly flat land. An enormous struggle then raged for it, but the Germans eventually regained all of it with the exception of its western slopes.

To add strength to their attack, which was set to begin at 6:30 a.m., the British had previously released poison chlorine gas for forty minutes in the early morning of the 25th with moderately successful results on the right. Elsewhere, however, an adverse wind had blown it back onto some of the attackers, including the 7th Battalion, KOSB. This forced the men either to don crude, suffocating smoke helmets in efforts to protect their eyes and lungs or simply take their chances without them.

Furthermore, matters were not improved for the men who had to crawl in the rain onto their slippery parapets and find what gaps they could in their own barbed wire in order to spread out in No Man's Land and begin their advance. In next to no time, an assault, which had seemed to promise success in its planning stages, began to turn into a disaster in its execution.

Although the Germans had known the assault was imminent, their army had failed to complete its third line of defensive positions, which the attackers might have penetrated with better luck. As for the poison gas, it caused an initial panic, but most of the enemy troops exposed to it were able to rally and settle down to a stubborn defense as their machine gunners traversed the battlefield with a torrent of lead.

Attacking British troops had been required to cross between 200 and 400 yards of open ground while German artillery spotters located in tall coal mining towers called down accurate ranges for their own guns. But this advantage was partially offset by smoke shells fired from British trench mortars, which limited the spotters' ability to observe the attack.

With the French Army reaching a depth of about two miles, this Allied assault had initially caught the Germans by surprise. Up to 8,000 yards of trenches were captured by the British, but no further major breakthrough was achieved, largely due to the exhausted condition of the attackers but also because of heavy overlapping enemy machine gun fire on the flanks. The Germans always relied heavily on their machine gun crews who characteristically used these fearsome weapons with great determination, skill and courage.

The Battle of Loos cost the BEF a total of 50,380 killed and wounded, and almost 23,000 officers and men were listed as missing. At its start, the 7th KOSB had numbered 950 rank and file but lost 611 men in just two days, this being over sixty-four percent of the battalion's strength.[55] All twenty of its officers who had been in the attack died, and only one non-commissioned officer survived. When withdrawn on September 27th, it was crippled as a fighting formation, although its morale remained surprisingly strong. One of its pipers had won the Victoria Cross, and his exploit is worth recounting.

At 6:30 a.m. on the battle's first day, 15851 Piper Daniel Laidlaw, a 39-year-old Reservist from Berwickshire, had jumped onto the parapet of his trench with Second Lieutenant M. C. Young to inspire the men of their company who were feeling some effects of the gas. Completely exposed to heavy enemy fire as well as to gas, Laidlaw calmly inflated his bag and began to march back and forth in the morning mist, piping the regimental quick march, 'All the Blue Bonnets Are o'er the Border.'

Hit in the leg and heel, he limped on toward the German lines behind his company, sufficiently composed to offer a second selection, 'The Standard on the Braes o' Mar.'[56] It was a miracle that he survived because the bag on his pipes was

---

[55] Records of the 19th Division maintain the battalion lost 656 men.
[56] Young died of his wounds on the following day, but Laidlaw survived the war and lived until June 2nd, 1950.

pierced several times, and all of its drones were shot off. Any one of the bullets and shell fragments hitting them might otherwise have killed him.

Among the battalion's officers hit on that day was its colonel, George de Wet Verner, who died on October 19th. At fifty-five, he had come out of retirement to lead the 7th Battalion from its beginnings one year earlier at Berwick-on-Tweed and had made the men into what they became. As a twenty-year-old subaltern, he had joined the regiment in 1879.

Remaining in billets behind the lines, the battalion trained and refitted, slowly being brought back up to strength by the periodic arrival of replacements. The need for second lieutenants was especially critical because eight subalterns had become casualties at Loos. Two officers of that most junior commissioned rank who had not been in the attack were now commanding A and C Companies, a responsibility normally reserved for captains and even junior majors. Another subaltern was serving as adjutant.

Unfortunately, these appallingly high losses suffered by British officers within the first fourteen months of war could no longer be offset by experienced replacements from regimental depots at home, almost all of whom had long since been committed to the inferno.

Instead, something new appeared on the scene—hastily trained and untried junior officers with little to be said for them beyond an unbounded enthusiasm and an eagerness to learn. These were largely the public school boys of Britain who had responded in 1914 to Lord Kitchener's appeal for a 'New Army' of 100,000 men. Some of these young officers would survive. A great many more would not.

On Friday, October 8th 1915, while the 7th KOSB was in billets in Lillers, three of these inexperienced second lieutenants turned up and reported for duty. One of them was Jeffery Bradley Penfold. At the age of twenty-nine, he was old to be a subaltern and, worse yet, he was not well.

133

On May 16th, 1886, he had been born in Folkestone, Kent, at 'Canadian Villa,' so named for his father's family connections in Canada. An only son, he had one sister, Susanna, who was known as 'Queenie.' He was called Jerry. His mother, the former Margaret Elizabeth Hall, was the daughter of Henry Acton of East Hanney in Berkshire.

Sir Stephen Penfold, his father, was a partner in a wine and spirits firm. For almost thirty years, he had held a commission in the Volunteer Corps, and at the time of his retirement in 1896, he was a major and honorary lieutenant-colonel with the 1st Cinque Ports Volunteer Artillery. In 1915 when he was knighted, he was a justice of the peace for Kent and had already been mayor of Folkestone for two years, a position he would retain into 1919.

In 1900, when Jerry was fourteen, he was sent to be educated at Uppingham in Rutland. Founded in 1584, this school had numbered not more than forty boys for almost 300 years, but in 1853 a dynamic headmaster had begun to raise its size and stature which, by Jerry's time, had reached a level second only to Rugby's, although Uppingham was generally better known for sports than for a high academic standard.

There was no one about when I wandered through the grounds of the school, admiring its fine stone buildings, but a faculty wife happened to come along and kindly unlocked the chapel door, enabling me to photograph the memorial alcove where Jerry Penfold's name is carved into one of the stone panels that displays the names of 448 additional former students who died in World War One.

Mr. B. Matthews, writing to me earlier from the school's records office, had explained that Jerry's academic career was 'remarkable for its lack of progress. He was placed in the second bottom form and came in nineteenth of nineteen in his first term.'

In the following term, while still in the same form, he finished third and was then moved up to the Army and Engineering Class II, which Matthews described as 'a haunt of those destined for the army or unlikely to profit from a classical education.' There poor Jerry languished for the following five terms, and upon leaving Uppingham in December 1902, he was once again at the bottom of his class.

On the surface, it would seem he was not especially bright, but there was much more to the matter than that. He had long expressed a desire to make the army his career, but he was acutely shortsighted, and one can see this was so from photographs taken of him. He squinted at the camera. Furthermore, a dangerous illness in boyhood had weakened him to the point where he was unable to pass the army medical examination.

Given these disabilities, Jerry might well have been a target for derision and the butt of countless pranks played on him by his peers at Uppingham. In those times, schoolboys could be unbelievably cruel to anyone who failed to be more like everyone else.

When war broke out in 1914, Jerry, still determined to serve his country, somehow managed to enlist in September as a private in the Public School and University Corps. He later applied for a commission in one of the so-called Service battalions then being organized throughout Great Britain.

As already demonstrated to everyone's satisfaction but his own, he never would have been accepted under normal circumstances. But by January 1915, circumstances had ceased to be even remotely normal, and so Jerry was gazetted second lieutenant to the 7th Battalion, The King's Own Scottish Borderers, which formed part of the 46th Brigade in the 15th (Scottish) Division.

So that is why this gaunt officer, who never should have been in France at all, was standing at attention in Lillers before Major J. C. 'Charlie' Connell, an outstanding Regular Army officer from the 2nd Battalion who had joined the regiment in 1901. He had only arrived himself to take command on September 17th, a mere two days after the disaster at Loos. With responsibilities for bringing the battalion back to its fighting form, he would have made a point to meet all new officers as soon as possible after their arrival.

Connell could hardly have been encouraged by the sight of Jerry, who had recently injured himself in England with a revolver, most likely another sign of his poor eyesight. Standing motionless, Jerry would have strained to bring his superior officer into focus, wondering, of course, what was in store for him.

Major-General F. W. N. McCracken, CB, DSO, commanding the 15th Division, also had a word with all battalion officers on that day, measuring them up for the deadly work that lay ahead. He was especially preoccupied with how soon the survivors of Loos would recover and how quickly these replacements could be made ready for the front line.

By then, the battalion had been in billets for eleven consecutive days and was needed desperately, but in the meantime the men's training continued. Four NCOs and twenty-eight privates left for a short course in grenade throwing at the divisional bomb school, while a dozen signalers were put through their paces with brigade instructors. The weather had been clear for a spell, but on the 19th it began to rain, quickly turning the ground into a sodden porridge.

By October 21st, the Borderers were in a grim and grimy coal mining town, its surface scarred by ugly chimneys, slag heaps and pit heads. It was known as Noeux-les-Mines, and it would later play a part in Jerry's destiny. The men soon moved on to trenches where they spent the next eleven days building two dugouts and improving their defenses, which in many places were only a few feet deep. Necessary, routine work, it would have been boring, too, except for the fact that in daylight the position was in full view of the Germans east of Loos.

As was so often the case, the enemy occupied higher ground, this time at the Hohenzollern Redoubt and a mine pit head. So in addition to resenting the German habit of draining rain water and sewage toward their enemy's trenches from their own, the 'Kosbies' had every reason to feel like insects under microscopes. Whenever German gunners bombarded the battalion's support line, they did so with deadly accuracy because this had earlier been their own front line, and they knew the distance to a yard. British guns, still limited to only a few rounds per day, hammered back sporadically at the enemy trenches only 250 yards to the east.

On one occasion in anticipation of an attack, the support company was called up to an uncompleted trench called 'The Milky Way.' A calm sector before the battle at Loos, this was now one of the most dangerous places on Earth. Skillfully concealed German snipers peered patiently into the dawn light through telescopic sights for the brief appearance of a head or a hand or anything else they could drill with a bullet.

During this time, 165 reinforcements arrived and were put to work with the rest of the battalion, which had gone into support trenches on October 27th. Daily tasks included the burial of British dead along with constant repairing and draining of trenches flooded by frequent torrential rain. As in Bleddyn Williams' battalion, steel helmets began to be issued to the KOSB, whose men were not pleased when ordered to put away their woolen bonnets which represented one of their regiment's cherished traditions. At first, the men refused to wear these new helmets and began to use them for every purpose other than the one intended.

Whenever there was time, men leafed through newspapers and magazines sent by their families. Among the latter was *The Bystander* with its illustrations of 'Old Bill' and other humorous characters in the trenches drawn by Bruce Bairnsfather, a Regular Army captain in the Royal Warwickshire Regiment. The men readily identified with these drawings that gave them a chance to forget the horrors of war for a spell and laugh at the absurdity of their lives along the front lines. This attitude played to a British tradition of never seeming to be too serious in whatever anyone was doing, even though beneath this veneer something very serious was often going on, such as killing other men in any way possible, both in France and Flanders and in many other parts of the world.

In France on November 1st, Penfold's battalion was relieved, having lost only four men wounded. At brigade headquarters, this total would have been callously marked down as little more that 'normal wastage.'

Jerry had survived his first days in the trenches, but the damp weather had been too much for him. Although he did his best to shake off a fever, he and two other subalterns were hospitalized on the 7th just as their battalion once more filed back up to the front line.

Returning on the 14th, Jerry most likely went up at night with a ration party to rejoin his battalion, stumbling in the mud along the communication trench where spent artillery shell cases, shattered wooden crates and derelict equipment formed macabre outlines in the glow of gunfire flashing from the east. As on all battlefields, paper was also strewn over everything as a constant reminder of the wastage of war.

During daylight in Jerry's absence, numerous but heavy bombardments had been accurately ranged onto the Borderers' position by German observers floating high above them to the east in baskets beneath huge 'sausage' balloons. This time, only 150 yards separated the two front lines. Enemy snipers remained active, but several were located and killed. About twenty Borderers had become casualties by the time the battalion was brought back for more than one mile to Philosophe on November 16th.

On the following day, an interesting character, Captain C. H. March, DSO, arrived to take over duties as the battalion's second in command. Although the KOSB regimental history makes no mention of him, he's worth a few lines here.[57]

As an officer of the British Indian Army, his temporary attachment to the battalion was further proof of the alarming scarcity of trained Regular Army officers. Marsh's tenure with the Borderers was brief but, by the end of January 1916, he had become their commanding officer and signed the war diary as such. Soon after, he left to command the 7th Battalion, The Queen's Own Cameron Highlanders.

As for Jerry, his health was failing him yet again. Even for short periods in the trenches or elsewhere, wind, rain and cold weather combined to wrack him with bronchitis. As if this were not enough, an imbalanced trench diet of bully beef, bread, jam and sometimes bacon, washed down with strong tea, whisky or ration rum, had brought on an attack of gastritis.

It was a trying time for all, and several officers who had also fallen ill were sent to a hospital well behind the front lines. But for Jerry, this time there was no alternative but to invalid him to England, and he reached his home on November 24th. The KOSB war diary makes no mention of this, but it is referred to in one of Penfold's two obituaries.

The time required between leaving his battalion and arriving home seemed endless to everyone because a train might easily take up to eighteen hours to travel just fifty miles. Dozens of delays occurred as tons of military supplies and equipment moved up each day by rail to huge depots. In the opposite direction came hundreds of sick and wounded men being taken down to French ports for

---

[57] Early in his military career, Cunliffe Hebbert Marsh had served in the Boer War with the 1st Battalion, South Lancashire Regiment. As a twenty-year-old subaltern he had been recommended for a Victoria Cross during the capture of Railway Hill on February 27th, 1900, one day before the relief of Ladysmith. Instead, he was awarded a Distinguished Service Order, a rare honor for such a junior officer.

embarkation to Britain, and the journey must have been dreadful for both British and French soldiers sitting squeezed together with neither heat nor light while facing each other on uncomfortable wooden benches.

Younger officers could look forward to the good times they would have with friends in London at the Alhambra, Savoy and Piccadilly Grill and also at shows in the West End. But regardless of rank, once a soldier reached his home, he still had to allow for the same delays in returning to his battalion at a specified time.

In the case of Jerry Penfold, one begins to wonder at the quiet courage of this frail man whose exposure to the vile French winter weather was just as likely to kill him as a bullet or shell splinter. There were any number of essential civilian wartime jobs he could have held, and given his physical disabilities, no one in good conscience would have sent him a white feather.[58] But instead of safety, he sought the firing line.

One can only speculate on what Jerry's family physician and a military doctor would have recommended for his recovery, but with the desperate need for officers growing steadily worse, he was once more passed as sufficiently fit to return to France after only six days. Bidding his family farewell, he caught the leave boat at Dover on the first leg of his journey back to the war.

On December 15th, Field-Marshal Sir John French, under pressure from Prime Minister Asquith, resigned his command of the BEF, which he had led to France in 1914. At sixty-three, he was little more than a corpulent caricature of the flamboyant Boer War *beau sabreur* who fifteen years earlier had galloped a force across the South African veldt to the Relief of Kimberley. Ever since Loos,

---

[58] In Britain during World War One and in earlier wars, gentlemen who were believed to be too cowardly to join up were sent a white feather attached to a calling card bearing the name of each sender. The recipient could expect to be shunned for life by his former friends.

confidence in his leadership abilities had been waning, and by December 15th he was gone, succeeded by his archenemy, General Sir Douglas Haig.

Sir John had never been the right man to command the BEF. As early as the immediate aftermath of Mons in 1914, his mood swings had ranged from unrealistic concern for the safety of his troops to overconfidence once the war became more fluid. This was followed by bad decisions based on such poor judgment that he became a liability to the BEF and the French with whom he was reluctant to cooperate.

The manner in which the war was progressing was sounding another sour note in London where Secretary of State for War David Lloyd George was scheming to topple the government of Prime Minister Herbert Asquith.

Lloyd George was a man of sparkling brilliance but had long carried with him a reputation for unsavory behavior and stunningly bad luck in investments. His speculations in gold and many other 'blue sky' schemes kept him constantly short of cash. As an active philanderer who lived apart from his wife, who resided in Wales, he outwardly kept an apartment in London with his mistress, a circumstance considered well beyond the pale by polite social standards of the day. His political career might well have been ruined had it not been for his friends at high levels in the press who arranged to keep his name out of the newspapers for being named correspondent in a number of messy divorce proceedings.

Fortunately for him, his ambitions to replace Liberal Prime Minister Asquith were substantially aided by a combination of Winston Churchill's eclipse for having insisted on the disastrous Allied offensive in the Dardanelles and Asquith's failure to deal firmly with the Western Front shell shortage scandal. These issues soured public opinion of both of these men and created the perfect climate for 'LG' to orchestrate a behind-the-scenes Labour coup. This would lead to Asquith's resignation and his replacement as prime minister by Lloyd George in December 1916.

Having been driven from his cabinet post of First Lord of the Admiralty, Churchill, to his credit, arranged to be sent to France to serve as a major with the 6th Battalion, Royal Scots Fusiliers. He soon earned the respect of all ranks by asking his colonel if he could sleep in the trenches with his men instead of at battalion headquarters. By December, he had become their colonel and soon after made himself instantly recognizable by affecting a bluish-gray French helmet!

In France at this same time, the 7th Battalion, KOSB, was in billets in Burbure, a town far enough behind the lines for the men to get a wash and relax after a day of kit inspections, rifle range practice and exhausting carrying parties. It might not have been as grand as Béthune, but to them it was heaven.

In its shops were cheap souvenirs to send home, while rough wine and watery beer flowed in floods from estaminets where *real* women were seduced in the imaginations of hundreds of weary, homesick men. Raucous songs shouted in unison helped to hide the horrors they had seen and would soon see again.

But even there they were not entirely safe, and they knew it. Shells from long-range heavy-caliber German guns often dropped on the town, randomly gutting a building here and abruptly atomizing a few men there.

On Christmas Eve, Jerry Penfold was riding his horse through the streets when, with a rising scream and a thundering crash, a shell killed the animal, which slumped beneath him. Thrown to the pavement, he was shaken but unhurt in a lucky escape from death.

Jerry then disappears from view until Monday, January 24th, when a friend of his, Charlie Hadbarry, joined him for lunch in his billet, then in Mazingarbe. Outside, Jerry's batman, Private Beaumont, had fetched his officer's horse, which he had ordered because he was needed that afternoon in a nearby village.[59]

Having finished their meal, Jerry and his guest walked down the road for a short distance, continuing their conversation. Suddenly, with next to no warning, an eight-inch German shell exploded behind them. When the dust and debris had settled, Jerry's horse lay still and Beaumont was dead. A French soldier with his leg torn off screamed and writhed in agony in the street. Another officer's batman was wounded.

That evening, to get his mind off this terrifying experience, Jerry attended a concert and mentioned in a letter to his family that it was quite good for something so close to the front lines. But his thoughts kept drifting back to the nightmare in the road.

'I was much attached to Beaumont,' he had written. 'He was a rough Yorkshire man, but a real good sort, honest as the day, and he did look after me so well.' Now, of course, it was Jerry's responsibility to write to Beaumont's mother, which he did.

At the funeral, which Jerry attended, Private Beaumont was buried with two other men. Carried on a gun limber, the three bodies sewn in cloth were brought into the cemetery where 7th Battalion pipers played 'The Flowers of the Forest.' Just as the third body was being lowered into the ground, the rising scream of a heavy German shell was heard.

'All of us, including the guards and the padre, dropped flat. It burst, and all the bits flew over us, but no one was hit,' Jerry's letter continued. 'So we can't even bury our dead in peace.'

He had a simple wooden cross made and inscribed, 'In Memory of Pte. J.

---

[59] A batman was a private soldier in an officer's company who was selected to be the latter's servant. His job was to clean his uniform and equipment and make life as comfortable as possible for him under all circumstances, even in the front lines where he always went with him. It was a cherished job because of the likelihood of small rewards for doing the job well. After the war, many officers remained in touch with their batmen and often helped them through difficult financial times, especially in the Great Depression of the 1930s.

Beaumont, Attd. 7th KOSB. Killed in action, January 24th, 1916. R. I. P.[60]

On the same day as this funeral, Lieutenant J. D. Proud, Royal Army Medical Corps, joined the battalion, replacing Captain T. H. Lawder, who had been posted elsewhere. Proud had only been mobilized from the Special Reserve in early July 1915. In the confusion of reaching a battalion ordered up to the line on the very next day after his arrival in France, he didn't even know he had been promoted to captain nine days earlier. His thoughts would have been centered on getting to know the stretcher-bearers who would soon be working with him.

On the 26th, three companies of the 7th KOSB fell in and began the march from their billets in Mazingarbe to the lower crest of Hill 70. As the late afternoon light began to fail, they felt their way out of the pulverized remains of Loos village where they dropped off their reserve company.[61] In the distance, irregular muzzle flashes from dozens of German guns formed brief, flickering shadows, while huge shells burst amidst the grotesque ruins around them.

Continuing east for about one mile while still under fire, the men moved on through the clinging mud in the long communication trench to the front line where shells were falling with shrieks and sheets of flame. Once there, they relieved the 8th Battalion, Seaforth Highlanders, in the front line. Quickly, efficiently, Seaforth officers handed over their trench sections to their Borderer counterparts. Wishing them luck, they disappeared into the evening gloom.

Men stood near the fire step in anticipation of an attack, and hunched signalers tested their telephone lines to brigade. Captain the Reverend T. S. Symington, the battalion's Presbyterian chaplain, worked his way around a traverse and down

---

[60] 14935 Private Joseph Arthur Beaumont was the son of George and Ellen Beaumont of Barnsley, Yorkshire. He was twenty-eight at the time of his death.
[61] It had become customary by this stage of the war for a battalion moving up to the front line to leave one of its companies in reserve. In the event of crippling losses, it was believed these survivors would be able to perpetuate the battalion's character and age-old traditions, thereby enabling it to be rebuilt along the proper lines.

another length of trench, encouraging a man here and there with a word or a Woodbine.[62] Jerry, anxious for his safety, offered him a steel helmet. By the early hours of the 27th, the battalion's position had been secured, but something ominous was brewing.

Fifty-seven years earlier to the day on a sunny afternoon in Berlin, a son was born to Queen Victoria's oldest child, the wife of Frederick William, Crown Prince of Prussia. Cannons in the Lustgarten fired 100 rounds to salute the future Kaiser Wilhelm II. Now, along the Western Front in France, another enormous celebration in steel burst upon the 46th Brigade's front at Loos, lasting throughout the night and well into the following day.

Several yards of trenches held by the 7th Borderers at the Hohenzollern Redoubt all but vanished beneath this hail of explosives. Covered by rapid fire from rifles and machine guns, the Germans put in an attack against the 10th Scottish Rifles to the left of Jerry's battalion, but machine gunners from the 6th Battalion, Royal Irish Regiment, and the 9th Black Watch, who were temporarily in the line on the Borderers' left flank, scythed the enemy down.

The Borderers' trench line was not assaulted, but the enemy barrage increased its intensity against it as black eruptions of muddy ground were sent skyward by the devastation of exploding shells. Men pressed themselves against the slimy walls of their trench, transfixed by terror and expecting to die at any moment.

Captain C. H. M. Horne, transport officer at Loos in the preceding year and now commanding A Company, was killed outright. So was Second Lieutenant Thomas Miller who had hastened to help one of his men who was wounded. One of Jerry's men was also hit. Pushing his way to him, he began to bandage his wound, and then he himself was badly wounded. The call went out for stretcher-bearers to carry him down to the battalion aid post located in one of the support trench

[62] Woodbines were a popular brand of cigarettes at the time.

dugouts. There Proud hastily did what he could to help him while many others were also being brought to him.[63] The massive bombardment ended as suddenly as it had begun, enabling what was left of the Borderers to prepare for a German advance, but no attack followed.

Bandaged but weakening fast, Jerry was carried toward the rear. It would have taken at least two strong stretcher-bearers to bring him down a communication trench while at risk if renewed artillery fire fell on them. On the following day, Jerry died at Number 37 Casualty Clearing Station at Noeux-les-Mines and was buried in the village cemetery,

Word reached Folkestone on the following day. Soon after, Jerry's fellow officers sent letters of condolence, one of which was written by a man whose name I will never know but who clearly had measured his comrade's worth in the trials of fire in France.

'. . . Dear old Jerry. We all loved him so much, with his quaint mannerisms, which were part of his loving self. He was, above all, a very fine officer when on duty in the trenches; never a minute late when his turn came for duty, often taking other people's watches. . .'

Sir Stephen's death in 1925 marked the passing of the Penfold male line in England. His daughter Queenie lived until 1949, having named in her will a relative, Frank Penfold of Upper Melbourne in Canada's Province of Quebec.

As a result of a taped appeal for help I made for the Canadian Broadcasting Corporation, I managed to make contact with a distant relative of Jerry's, Mrs. Jocelyn Penfold Tetley Call, whose mother had known Queenie. Unfortunately, she could add nothing to the story of a young officer who had died in France in 1916.

---

[63] John Dover Proud became an acting major in 1918, having won a Military Cross and bar for a second award in the space of just two months in 1917. On August 1st of the following year, he died of wounds at the age of twenty-five.

What was once Hill 70 now forms part of an airport. Near its summit, shallow dips and hollows—the remains of trenches and craters made by mines—still mark the horrors that happened there to so many young men who died so many years before their time.

BIBLIOGRAPHY:

Carew, Tim, *How the Regiments Got Their Nicknames* (Leo Cooper, Ltd., London, 1974)

Folkestone Express, Sandgate, Shorncliffe and Hythe Advertiser (February 5th, 1916)

Folkestone, Hythe and Cheriton Herald (February 5th, 1916)

Gillon, Captain Stair, *The KOSB in the Great War* (Nelson, London, 1930)

Greenwell, Graham H., *An Infant in Arms, War Letters of a Company Officer, 1914-1918* (Lovat, Dickson & Thompson, Ltd., London, 1935)

Kraus, René, *Winston Churchill, a Biography* (J. P. Lippincott Company, New York, 1941)

Official History, Military Operations, France and Belgium, 1915 (Macmillan and Co., Ltd. London, 1928)

B. Cory Kilvert Jr.

War Diary of the 7th Battalion, King's Own Scottish Borderers, 24 September 1915- 31 January 1916 (Public Record Office, Reference WO97/1953)

Warner, Philip, *The Battle of Loos* (Wordsworth Editions Limited, Ware, Hertfordshire, 2000)

Wickes, H. L., *Regiments of Foot, A Historical Record of All the Foot Regiments of the British Army* (Osprey Publishing Ltd, Reading, Berkshire, 1974)

Woollcombe, Robert, *All the Blue Bonnets, The History of The King's Own Scottish Borderers* (Arms and Armour Press, 1980)

Second Lieutenant Jeffery Bradley Penfold prior to leaving for France in 1915. Faintly visible in the photograph is the monocle in his right eye, a clear indication of his poor vision, which might have enabled him to avoid military service.

Penfold's parents received news of their son's death while living in this house at 70 Cheriton Road in Folkestone, Kent.

Lieutenant Penfold's headstone in Noeux-les-Mines Town Cemetery in France.

CHAPTER 7

1890-1917

Second Lieutenant William McNally, MC

3rd, 10th, and 4th Battalions, The Worcestershire Regiment

My medal collection includes a Military Cross and three World War One medals named to W. McNally who served in the ranks of the Worcestershire Regiment and later was commissioned as a second lieutenant. These medals are especially interesting to me because of one of the regiment's 18th century experiences in Boston, Massachusetts, where I had once lived.

Raised as the 29th Regiment of Foot on February 16th, 1694, the Worcestershire's men would be nicknamed 'The Vein Openers' seventy-six years later for having been ordered against their wishes to fire on a crowd of colonists at what would become known as the Boston Massacre. A plaque laid into the pavement outside the city's Old State House has long marked the spot where this shooting occurred.

The regiment's 667-page history of its record in World War One is remarkable for the comprehensive accounts of its twelve fighting battalions in which 9,000 officers and men died between 1914 and 1918. It includes two footnotes relating to McNallys, the first of which shows that Company Sergeant-Major W. McNally,

10th Battalion, was awarded the Military Cross for an exploit performed in the Somme area on July 30th, 1916. The second mention indicates that W. W. McNally, MC, was among two second lieutenants killed in the 4th Battalion during the Battle of Poelcappelle in Belgium on October 9th, 1917.

Assuming these two McNallys were probably the same man, I asked Pat Wolfston to obtain his birth certificate and will. The former showed he had been born on July 4th, 1890, at The Castle in Dover. His father was Battery Sergeant-Major William McNally, and his mother was the former Elizabeth Jane Wright, who had been born in 1861 in Blue Town in Sheerness, Kent. The latter document indicated that McNally's beneficiary was his mother, then living in Chatham, Kent.

Armed with these fragments of information, I sent a letter to the postmaster of Chatham, outlining my interest in locating relatives of this Great War soldier. In reply, he told me my letter had been passed on to his local newspaper and also to the manager of BBC Radio Medway.

Less than one month later, I received a letter from Mr. Desmond McNally in Rochester. He had read my newspaper notice and told me he was William McNally's nephew. Although he was unsure of his memory on a few points, his recollections presented the chance of finding someone else who might know more, and the threads of a story then began to unwind.

He told me that McNally's sister Edith had married a man named Cook by whom she had a son and daughter, both of whom had been born in Luton, Kent. He could not recall his cousins' names but stated that Edith had remarried and moved in the 1920s to Harwich where her second husband served as a civilian instructor on a Royal Navy training ship. Pat discovered this might have been H.M.S. *Ganges* at Shotley.

Pat also found the marriage certificate of Edith McNally and John W. Cook in 1917 as well as the birth certificate of a child, Bettine E. Cook, born in 1920. Anticipating one of my habits, she also sent me the names of two newspapers in areas in which Bettine Cook might still be living.

In this particular case, attempting to locate a woman who might—or might not—still be living somewhere in Essex or Suffolk by sending letters to newspapers seemed so far-fetched to me that I delayed doing so for almost one year. But as other possibilities of making contact with this woman withered, I finally mailed requests for help to newspapers in Harwich, Colchester, Halstead, Sudbury and Ipswich.

Clearly, finding this woman would be a one-in-a-million long shot, but I had no alternatives left. The telephone directory for the Colchester area alone listed almost 700 Cooks, and the thought of mailing letters to even one-quarter of them was a forbidding prospect. Fortunately, I already knew a few details in the life of Battery Sergeant-Major McNally because Pat had sent me a copy of his army record which showed he had been born in Bishop Auckland, Durham, in 1857 and had served in India and in the Second Afghan War in 1878-80.

In the spring of 1892, before Mrs. McNally's baby boy had reached the age of two, her husband announced they were due to sail in May for Cape Town, South Africa. He was to serve there with the 25th Company, Western Division, Royal Artillery. During this posting, they brought two more children into the world at 83 Church Street—Edith in 1893 and in 1895 Harry, who was to become Desmond McNally's father.

In 1896, after almost twenty-four years of service, which had begun in 1872 when he was fifteen, the sergeant-major requested his discharge. An exemplary soldier, he had qualified as a third class master gunner, held a Long Service and Good Conduct Medal[64] and also the Second Afghan War Medal. He asked that his pension be sent to him at his mother's home at 1 Mark Lane in Leeds.

---

[64] At the time of this award, twenty-one consecutive years of exemplary service were required. Through the years, this time span would be reduced.

In an effort to trace someone at that address who might be helpful, I learned the entire area had been occupied by a huge department store since 1934. So I then was left with only one remaining hope of finding William McNally's niece, but as more than two months passed by with no word, I began to lose hope. But in September 1984, the one-in-a-million miracle happened with the arrival of a letter from a Mrs. Hunt in Ipswich.

'I am the Bettine Hunt you are hoping to contact, the niece of Second Lieutenant William Wright McNally, MC,' she wrote, adding that one of my newspaper letters had been seen by a former school friend. 'It is really quite extraordinary how quickly I was traced,' she continued, 'as several of the facts were not altogether accurate.'

Mrs. Hunt explained that she had moved from Chatham to Ipswich when her stepfather was appointed to the Royal Hospital School Holbrook, and that it was *she* who had served on H.M.S. *Ganges* during seven years' service in World War Two as an officer in the Women's Royal Naval Service.

She recalled that her mother's earliest memories were of great happiness in South Africa. Edith could recall many carefree days of sunshine, Table Mountain, a black nanny and many pleasures of play with her brother Will. After returning to England, their sister Florence was born in 1898, but sadness would soon cloud their young lives when their father died of pneumonia in 1901 at the age of only forty-four.

With the exception of Florence, whose health was never good, the children were sent to boarding schools near Leeds, which were administered by the army. Will, in particular, flourished in this environment, doing especially well at sports, an interest he retained after he enlisted in the Worcestershire Regiment on August 21st, 1906.

Responding to a letter I sent to Lieutenant-Colonel K. G. Allen, a retired officer then serving as curator of this regiment's museum, he explained that McNally 'would have done his recruit training here at Norton Barracks. He would probably have spent six months at the Depot, but it could have been less.'

Colonel Allen added that, normally, when a recruit completed his training, he was posted to the Home Service Regular battalion. In 1906-07, two of the four Worcestershire Regular Army battalions were 'home,' the 1st being in Ireland and the 3rd at Aldershot. So McNally could have been posted to either, although it seemed to me likely that he was sent to the 3rd, for reasons that later will become clear.

Since 1903, the 3rd Worcestershire had developed an impressive reputation for marksmanship, and by 1907 they were universally considered the best shots of any battalion in Great Britain. They won the coveted Queen Victoria Cup in 1903, 1904 and again in the following year.

While stationed at Tidworth, Will represented his regiment in field hockey and track events, winning a Royal Army Temperance Association gold medal in 1913 for coming in first in a cross-country race. At twenty-three, he was fit and anxious to do well in his chosen career, which all too soon would call him forth to war as thunderclouds began forming over Europe.

Germany's dread of encirclement, aggravated by the Franco-Russian Alliance of 1894, was increased still further by Great Britain's diplomatic agreement with France, the *Entente Cordiale*, signed in the spring of 1904. An additional threat seen by Germany was presented by the Anglo-Russian agreement of August 1907, which created the Triple Alliance.

Britain, however, emerged from these understandings with no obligation to support either France or Russia if Germany attacked them, although the Royal

Navy was committed to cover French ports along the English Channel to protect them in the event of a German naval assault.

No other naval or military responsibility was either stated or implied in this masterstroke of British diplomacy. So it remains one of the greatest ironies in modern history that Germany adopted the quickest and surest means of destroying her security in Europe by attacking France through Belgium. Britain and also the Prussians had twice by treaty guaranteed Belgian neutrality, once in 1831 and again eight years later. So with German troops across the Belgian frontier by the morning of August 4th, 1914, Great Britain was at war with Germany by midnight of the same day.

At 5:45 p.m. on that day, the 3rd Worcestershire received orders to mobilize. By the 9th, 724 officers and men from the Reserve had arrived at Tidworth, and the next few days were spent in route marching and musketry drills. On the 14th, the battalion embarked at Southampton aboard s.s. *Bosnian* which headed for Le Havre and then steamed up the River Seine to Rouen. Early on the 17th, the men marched through its streets but left soon after by train on their way toward the front lines. In command was Lieutenant-Colonel[65] Burleigh Francis Brown Stuart, a forty-six-year-old officer who had joined the regiment as a young subaltern almost twenty-five years earlier.

The battalion spent the next week moving up to Ciply, Belgium, then a separate village about one and a half miles south of Mons but now an extension of that city. The men formed part of the 7th Brigade, 3rd Division in General Sir Horace Smith-Dorrien's II Corps.

On August 23rd and on the following afternoon, they would hear guns booming to the north along the canal stretching west from Mons where battle had been joined with the Germans. By nightfall of that day, the 3rd Worcestershire were well

[65] Later Colonel (temporary brigadier), CB, CMG.

dug in at Ciply. Being in the second line behind the front, they were not attacked until early the next day.

Although they shot their foe to a standstill, the battalion and the rest of the 7th Brigade were soon forced to conform to the general retirement from Mons. McNally's mob sustained twenty-one casualties, including two men killed, but they were not seriously threatened until the 26th, by which time the bulk of II Corps was exhausted by two days of almost endless marches and frequent rear guard fights in efforts to escape destruction.

In the small hours of that day, Smith-Dorrien made his gallant stand near Le Cateau as described in an earlier chapter. Sir John French, in a later attempt to justify his specious claim that nothing should have slowed up the withdrawal, released false casualty figures, but Sir Horace's stand went far toward discouraging the Germans from pressing their foe south with the speed and determination they might otherwise have shown.

On the 26th, while manning an outpost line west of Bavay at dawn, members of the 3rd Worcestershire's D Company observed a German Uhlan patrol trotting toward them out of the mist. Like Private Arthur Small's battalion of Cornwalls along the Mons-Condé Canal, they repelled these enemy horsemen. The rest having scattered, the men calmly brewed tea over tiny fires, but this would be no day of rest.

What followed was to blur memories and blend events into a series of long marches with short rests similar to those experienced by Corporal Kirkham of the 1st King's. Defensive positions dug into the ground were usually evacuated almost as soon as they had been started, and this exhausting work was performed under a blazing sun. High in the air, flimsy, kitelike enemy aircraft were sometimes seen spotting the battalion's movements, and from the east was heard sporadic gunfire from the huge German right wing that menaced the BEF's very survival.

General von Kluck was pressing his German masses to break the BEF by getting their huge force between II Corps' right flank and the vanguard of Haig's I Corps that was hastening south from Landrecies to close a dangerous eight-mile gap.

After only two hours' sleep, McNally's battalion was called forth at 2:30 a.m. on August 26th to occupy shallow, inadequate trenches to the west of Caudry. There the men dug for their lives before catching what additional sleep they could, which seldom lasted for more than a few minutes. At dawn, a firefight developed rapidly in which B and C Companies, in particular, were assailed by machine gun and artillery fire.

Patiently and with their deadly aim undiminished, the men systematically picked their targets, their rapid fire taking a heavy toll of Germans attempting to cross the Cambrai road. Later that morning, a heavy German shell pitched into 3rd Battalion headquarters, recently located near a railway embankment in Cambrai. Exploding with a deafening roar, it instantly killed several men on orderly room duties and injured several others. Major W. R. Chichester, battalion second-in-command, and Captain C. V. Beresford, the adjutant, were severely wounded and soon to be taken prisoner in a makeshift hospital.[66]

Before daybreak on the 27th, the battalion moved off once more, their route as staggered as the steps they took for another twenty-one miles before stumbling into Vermand, six miles northwest of St. Quentin, which they reached at 4 p.m.

And so it went for another day and another twenty miles to Tarlefesse, which some of the men entered in bare feet, their boots having worn out completely in the thirteen days since they had landed in France. But here, at least and at last, a long rest awaited them. The worst was over, although their retreat continued until September 5th.

---

[66] The Army list for 1920 shows that both of these officers survived the war as German prisoners.

No one in Great Britain with sons, husbands and brothers in the 3rd Worcestershire would have known anything even half as specific about the retreat as the few details written here. This was a time of widespread confusion and of the wildest rumors for the men of the BEF as well as for their families at home who were starved for war news.

About eight years earlier, Will McNally's mother had bought a home in Chatham, Kent, which she was now operating as a hotel. Located at 6 Ordnance Terrace, the building would have been known to Charles Dickens because he had once lived as a boy at what became Number 11.

It was not a large place, having only three apartments. In the daytime, according to Mrs. Hunt, the family lived in the basement, which consisted of several rooms, including a kitchen and food store. Florence and Edith had a bed/sitting room in the attic, as did Harry, and there would be space made for Will, too, whenever he might get leave.

Of course, at this desperate stage of the war, leave was out of the question. But following rest, reinforcement and a good bit of reorganization, the BEF again began to take shape as it became the hunter instead of the hunted in pursuit of its foe to the heights about the River Aisne. And it was there that William McNally was first to make a name for himself in the regiment.

For unspecified services rendered, he was mentioned in General Sir John French's despatches for October 8th as a member of the Worcestershire's 3rd Battalion. Because these documents related to operations from the evening of September 10th, Will's exploit probably occurred during his battalion's most serious engagement in the fighting just north of the Aisne.[67] This took place on

---

[67] These same despatches also honored Major George Cory, the author's Canadian cousin mentioned earlier in this book. Cory was then serving as a General Staff officer, 2nd Grade, at General French's headquarters.

September 20th, the same day that Albert Armitage and his East Yorks' mates were also fighting furiously in the same general vicinity.

In the early morning of that day, a fierce German bombardment was followed by an attack on the 7th Brigade north of Vailly. Two platoons of the 3rd Worcestershire were rushed to the left where the enemy had broken the front line and stormed through to headquarters of the Wiltshire Regiment's 1st Battalion, where they took several prisoners.

Even further to the left, the line held by the 2nd Royal Irish Rifles was in danger of cracking from a steady pounding by German guns. Huge explosions echoed along the riverbanks behind the 7th Brigade's positions, while showers of soil and stone rained down upon the British trenches. To make matters even worse, the right flank of Will's battalion, which rested on a thick wood, was soon involved in a desperate struggle amidst the trees where D Company led by Captain Jefferies fought a stubborn delaying action while falling back gradually by twos and threes.[68]

Once more, rapid and accurate British rifle fire decided the issue, and the Germans withdrew, leaving behind more than forty dead. Losses in Will's 3rd Battalion were even worse—sixty-one killed and wounded and a large number of missing.

Elsewhere on September 20th, the war was escalating. *The Sunday Times* reported the early morning landing of the Royal Marine Brigade at Dunkirk. A second contingent of British Indian Army troops had left Bombay for France, and off the coast of Zanzibar, the ancient H.M.S. *Pegasus* had been sunk by the fast German cruiser *Königsburg*.

---

[68] Hugh St. John Jefferies survived the war as a major, having won a Distinguished Service Order in August 1917 for gallantry north of Hooge, Belgium, while commanding the 2nd Battalion, West Yorkshire Regiment.

From the beginning of the fighting in Belgium and France, Secretary of State for War Lord Kitchener and Prime Minister Herbert Asquith had been among the very few voices of authority in all combative nations to predict a long conflict. Kitchener was convinced from the start that the war would require far more soldiers than could be supplied either by Britain's standing army or by the Territorial Force, both of which had already taken heavy casualties. Almost overnight, his call for volunteers resulted in long lines outside recruiting centers throughout Britain, and chaos prevailed before these enthusiasts could be properly clothed, sheltered, fed, equipped and, above all else, trained.

Soon to be organized into 'New Armies,' each battalion enjoyed a direct link to its Regular Army battalion already in the field. And while the ranks were being filled with inexperienced young, and not so young, men—bankers, brokers, shopkeepers, clerks and those from other civilian vocations—command of these new battalions fell largely onto the shoulders of older officers of experience, most of whom were recalled from retirement.

The 10th (Service) Battalion, Worcestershire Regiment, was one of those units. Organized at Worcester in September 1914, it was commanded by Colonel Alexander George Chesney, a fifty-seven-year-old veteran who had retired in 1905, five years after he had raised, trained and commanded the 4th Battalion. Well qualified to lead the 10th, he was, however, hampered by a problem which plagued all New Army battalions, a growing shortage of experienced officers and non-commissioned officers.

To partially overcome this deficiency, a small percentage of officers and men from the Regular Army, veterans of the recent fighting, were distributed throughout the New Army battalions to impart their knowledge and skills to the newcomers. It is almost a certainty this is how William McNally came to serve with B Company of the 10th Worcestershire, which had landed in France in July 1915.

161

As part of the 57th Brigade, 19th Division, the 10th Battalion had gradually been exposed to the hazards and terrors of trench warfare, and by January 1916 its members were spending time in and out of the line at Neuve Chapelle, the scene of a costly British attack in the preceding March in which almost 13,000 officers and men had become casualties within just three days.

Will's experiences in France are unknown until January 14th, 1916, when he sat down and wrote out his will while his battalion was resting in billets at Croix Barbée. It stated, simply: 'In the event of my death I give the whole of my property and effects to Mrs. E. McNally, No. 6 Ordnance Terrace, Chatham, Kent. W. McNally, 10099 Sergt., B Coy, 10th Worcestershire Regt., BEF.'

On February 10th, the war at sea brought a German warning that, as of March 1st, all armed merchant ships of any nation would be considered belligerents. Five days later, the United States summarily rejected this declaration, inching it closer to entering the war in 1917.

In 1989, I received a letter in a shaky handwriting from Mr. E. A. Cave, a ninety-two-year-old man in Emsworth, Hampshire, who told me he had read an article on McNally by me which had recently been run in a journal published by The Western Front Association. Cave had served with McNally in the 10th Battalion and had retained his high regard for him over the next seventy-three years.

Cave had enlisted in March 1915 when he was only seventeen years old, and he told me that Will was interested in him because he had already seen active service with the 9th Worcestershire and been wounded at Gallipoli.

'He was a very strict disciplinarian,' Cave wrote. 'My clearest memory of this [involved] a certain private in the platoon—a big, bullying type of man who took a dislike for some reason to a corporal in the platoon and was in the habit of hurling abuse at him. The corporal was physically afraid of him.' Cave explained further that McNally once overheard this abuse and immediately had the private sent to the Guard Room and put up on a charge.' Readers will shortly learn more about who this bully may have been.

In May 1916, the 10th Battalion arrived in the Somme area to begin strenuous brigade training until the end of the month. During that time, half the battalion occupied a 15th century farm where nineteen-year-old Joan of Arc had been imprisoned prior to her trial for witchcraft.[69]

During this 1916 spring in London and Paris, astronomical losses in killed, wounded and missing in the Czar's forces on the Eastern Front were sounding Allied alarm bells regarding Russia's ability to remain in the war. Should its collapse occur, millions of German troops could quickly be transported by rail to the Western Front to provide an overwhelming military supremacy with more than enough manpower and artillery to drive through the British and French lines to victory.

As a means of shoring up Russian morale, it was decided to send Lord Kitchener to St. Petersburg to see if he could stiffen the Czar's resolve to carry on the fight. So on June 5th, five days after the huge but inconclusive battle off the Danish peninsula of Jutland between ships of the Royal Navy and Germany's High Seas Fleet, he left on H.M.S. *Hampshire*. This cruiser soon ran into the teeth of a gale with such power that two accompanying British destroyers were ordered to escape destruction by returning home. The seas were even more threatening to submarines but could not have been better for mines sown earlier by the German submarine U-75 onto what would prove to be the cruiser's course.

Having hit one of these powerful explosive objects, the ship went down within fifteen minutes, taking Kitchener and all but twelve of its 600-man crew with it. All of Britain was stunned.'K' killed? Impossible!' But Winston Churchill heard it being shouted by a news vendor outside his London home, and King George

[69] Condemned, Joan was burned at the stake in Rouen on May 30th, 1431.

V would be overwhelmed by the loss of a close friend he had admired for thirty years.

On the Western Front, everyone from Field-Marshal Haig down to the lowliest private was affected by the passing of this larger than life national icon. Among his most memorable achievements had been his systematic destruction of a huge Dervish army in the sands of Omdurman in 1898, bringing an end to the cruel reign of an African despot. Haig first got word of the tragedy when he was handed an intercepted German report. But while Great Britain mourned this loss, the war continued to claim many more thousands of victims.

During the morning of July 1st, the British launched their massive, cataclysmic offensive, which would be remembered forever after with horror as the Battle of the Somme in which 57,000 British and Commonwealth soldiers were killed and wounded on the first day alone. However, there was justification for this massive assault because it was Haig's response to a frantic French appeal for help in easing relentless German pressure on their forces at Verdun. By the time this offensive was called off more than two years later with no meaningful gains, it had left 420,000 British soldiers killed, wounded and missing. German and French losses came to 650,000 and 195,000, respectively.

Sergeant McNally's battalion was not committed to the Somme front lines until July 3rd when shortly after 3 a.m. the order to advance was heard with whistles and hunting horns blown by its officers along their sector. Jumping 'over the bags,' the men quickly dashed across No Man's Land and went straight at their foe entrenched in the remains of La Boiselle.

Few activities in warfare are more hazardous than those spent fighting in towns, even those in a state of ruin. In this instance, the Germans, having reinforced cellars and dug deep pits, rose from these shelters like hornets to confront their foes. Savage hand-to-hand fighting ensued with clubbed rifles, bayonets, grenades and bare hands. By this stage in the war, some men preferred a short-handled entrenching spade to a rifle. When brought down with force onto an enemy's shoulder, the blade could make a dreadful wound and be ready to slice deep into the next German's neck, as well.

While the outcome still teetered in the balance, the 10th Battalion's commanding officer, Lieutenant-Colonel G. A. Royston-Piggot, came forward to assess the situation with his adjutant, Captain H. A. Gillum-Webb. Almost at once, the former was shot through the heart, and the adjutant was hit within another few minutes. But as more defenders were killed, several small groups of Worcestershire men pressed on through the village and into open country beyond it to the northeast.

Lieutenant Richard William Jennings was among those pursuers. He called to several men to follow him, one of whom was Private Thomas George Turrall, a giant of a man from Small Heath, Birmingham, and somewhat of a troublemaker. A footnote on page 170 of the Worcestershire Regimental History states that Turrall *'had been freed from the Guard Room specially to take part in the battle'*[70] because he was a member of a specially trained and badly needed squad of Mills bombers led by Jennings. Readers may decide for themselves if this was the same man as the one McNally had arrested earlier.

Regardless, no one can deny that Turrall would prove to be an extraordinarily brave man. While advancing, he was fired on by a hidden machine gun but escaped injury by hurling himself to the ground. Nearby, he could see that Jennings was badly wounded. Dragging him to a shell hole, Turrall splinted his shattered leg with the handle of his entrenching spade, which he secured with a puttee unwound from one of his own legs.

Spotted and attacked by Germans hurling grenades, Turrall shot two of them before an enemy counterattack swept over them. Jennings had fainted, and Turrall

[70] Author's italics.

165

lay still beside him, feigning death while German bayonets poked at him until the attackers moved on. While daylight lasted, Turrall succored and protected his officer, and when night fell he carried him to safety on his back, earning a well-deserved Victoria Cross. Jennings died within a few more hours at a dressing station in Dernancourt,[71] but Turrall survived the war.[72]

In Cave's letter to me, he recalled seeing Sergeant McNally at one point walking calmly up and down a trench during a tremendous German artillery bombardment. 'I think this was at Ovillers and just after the attack at La Boisselle,' he wrote. 'This was before his promotion to company sergeant-major,' he explained further. Cave noted in his second letter that while still in the front line on the Somme, 'one shell fell right in the trench of the platoon on our right, killing at least six men and wounding many others.

'While we were crouching against the parapet, getting what cover we could, McNally was giving us words of encouragement and making no attempt to get into any shelter for himself. I served with many non-commissioned officers,' he added, 'but nobody to touch McNally. He was always very cool in the most trying circumstances. A very great man, liked and respected by everyone, senior and junior.' Will was only twenty-six at the time but an experienced and thoroughly reliable veteran of the old Regular Army whose outstanding leadership qualities would soon be revealed once more in the days that lay ahead.

In the haze of dusk on the evening of July 29th, the land was a moonscape of shell holes and destruction. Ahead of the British front line, the Germans had connected many of these craters into a new defensive position which could not be seen because of its clever siting on the reverse slope of a slight rise. This elevation

---

[71] Jennings was buried in Row D, Grave 324 in Meaulte Military Cemetery, which is south of Albert. The son of a Gloucestershire minister, he had studied to be a solicitor at Cambridge and was a boxing champion while there. He was twenty-seven years old at the time of his death.
[72] In 1964, Turrall died in Birmingham at the age of seventy-four.

was still clearly visible in 1984 when I photographed what anyone else would reasonably have dismissed as nothing more than a potato field.

After dark, patrols probed silently forward with eyes straining into the gloom to locate enemy positions on the far side of the slope. Edging along the broken ground like rats, the men froze in the light of flares sent up to betray their presence. Briefly, traversing enemy machine guns barked on the flanks, randomly searching for victims. Well before dawn, the patrols slipped back through their own wire with important information. The Germans were located only 120 yards north of the British line.

The 19th Division's assault was planned for the evening of July 30th. This was unusual because British attacks had most often been made in the morning. So perhaps surprise would play a part and catch the enemy off balance. In anticipation of this, the first wave of attackers had silently moved forward to points near the top of the rise, ready to race toward the German trenches. At 6:10, British guns pounded the ridge and the ground beyond it for a mere five minutes and then lifted to more distant targets. The attack went in.

On the right, the 10th Royal Warwickshires and the 7th King's Own crossed No Man's Land in one great bound and jumped into the enemy line, bayoneting and gunning down their foe before they could respond with rifles and grenades. Prisoners were rounded up and hurried to the rear under guard.

But on the left, disaster struck the 8th Gloucesters and McNally's battalion. Almost as soon as they began to move forward, they were hit by murderous enfilade machine gun fire. Struggling ahead to the crest of the ridge, they were caught by even heavier fire ahead of them, which forced them to withdraw to their starting point while pursued by hostile shelling. Within little more than two hours, the two battalions suffered losses totaling eleven officers and 247 men. That night heavy artillery fire fell on their front and support trenches and also behind them in Bazentin-le-Petit, now little more than a pile of broken bricks.

McNally lived through this dreadful day and was recognized for bravery. The specifics are long forgotten, but his regiment's history starkly declares: 'For gallant conduct in that attack, CSM McNally was subsequently awarded the Military Cross.' I like to believe that he rescued one or more of his men in this action because it was the sort of thing he would have done without hesitation. But whatever the reason, his superiors held him in high regard, as indicated by the conditions under which this award could be earned by officers and warrant officers.[73]

On the preceding day near Ypres, Lieutenant Sydney Baker Harris of the CEF's 27th Battalion, another of the author's Canadian cousins, had distinguished himself during an action and would also receive a Military Cross. This was the younger brother of the two officers mentioned in an earlier chapter. The citation read as follows: 'For conspicuous gallantry during a raid on the enemy's trenches. He killed two of the enemy with his revolver and three with bombs [hand grenades]. Finally, he helped to carry a wounded sergeant back to our lines under heavy fire.'

Like the Australians, the Canadians excelled at this activity, which was usually launched in an effort to capture and interrogate a few prisoners and keep the others as nervous as possible. It was dangerous work, and once men were able to enter a section of enemy trench, their troubles had just begun. They still had to block both sides of it and hold the space between, while fighting with knives, clubs, rifle butts and their bare hands until their captives had been removed or killed.

At the time of his exploit, Harris was not yet eighteen years old, and in the course of the raid, his arm was badly broken. Treated at a casualty clearing center

---

[73] Out of a total of 40,261 MCs awarded between 1914 and 1920, only 781 (less than two percent) were won by warrant officers.

in Poperinghe,[74] he was sent soon after to a London hospital and later to Canada for additional care, but his wound would prove to be too serious to allow him further active service. Thousands of Canadian soldiers would also be partially or seriously incapacitated for the rest of their lives, a condition that would affect millions of other men on both sides of the war.[75]

In the trenches and back areas, one of the few comforts a fighting man could look forward to was the infrequent chance to go home on short leaves, and Will McNally was known to have had more than one of these welcome respites. His sister Edith remembered how filthy he looked and how everyone insisted he remove his lice-infested uniform in the garden before coming indoors. Most men burned their clothes because a new uniform could be obtained at no cost at any military depot whether it was his own regiment's or not.

Once home, men cleaned themselves up while savoring the good times that lay ahead. But too often, they found it difficult to discuss the realities of war with civilians, and many were unable to sleep in their old beds, preferring a corner of the floor. Having longed for home, once there they missed the rough comradeship of those still in France or Flanders with whom they had witnessed a multitude of horrors. Somehow maintaining their sanity with crude jokes and silly songs beneath which lay an unspoken feeling of affection, these men were indeed a family of brothers. Having spent brief periods in England with their parents and wives, they were often relieved to return to the front, even though the war was

[74] 'Pop' had become a huge Allied supply base. Although it was considered a back area, heavy-caliber German guns could, and did, shell it late in the war. To thousands of Allied officers and men, it was perhaps best known as the site of Toc H, a club established by a British Army chaplain, the Reverend Phillip 'Tubby' Clayton, in what he called Talbot House. Once through the door, soldiers could relax with a cup of tea or a newspaper without considerations for differences in rank. This three-storey building survived the war, but in the war to follow, the Germans attempted to burn it after the Allied invasion forced them to leave Poperinghe. It was saved by local inhabitants and may be seen to this day.
[75] My father once told me when I was a boy that he knew Canadians who had received such disfiguring facial wounds that they covered their faces with cloth hoods with holes for their eyes, nose and mouth whenever they left their homes.

not going well in 1917, especially for the French. As will be seen, this would put increasing strain on the BEF to assume greater responsibilities in the front lines to take German pressure off their hard-pressed ally.

It now becomes necessary to put aside the story of Will McNally for some considerable time in order to concentrate on certain aspects of the war's more significant events, the perils which some of them posed and the effect they would have on the course of the conflict and on McNally, in particular.

Haig's moment for glory had arrived in September 1916 but would quickly evaporate as a result of his impatience and stubbornness. Earlier in England, the few military and civilian minds still able to think beyond the front line stalemate began to experiment with an entirely new concept for breaking the Western Front wide open. By manufacturing a heavy steel enclosure mounted above tractor treads, they ran numerous tests until convinced they had a fearsome weapon with huge tactical potential. Code-named 'tanks' for the sake of secrecy, the first models were designated the Mark I but were also known as 'Big Willies.' It remained to be seen if they would perform as well in battle.

Once finalized in England and shipped to France in great secrecy, these steel monsters weighed 22 tons and were able to crush barbed wire entanglements. They could also cross trenches that were nine feet wide, but their top speed was less than four miles per hour, making them easy artillery targets. Their main strength included two six-pounder guns and two machine guns, and each crew consisted of one officer and nine other ranks.

Once inside these huge machines, the men lived in a unique hell. There was no engine muffler, and the noise was so overpowering that commands had to be shouted as loudly as possible. In addition, what could be seen outside was so limited that effective fire control was almost impossible. The smell of gravity-fed fuel was everywhere, and if a tank pitched nose down into an enemy trench, its gas had to be fed by hand to the engine—a hazardous process, especially while under fire. Worst of all, the fuel range of each tank was limited to less than ten miles and if stalled in front of a strong German position, it might easily cost the lives of its crew. But for all these drawbacks, the men who operated tanks willingly served in them and were given extra comforts when behind the lines.

Haig, who was anxious for a significant victory, foolishly decided to commit these machines to the Somme battlefield almost as soon as they reached him. This proved to be a costly mistake. Had he awaited the arrival of many more tanks, his dream of a major breakthrough might well have been realized.

Of the forty-nine Big Willies chosen for an attack to be made shortly before dawn on September 15th, only eleven managed to move beyond the German front line, but one of them reached an enemy trench, got behind it and took 300 prisoners. However, Germans who were still holding their positions elsewhere soon realized that these lumbering machines were vulnerable to heavy-caliber artillery fire.

Haig's second mistake was equally fatuous because he should have decided to use tanks almost anywhere but along the Somme. The ground there had long before been churned into a vast bog, and heavy enemy artillery stood ready behind enormously strong defensive systems.

On that same September day of the tank assault, the Canadian Corps had been in the front line for the past two weeks, rotating its divisions while awaiting the start of the massive attack. In the 2nd Division was a 23-year-old officer from Hamilton, Ontario, Lieutenant John Chilton Mewburn, who was another of the author's cousins. Serving with the 18th (Essex and Kent Scottish) Battalion, he and his men were ordered to capture a strong German position called 'Candy Trench,' which was to the east of Thiepval along a three-mile line extending west to east from Courcelette to Flers.

B. Cory Kilvert Jr.

The younger son of Major-General Sydney Mewburn, CMG, VD,[76] and his wife, the former Rachel Amanda Cory, he was killed on that day somewhere within the Flers-Courcelette sector. Today, his gravestone may be seen at the Canadian Memorial in Courcelette.

Gloom persisted along the Western Front toward the end of 1916. The French government had become disenchanted with General Joseph Joffre's stubborn policy of forcing his troops to make frontal attacks against strongly held German positions. Time after time, these assaults of a nineteenth century nature had sacrificed many thousands of lives with nothing to show for them in terms of breaking through the enemy's lines in force. On December 12th, Joffre was replaced by General Robert Georges Nivelle, an artilleryman but with the dash and panache of a cavalry leader, who claimed to have all the answers required for ending the Western Front deadlock.

This appeared to make sense in the light of his service record to date. He had been Pétain's assistant at Verdun where his capture of Fort Douaumont had led to his being given command of the entire sector. On April 16th, 1917, he was also credited with a solid victory along a thirty-two-mile front between Soissons and Rheims where he had taken 10,000 German prisoners and much war material. Radiating optimism while surrounded by gloom in both Paris and London, he seemed to offer a simple solution for creating some new found momentum with victories to follow it.

Bilingual because of an English mother and upbringing, Nivelle was polished, politically adept and manipulative, traits which had helped his rapid rise to high rank. His tactical plan had quickly caught the ear of Lloyd George whose efforts to replace Haig were being frustrated by the latter's friendship with the King. Lloyd

---

[76] Major-General Mewburn served as Adjutant-General in 1917 and having succeeded Sir Edward Kemp as Minister of Militia and Defence, he directed Canada's war effort from 1918 to 1920.

George also lacked sufficient support in the Imperial War Cabinet to effect Haig's replacement. So all he could do was insult Sir Douglas by subordinating him to this new self-styled Gallic Messiah, who had quickly become the senior Allied officer for Western Front operations. Haig, ever the perfect gentleman, bowed to being treated in a peremptory manner whenever Nivelle sent him orders, but disgust for the man's rude behavior simmered within him.

The year ended on the usual depressing note as the people of all warring nations wondered with trepidation what still lay ahead. To underscore their apprehension, word of an especially painful event had emerged which had its start on October 23rd, 1914. On that day, British Indian Army forces garrisoned in Bahrain to protect its oil refineries invaded southern Mesopotamia (now Iraq), moved up the Tigris Valley and captured Basra on November 23rd. This would prove to be the beginning of the first war fought for control of the Middle East oil fields.

While advancing further toward Baghdad, this force under Major General Charles Townshend was stopped, pushed back to Kut-al-Amara, surrounded and forced to surrender on April 29th, 1916, to Turkish troops fighting on Germany's side. Having held out for 143 days, these already exhausted and starving men were subjected to a merciless 1,200-mile death march while being lashed, kicked and killed by their Kurdish guards.

As for Townshend, he had sent fawning letters to the Turkish commander throughout the siege and messages to his superiors requesting promotion, and after being forced to surrender, he readily accepted treatment as a celebrity. The Turks' highest-ranking officer, Mustafa Kemal, provided elaborate dinners for him in Baghdad, later furnished him with an island villa perched above the Sea of Marmara and even arranged for him to be reunited with his dog!

While this unfeeling man spent comfortable months seeking ways to gain his release from confinement, his men continued to rot and die from brutality and neglect. But among his command were eight soldiers who managed to escape from their captors. Having somehow traversed 450 miles of harsh, desolate country and reached the Mediterranean in a state of near collapse, they stole a small boat, avoided a large Turkish military camp and eventually reached Cyprus and freedom. They arrived there half dead but with their honor intact.[77]

A weary world could not have anticipated that 1917 would prove to be pivotal in world history. But at its start, a scent of optimism was in the air because of Nivelle's appointment. Clearly, here was the right man with the right answers for all that had gone wrong before, but he was being seen through rose-colored glasses. In London, major concerns over the course the war was taking were being felt by many, including Lieutenant-Colonel Charles Repington, a former army officer and now an influential military correspondent for the *Times*. On January 18th, he had a conversation in London with Field Marshal Lord French, who had been named commander, British Home Forces, following his dismissal from command of the BEF in France.[78]

French told Repington he did not think the British were making proper arrangements for winning the war in 1917 and added that "Haig and others, including Nivelle, believe that the Germans are demoralized and that we can walk over them." He then made the sobering observation that the British Army had sufficient "infantry drafts for [only] two months' normal casualties."

Repington would have been comfortable in the relaxed morality of the 21st century. A gifted, bilingual journalist with both friends and enemies in high places,

---

[77] Upon his return home, Townshend's fate was to be rendered invisible to everyone in government, the army and society. He died in France on May 16th, 1924, and, fittingly, no one from either the War Office or the British Government attended his funeral.

[78] French was sent home in December 1915 because of his leadership failures in France and also due to his heavy drinking, which was interfering with his command judgments. Sir Douglas Haig, one of his major enemies, planned this banishment but was supported in his efforts by General Sir Henry Rawlinson and other senior British officers.

he was also a social butterfly who appeared to know virtually everyone in both British and French government and society. Clever, articulate, chatty and often indiscreet, he had reached his social low water mark in 1902 when he was publicly named in a divorce case for having had an affair with the wife of a Colonial Office official—a major black mark in its day which forced Repington to resign his commission in the Rifle Brigade.

His most injudicious moment in the war had occurred when he ignored an army gag order with his article in the *Times* on May 14th, 1915, in which he claimed, 'The want of an unlimited supply of high explosive was a fatal bar to our success at Festubert.' This revelation had not only led to the downfall of Asquith's Liberal government but also to the eclipse of Sir John French, the very man Repington was speaking with in London on that January day in 1917.

Sir Douglas Haig, who still maintained his dislike and distrust of the press, would long before have wasted no time adding Repington's name to his list of cads. As for Minister of Munitions Kitchener, whom the *Times* had raked over the coals because of the shell shortage, he had seen to it earlier that Repington was prevented from generating new information on the war from officers on the Western Front until the spring of 1916.

Remaining in character, Repington, who defected to the *Morning Post* in 1918, plumbed another depth by being found guilty and fined for leaking secret information in violation of the Defence of the Realm Act. But always a survivor, he published two best selling books after the war ended and lived until 1925.

On the Eastern Front in 1917, a huge casualty rate and wretched treatment of a largely peasant Russian army would lead to revolution against the Czarist regime on March 12th, the Czar's abdication three days later plus the establishment of a Bolshevik state and ultimate surrender to Germany. Nicholas and his entire family were murdered at Ekaterinburg on July 16, 1918. As the Allies had feared earlier, this eventual Russian collapse enabled Hindenburg and Ludendorff to transfer masses of fresh troops to the Western Front and concentrate on the destruction of the Allied armies before the weight of America's strength could be felt in the front lines.

While Nivelle was finalizing his attack plan, the Germans shortened their front in early April 1917 by withdrawing for twenty miles to the recently completed Hindenburg Line, a defensive position of enormous strength. The vast area evacuated was subjected to total devastation to prevent it from offering shelter to anyone. Every house and barn was completely demolished, trees were felled, food confiscated, all livestock killed and every well, lake and pond was poisoned.

This formidable new German line was where Nivelle, in choosing to maintain French military dogma that called for attacks at all times, orchestrated another grotesque failure with severe consequences. In short, Joffre's policies were maintained almost to the letter. But not quite.

Because Nivelle now controlled both the French the British armies on the Western Front, he was able to claim all the anticipated glory for himself by canceling Haig's plan for encouraging the British to assume the leading role in this latest attack. This was a deliberate slap in the face to Haig whom Nivelle would continue to treat in a peremptory manner when issuing orders to him.

For the time being, Nivelle was free to finalize another huge assault without the slightest consideration for the hundreds of thousands of casualties already suffered by the French army whose low morale had seriously weakened both its capacity and willingness to fight any longer. But before this offensive was launched, Haig was instructed to make an attack on Vimy Ridge on April 9th. Essentially a Canadian-planned assault, in contrast to so many French failures, it was a thundering success from the start, and its ground gained would be held for the rest of the war.

This achievement caused Allied spirits to rise as they had three days earlier when it was learned that the United States had finally joined the Allies. This was largely the result of Germany's ham-handed effort three months earlier to bring Mexico into the war on the side of the Central Powers in return for U.S. territory. British cryptanalysts had deciphered a telegram to this effect from German Foreign Minister Arthur Zimmerman. Incoming President Venustiano Carranza was not interested and was yet to be sworn into office, but the United States was justifiably outraged.

Nivelle's preamble to what would become known as the Second Battle of the Aisne was to try shoring up the spirit of his French troops by convincing them that this offensive by twenty-seven divisions on a forty-mile front would win the war within two days. But when the assault began on April 16th, their ranks were decimated by customarily accurate German artillery fire. Undeterred, Nivelle resisted efforts by both Chief of the General Staff Henri Pétain and the French government to call off what would result in 187,000 casualties by May 5th.

Success had never been possible from the beginning. In fact, the battle had been lost by the end of the first hour because German Military Intelligence had known exactly what to expect from having captured an outline of the attack during a raid on a French trench. Its agents had also overheard many of Nivelle's earlier indiscretions while revealing his battle plans to adoring women with whom he had dined in London restaurants.

This catastrophic failure proved that Lloyd George had hitched his wagon to the wrong star. It would also serve as the last straw for large numbers of mistreated *poilus*, some of whom when going into battle had begun to 'baa' like sheep, which indeed these poor devils had become. And when a single French regiment mutinied on April 29th, the act spread rapidly through the army, affecting 23,000 soldiers who refused to fight any longer. News of this outbreak was suppressed, but while it lasted for two weeks, the entire Western Front was practically devoid of a French Army presence while grievances were addressed and authority restored.

The only salutary events to follow this defeat would be Nivelle's removal from his command on May 15th and banishment to a French military backwater in North Africa for the rest of the war.[79] In addition, Pétain managed to stop the rot of mutiny from spreading further through the French Army by combining compassion with firmness to restore order in the ranks more rapidly than might have been expected.

Although thousands of French soldiers were tried and found guilty of mutiny and another 432 were condemned to death, only fifty-five went before firing squads, while the remainder who had been condemned were transported to penal colonies at Devil's Island and elsewhere. During this dangerous time on the Western Front, a weakened BEF stood alone with the pitifully small Belgian Army on its northern flank.

Prior to Nivelle's departure for oblivion, Repington spoke with him at length on May 2nd and again on the following day, and the former's comments revealed the depth of his dishonesty. Insisting that his losses were far lower than reported, he also made the absurd claim that he had "imposed our will upon the enemy, had taken the initiative and could claim a victory by occupying the enemy's first lines on the fronts attacked, contrary to the enemy's will." He also speciously maintained that the Germans had suffered so severely from French artillery fire that their ability to remain on the offensive had been seriously affected for a long time.

During these momentous events in the spring of 1917, Will McNally's 10th Battalion, Worcestershire Regiment, had moved up from the Somme to Flanders

---

[79] French generals who had failed the tests of war were usually banished to Limoges in the southwest of France. That Nivelle was required to leave France altogether is indicative of the government's reaction to his shocking failures.

on March 18th with the rest of the 19th Division. On the 27th, the battalion occupied trenches north of the Vierstraat-Wytchaete Road for four uneventful days. For men who earlier had been through such fierce fighting on the Somme, this relatively quiet area would have been a blessing. It was also an indication of their division's understanding of how tired and depleted the 10th Worcesters had become after the heavy fighting its men had seen. Clearly, they were in need of a rest.

April and May would bring the battalion even safer activities involving training and working parties with only brief time spent in the front lines, including duty near Hill 60—a hot spot like all other elevations on an otherwise flat landscape and one that would grow even hotter.

Lieutenant General Sir Herbert Plumer was charged by Haig with the task of planting mines deep in the earth below Messines, which was enabling the Germans to observe for miles beyond them virtually everything the British and French were doing. On June 7th, this elevation gave its name to a battle planned eighteen months earlier when German forces began to drive mine shafts and tunnels extending beneath the British lines. Each tunnel was large enough for enormous amounts of high explosives to be packed into them.

On the receiving end of this activity, British underground listening devices had detected the sounds of digging, and British, Canadian and Australian tunneling companies began to drive their own tunnels below those of their enemy at twenty-two places from Hill 60 south to a point immediately east of Ploegsteert Wood. At all times, both British and German tunnelers had to face the possibility of an enemy breakthrough, which would result in savage fights with knives, pistols, clubs and grenades plus picks and shovels. Sometimes, enemy tunnels were collapsed with explosives that entombed those working in them.

Mines had been detonated before, but this effort was something far more ambitious and deadly. Each of these twenty-two British tunnels that varied in length

179

from 200 to more than 2,000 feet were packed with 600 tons or more of explosives for a distance of just over one mile along a line roughly resembled an irregular letter C. The Germans discovered one mine near the River Douve and blocked it. So it then became a race to see who could finish the task first. In the meantime, a devastating seventeen-day British artillery bombardment wreaked havoc on the German trenches and troops manning them.

The enemy lost the race. At 3:10 a.m. on June 7th, 1917, nineteen of the twenty-one remaining British mines were detonated to coincide with an attack that would capture Wytschaete and Messines below it. The cataclysmic blast of a million pounds of ammonal and the sheets of flame that followed it were unlike anything the world had ever experienced before. So violent were the sights and sounds that they were seen and heard across the Channel in Kent and also heard 130 miles away in London.

An estimated 10,000 Germans were buried alive or killed by millions of rounds of shrapnel, high-explosive and gas shells, and many of those who survived were turned into numb or babbling wrecks. At once, a tidal wave of British and Empire troops rose from their trenches, moved forward, and six hours later, the ridge was in Allied hands, but at a high cost in killed, wounded and missing..

Within less than seven hours, the German first and second lines were in British hands, and a German counterattack failed. In addition to enemy killed, many more were taken prisoner, and large numbers panicked in a rush to the rear. Further enemy counterattacks over the next seven days were also unsuccessful.

Of the two mines that failed to explode, one was set off near Ploegsteert Wood during a thunderstorm in 1955, killing a lone cow. The remaining mine is known to be in the same general location and is believed to be fifty to 100 feet deep.

Hill 60 where Will McNally had fought in the spring, and where the northernmost mine was blown, changed hands four times in the war and is now owned by the

Commonwealth War Graves Commission. A plaque tells the story of the fights for this uneven terrain with its small craters and irregular rises on which sheep were grazing when I visited it. Only heaven knows how many brave men on both sides remain buried beneath it.

Beyond these generalities about Warrant Officer McNally on Hill 60, nothing specific is known about him except for the sparse information in his service records which I had asked his nephew to apply for. Having survived the London Blitz, they showed he had been commissioned a second lieutenant on September 15th, 1917.

At that stage, the war had killed and maimed so many British officers that commissioning of men from the ranks had accelerated appreciably. Often looked down upon as 'ranker officers' by those who had never served as privates or sergeants, these 'temporary gentlemen' were often sent to battalions of regiments other than their own where their presence would be less likely to ruffle sensitivities.

But in Will McNally's case, his own regiment wanted him, which was one more tribute to his stature as a front line soldier. Furthermore, he was to go to one of the Regular Army battalions, the 4th, which had also been training for most of September.

Soldiers commissioned from the ranks often received a respite from the fighting with a few weeks of training in England, but Lieutenant McNally was not among those so lucky. In any case, there was precious little he could have been taught that he had not learned from practical experience over the past three years. Furthermore, the immediate need for more officers at the front was reaching crisis proportions.

Leaving the 10th Battalion at the village of Moolenacher, about three miles east of Bailleul, Will was given less than a day to report to his new battalion. Perhaps he got a ride north to a point near his destination in an Army Service Corps vehicle carrying supplies and ammunition from a dump behind the lines. It was only a ten-mile journey, at most, to 'Piccadilly Camp' near Proven in Flanders.

For some days, he had been carrying with him a letter from his sister, which she had written on September 7th. 'Having not heard from you for a fortnight,' it began, 'we are naturally very worried about you. We read about this terrible battle and wonder are you all right. Do try to write Ma a line as she is quite ill. She has not heard from Harry, either.[80]

At Will's destination, the 4th Worcestershire were preparing for front line duties. They had been in France and Flanders since March 1916, having served earlier at Gallipoli. Their brigade was the 88th, and their division, the 19th, was widely recognized as the best in the BEF. Its senior officer was Major-General Douglas Edward Cayley, CMG, DSO, who had commanded the 4th Battalion at the start of the war and later the 88th Brigade. His adjutant would have known that an outstanding soldier was on his way to him.

The Third Battle of Ypres, launched on July 31st, 1917, and destined to last until November 10th, was a series of British attacks which came to be known collectively by the sorrowful-sounding name of a single village on the vast Flanders battlefield—Passchendaele. By this or any other name, it was an offensive forced upon the BEF by one ally recently shaken by mutinies in its army and by another whose forces from America were still not sufficiently trained or equipped to play a meaningful role in the front lines. Equally urgent at this time was the need to capture North Sea harbors being used by German submarines and surface craft to prey on the Allies' shipping lanes.

For three years while British staff officers busied themselves by sticking pins into maps while comfortably ensconced at safe distances behind the lines, few of

---

[80] Will's brother Harry had enlisted in the Essex Regiment and served with its 10th Battalion. He survived the war, having won a military Medal in 1918 for bravery in the field.

them ever came up to see what an appalling area it was for men on the war's cutting edge. To British and German soldiers alike, it was a Calvary of systematic misery and murder fought out in a poisoned swamp in which men sometimes stood for days in cold mud and water up to their waists. There was almost nothing of Nature left to be seen there while men died by the thousands. For British forces and their Empire allies, Passchendaele was especially dreadful because it formed a salient, which allowed for torrents of enemy flanking fire. But Allied attacks went on under conditions that modern minds can scarcely believe could have been demanded. However, it must be remembered that the masses had been used to obeying orders all of their lives, and they and their officers also had too much regimental pride not to obey them

From the time Lieutenant McNally joined his new battalion until October 7th, only four days were spent in the front line. The remainder of the men's time was spent in training for the next big push scheduled to begin on the 9th.

On the evening of the 7th, the battalion moved east once more along duckboards laid on the muck of Pilckem Ridge. It was raining, and their progress was slow. At best, the wooden track offered a firm but slippery footing to soldiers burdened by sixty pounds or more of equipment. At any moment, sections of it could be blown apart by enemy shellfire, but to leave it was to court disaster of a different sort. Once in the mud, men could easily lose their balance and slide into shell holes. Filled to the brim with putrid, opaque water, each crater could be two feet deep or twenty. If the latter, drowning was all too often the doom of those whose mates were unable to reach them in time.

As Will trudged up the track in the darkness and rain, there would have been time to muse about his latest link with home—the letter from his sister, which was still in his pocket. With it had come a photograph of a pretty young woman with bright eyes and an intelligent face.

Edith was twenty-four. In January, she had married an officer in the Royal Navy, and she was expecting their first child in late October. 'I myself am fairly well and expect to go into the nursing home at Gillingham about the 20th of this month,' she had written. 'I hope everything will turn out A1. . . . Well, dear Will,' she continued, 'I do trust you are spared through this terrible war as poor Ma seems to look back on you so. I know you will help her all you can as she is beginning to age now. But we will talk things over later, as I hope you will get leave soon. . .'

The guests at Elizabeth McNally's hotel were now all married doctors from St. Bartholomew's, a military hospital in the New Road. Undoubtedly, she would have asked them for advice about Florence, whose health had deteriorated steadily. But there was nothing anyone could do, and in June she had died of tuberculosis at the age of nineteen.

This tragic loss added to constant anxiety over the safety of her sons had led Will's mother into periods of deep depression. To make matters worse, German aircraft had dropped forty-six bombs on Chatham, Sheerness and Margate on the night of September 3rd, killing 132 people and injuring another ninety-six.

'We were all terrified,' Edith had reported in her letter, adding encouragingly, if inaccurately, 'but our guns kept them off.' Clearly, she was trying not to worry her brother.

Air raids like these were nothing new. The first Zeppelin attack had taken place over East Anglia on January 19th, 1915. Since then, fifty-three more assaults of this type had been made by these dirigibles or huge Gotha bombers as far north as Edinburgh, during which over 70,000 pounds of bombs were dropped, causing over 1,800 civilian casualties. The last Zeppelin raid on British soil would not take place until April 12th, 1918.

In closing her letter, Edith asked Will to write soon 'and take care of yourself and you will have a fine fat nephew. With tons of love and XXXXXXX, Your Loving Sister, Edie.'[81]

Before dawn on October 8th, the 4th Worcestershire had filed into their allotted sector of the front line about 1,000 yards north of the village of Langemarck and less than three miles southwest of Ypres. Patrols crept forward to find suitable crossings over a stream, while over their heads a storm of fire boomed from British guns. By noon, it was pouring rain, which lashed the men until evening.

Immediately after dark, the assault companies began to move up to their jumping off points. A ration party, suffering its way through the clinging mud, brought up packs filled with tea and rum kept hot by straw tied around them. The rain came down once more and continued until shortly after midnight.

In the first few moments of dawn on October 9th, the two leading companies commenced their attack, while artillery fire pounded German concrete blockhouses and fortified farms, the latter with innocent-sounding trench map names like Olga Houses and Kortebeek Farm. Fording the stream without difficulty, men pushed on to neutralize the blockhouses, which generally required a direct artillery hit to be destroyed.

Heavy enemy shelling began to range onto the assault troops about ten minutes after they had left their start line, and men began to drop. Within half an hour, those who survived had advanced about 1,200 yards and reached their first objective. The attack was going well, but a machine gun in a solitary blockhouse continued to cause heavy casualties. While waiting for Stokes mortars to be brought up to deal with it, the men suddenly realized the gun had stopped firing.

Beyond their vision and outside the rear doorway of this fearsome obstacle, a thirty-eight-year-old native of Barbourne, Worcester, Private Frederick George Dancox, was

[81] Sadly, Edith's baby, born of October 25th, died within one month. This may well have been due to the malnourishment of many British expectant mothers whom German submarines were depriving of a sufficiently balanced diet.

standing with a Mills bomb held above his head in his right hand. Unnoticed, he had approached the blockhouse from one shell hole to another with ten other men, entered its door and now was threatening its terrified occupants with extinction. Having rounded up forty Germans and started them off toward the British lines, he returned to the concrete structure, removed its machine gun and used it to considerable advantage for the remainder of the day. He was awarded the Victoria Cross.

At about 7:15 a.m., a renewed British bombardment dropped shells on the second objective about 750 yards ahead. The two companies held in reserve then moved into position to continue the advance. Carrying a Stokes mortar with them, they scored four hits on a blockhouse, surrounded it and took its survivors prisoner. Pascal Farm fell next, after twenty-five mortar rounds had blown it to pieces. By 9 a.m. the attackers had reached their goal. Digging frantically, they consolidated their position as once again their own artillery lifted onto more distant targets.

The 29th Division's history refers to the many German snipers who caused casualties during this advance to the second objective. Somewhere during this second phase, one of these marksmen brought Second Lieutenant McNally into his telescopic sight, held him there and shot him dead. He was one of seven officers and 167 men of the 4th Battalion killed, wounded and reported missing on that day, in which 200 Germans and five machine guns were captured. Rated a significant success, this attack was just one of dozens of costly actions fought in Europe in 1917 as the war continued to engulf more nations throughout the world.

Italy, for example, had been allied with Germany and Austria-Hungary by the Triple Alliance of 1882, but her partners' unprovoked aggressions enabled Rome to claim neutrality. Looking for greener pastures, she turned to Britain and France in 1914, and Prime Minister Antonio Salandra was gratified by their offer to expand Italian colonies in Africa on the assumption that Allied holdings would also grow larger there. Still playing both ends against the middle, Italy come into the Allied camp on May 23rd, 1915, shortly after her demands on Germany and Austria for more postwar territories had been agreed to but too late to suit Rome.

Neither side should have dealt with Italy, and events would prove she would have been far better off to sit out the war. Instead, her army began immediate attacks along the boundary she shared with Austria-Hungary.

Between late June, 1915, and mid-September, 1917, there would be numerous battles fought along the Isonzo River in the difficult mountain terrain along the eastern Austria-Hungary border where some elevations reached 3,000 feet. This activity would command little of General Ludendorff's attention until August 6th, 1916, when in eleven days, General Luigi Cadorna's army of fifty-two divisions and more than 5,000 guns punched holes up to five miles deep along a front of forty-five miles extending north from the Gulf of Trieste.

This achievement and its potential for causing the loss of the important Bainsezza Plateau prompted Ludendorff to give General Otto von Below seven German divisions to help the Austrians smash the Italians at Caporetto on October 24th. This one-day triumph created a panic of such magnitude that the rout lasted until November 10th when Italy's depleted forces finally reached the Piave River, seventy-five miles from the battlefield they had abandoned and less than twenty above Venice.[82] Soon after, the 23rd and 41st British Divisions would be rushed to the aid of their ally and more would follow to prevent a total Italian collapse.

Of Italy's military manpower at the start of hostilities, her war casualties total would reach over 600,000 for no appreciable gains except for its one successful offensive. An additional 22,000 Italians would also be captured.[83] But to this

---

[82] During this pursuit, an enterprising German lieutenant captured 8,000 Italians in a single day. In World War Two as General Erwin Rommel, he would prove to be a master of armored tactics in the desert sands of North Africa.

[83] Among the Italian casualties in 1917 was a newspaperman and ardent socialist who was severely wounded by a premature explosion of a mortar shell. Had he been killed instead, Italy would have been spared Benito Mussolini, who in World War Two would take his country down another dark path to ignominious defeat.

country's credit, she remained in the war and managed to prevent the Germans from moving large numbers of troops back to the Western Front.

Although Italy's representatives would sit at the peace table as victors, they would dine only on the crumbs of empire. Having learned little from more than three years of folly, this nation's dreams of glory would eventually blossom into its ill-advised involvement in World War Two.

During the war in France and Flanders and in many other places where British fighting men had died, their bodies had been buried in makeshift cemeteries, many of which had been blown to pieces by enemy artillery fire, leading to a rapidly rising number of men whose bodies would never be found. Britons in positions of authority were sensitive to this tragedy, and in 1917 the Commonwealth War Graves Commission was established by Royal Charter to obtain land in 150 countries on which cemeteries and memorials to the missing could be maintained for all time. Today, these plots remain beautifully planted with trees, shrubs and flowers and with lawns kept well mowed and clear of weeds.

Four miles southeast of the one-time cow pasture where William McNally had died now stands the largest such cemetery in the world. The area it occupies formed part of a German redoubt on Passchendaele Ridge, which was finally captured by Commonwealth soldiers in November 1917. Men of the 50th Northumbrian Division who fought there called this space Tyne Cot.

In addition to its many thousands of graves, Tyne Cot British Military Cemetery to the Missing at its northeastern end enshrines an even greater number of names carved into stone of United Kingdom soldiers whose remains may be lost for all time. Among the latter is the name of 2nd Lieutenant W. W. McNally, MC.

I arrived there on a gray August afternoon with skies that threatened rain. There wasn't another soul in sight and nothing to be heard but a damp wind that moaned among the headstones. The scene, though one of dignity and reverence, presented a jarring reminder. Incorporated into the design are three concrete German blockhouses, one of which is almost completely covered by the base of the Cross of Sacrifice. The other two, surrounded by graves, squat like sightless monsters with ugly mouths that once spat streams of death.

BIBLIOGRAPHY:

Bruce, Anthony, *An Illustrated Companion to the First World War* (Viking Penguin, New York, 1989)

Coombs, Rose, E. B., MBE, *Before Endeavours Fade, a Guide to the Battlefields of the First World War* (Battle of Britain Prints, International, London, 1977)

The Despatches of Lord French (Chapman & Hall, London, 1917)

English Heroes ('This England,' Summer, 1981)

LaFore, Laurence, *The Long Fuse, An Interpretation of the Origins of World War I* (Lippincott, Philadelphia, 1945)

Gardner, Brian, *The Big Push, A Portrait of the Battle of the Somme* (Morrow, New York, 1963)

Gilbert, Martin, *The First World War, a Complete History* (Henry Holt and Company, New York, 1994)

B. Cory Kilvert Jr.

Gillon, E. Norman, *Ypres 1917. A Personal Account* (Purnell Books Services Limited, Abingdon, Oxfordshire, by arrangement with William Kimber and Co., Limited, 1967)

Gliddon, Gerald, *VCs of the First World War, the Somme* (Budding Books, an imprint of Sutton Publishing Limited, Phoenix Mill, Thrupp, Stroud, Gloucestershire, 1997)

Lawson, Henry, *Vignettes of the Western Front, Reflections of an Infantry Subaltern in France and Belgium: 1917-1918* (Positif Press, Oxford, 1979)

Official History, Military Operations, France and Belgium, 1914 (Macmillan, London, 1926)

Owen, Edward, *1914, Glory Departing* (Buchan & Enright, Publishers, Limited, London 1986)

Pollock, John, *Kitchener, Architect of Victory, Artisan of Peace* (Carroll and Graf Publishers, Inc., New York, 2001)

Repington, Lieut-Colonel C. à Court, CMG, *The First World War 1914-1918, Personal Experiences, Volumes I and II* (Houghton Mifflin Company, Boston and New York, 1920)

Spears, Brigadier-General E. L., CB, CBE, MC, *Prelude to Victory* (Jonathan Cape, London, 1939)

Stacke, Captain H. FitzM., MC, *The Worcestershire Regiment in the Great War* (Cheshire, Kidderminster, 1928)

Taylor, A. J. P., *The First World War, an Illustrated History* (Penguin Books, Ltd., Harmondsworth, Middlesex, England, 1966)

Terraine, John, *The Road to Passchendaele, the Flanders Offensive of 1917: A Study in Inevitability* (Cooper, London, 1977)

Times of London (September 20th, 1914)

War Diary of the 3rd Battalion, Worcestershire Regiment, August 4th-October 31st, 1914 (Public Record Office, Reference WO 95/1415)

War Diary of the 4th Battalion, Worcestershire Regiment, October 1st-9th, 1917 (Public Record Office, Reference WO 95/2309)

War Diary of the 10th Battalion, Worcestershire Regiment, July 23rd-30th, 1917 (Public Record Office, Reference WO 95/2086)

This faded image of William McNally as a young soldier with the 3rd Battalion, Worcestershire Regiment, was worn in a locket by his sister, Edith. It was taken at an army athletic event in 1913.

CHAPTER 8

Private Arthur Horner
3rd, 1st and 1/7th Battalions, The West Yorkshire Regiment

For Christmas 1914, arrangements were made for all British Army, military nurses and Indian Army forces personnel in France and Flanders to receive a special gift. Sponsored by Princess Mary, the only daughter of King George V and Queen Mary, this gift, a small, embossed brass box with a hinged lid, was funded by public subscription that raised a considerable sum of money. Contents of the box varied, but the majority contained a briar pipe, one ounce of tobacco, twenty cigarettes and a lighter plus a photograph of the donor and a greeting card. For non-smokers, acid tablets, a pad of writing paper, pencils, paper and envelopes were enclosed along with the photo and card. Indian Army troops received various different gifts, but military nurses ended up with the short end of the stick by receiving the box containing only some chocolate and the card because smoking was not then deemed appropriate for women.

Among the more than 426,000 of these boxes to be distributed was one received by a private with the 1st Battalion, West Yorkshire Regiment, then in billets at Erquinghem near Armentières in France. His name was Arthur Horner. A native of

Yorkshire, he had been born on December 7th, 1884, in the Bishophill section of York, but by 1914 his family had been living in nearby Acomb for some time.

His father, John Horner, was a painter who applied delicate and ornate striping to carriages and each year was known to demonstrate this talent on his own front door. He was sixty-one in 1914 and his wife was fifty-three. Besides Arthur, they had five other children, three boys and two girls.

Like many other soldiers, Arthur was pleased with his Christmas gift and decided to send it home to one of his sisters. So he sewed it carefully into a khaki army handkerchief which he addressed with a pen to 'Miss Lily Horner, 47 Gladstone Street, Acomb, nr. York, Yorks' and let it be known that it was from '6493 Pte. A. Horner, Stretcher Bearer, Headquarters, 1st West Yorks, British Exped. Force.'

Several years ago at a convention for medal collectors in Canada, I saw that handkerchief. A dealer had it on his table along with the brass box and five medals awarded to this soldier. The handkerchief offered its own clues. Because Horner was a stretcher-bearer, it seemed almost certain that he had been a bandsman as well because the wartime role of British Army musicians was to aid the wounded.

From a collector's standpoint, the five medals were interesting because they represented one man's service to three sovereigns. Although all were named to Horner, the three issued for service in World War One were as mute as ever about the experiences of the soldier who had earned them.[84] But the other two were prepared to tell at least some of their story.

The first of these, the silver Queen's Mediterranean Medal, was for service by men at garrisons within the boundaries of that sea who had replaced Regular Army battalions that left to serve in the Boer War. Enemy prisoners were guarded in these

---

[84] Prior to World War One, British military medals awarded for active service usually carried thin silver bars on their ribbons, which bore the names of battles or regions in which several battles were fought. This became no longer practicable for the 1914-1918 period because of the great number of battles and the different places in which they were fought.

establishments by the 3rd battalions of nine regiments, including members of the 3rd West Yorkshires. The remaining medal, also in silver, was the Indian General Service Medal with a silver bar for active service on the North West Frontier of India in 1908.

Along with numerous British Indian Army formations, six British infantry battalions, including the 1st West Yorks, and one cavalry regiment of the Regular Army are known to have served in this brief but taxing campaign.

Assuming that some information on Private Horner might be available, I wrote to the secretary at Regimental Headquarters, The Prince of Wales's Own Regiment of Yorkshire, at Imphal Barracks, York, and received a reply from Major R. F. Tomlinson (retd.). He told me that the only information he had on Horner was that he had died at home on November 16th, 1918, five days after the end of World War One. He added that the regiment's 3rd Battalion had been embodied in May 1900 and that its members had served on Malta in that year and until 1902.

Malta. What a different world this would have been to a lad from Yorkshire who had joined up before his sixteenth birthday. Proud of his new uniform, he had walked to Cuthbert Brothers in Davygate to be photographed in it before leaving home on a transport with 721 other members of his battalion.

Standing midway between Gibraltar and Suez, Malta had been confirmed as a British possession in 1814 under one of the terms of the Treaty of Paris. This document was written after Napoleon Bonaparte's abdication in April of that year, and it reduced France's frontiers to where they had been in 1792.

This 120-square-mile island of limestone rock compensated for its few shade trees with a wealth of oranges, melons and other fruit that thrived in a hot summer sun. The Babel of foreign languages in its streets added vibrancy to a setting in which countless church bells seemed never to stop ringing.

195

As a natural crossroads along many trade routes, Malta's history extended deep into the gloom of antiquity. Its earliest people are thought to have descended from the Phoenicians, and St. Paul was believed to have been imprisoned at its old Roman capital of Medina after the ship carrying him to Rome was wrecked. Its later capital at Valetta had been built by the Knights of St. John of Jerusalem, who fortified it and in 1565 successfully resisted a four-month siege by a huge Turkish force. But as a Boer War military outpost, the island's importance began to wane as a peace treaty became a likelihood, and the 3rd West Yorkshires sailed for home in the late winter of 1902.

Prior to being disembodied at York, the men served in Chatham, Kent, for seven months, and it was there that Arthur Horner joined the Regular Army, being posted soon after to his regiment's 1st Battalion at Quetta in Baluchistan, then under British jurisdiction. He was just eighteen.

Quetta, a large fort located almost 450 miles due north of Karachi, stood on the left flank of the North West Frontier, a province extending for more than 650 miles along the southern boundary of Afghanistan. Studded with military posts along its mountainous terrain, this vast area served as a political barrier to Imperial Russia's designs on the riches of India and as a military deterrent to the local ambitions of its fierce Pathan tribesmen.

During interludes of peace in the early 20th century, life on this frontier for a British private soldier offered little beyond a monotony of training, drill and sentry duty broken only by occasional active service against the tribes, but there were compensations unknown to soldiering at home. Paid in Indian coinage at the rate of one shilling fourpence per day, a private could easily afford the farthing it cost him for enough milk for his tea. For onepence, he could dine on tasty, if tough, beefsteak, and an entire chicken could be his for fourpence or less.

At rates like those, he could avoid army fare entirely, as most men did, except for those unfortunates who sometimes were unlucky at Crown and Anchor and other illicit forms of barrack room gambling. And even they usually managed to be shaved in bed by native barbers paid a pittance for their services.

Arthur would spend about nine years in India, and during that time he became a bandsman. Regimental archives at York include an unpublished album containing a group photograph of the 1st West Yorkshire Drums taken in 1906 at Mian Mir. This was near Lahore where the battalion was stationed from 1905 to 1908, with intervals at the hill station of Kuldana during the hot season.

Although this photo is not captioned, I was able to identify Arthur in it because of some good fortune early in my search for his relations. That search began in the early 1980s when I sent a letter of query about the Horners to the current resident of 47 Gladstone Street in Acomb whose name I did not know.

In return, I received a reply from a Mrs. Peter Watson who declared she had never heard of the Horners. But she took my letter to an eighty-year-old man named C. H. Wigley, who had lived all his life in a house several doors down from the one the Horners had occupied.

I exchanged several letters with Mr. Wigley, whose memory was remarkably clear. He told me that Lily Horner was deceased but that her seventy-six-year-old nephew, George Horner, was living in York. Mrs. Watson telephoned him on my behalf and reported he would be pleased to help me if he could.

Although he knew very little, he suggested that I write to his first cousin, Raymond Vipas, who also lived in York, who would know much more because he had lived with the Horners for seven years as a boy and was Arthur's godson. 'I know Ray has a photo,' he concluded. In fact, he had two likenesses of Arthur, and after we had exchanged a few letters, he agreed to lend them to me so I could copy them.

Raymond Vipas was the son of Edith Horner, Lily's older sister. Due to a serious illness, Edith had been forced to send young Raymond to live with the Horners in the autumn of 1916, and when his mother died two years later, he had stayed on for another five years until his father remarried.

Mr. Vipas wrote to me that, as a boy, Arthur had always had an ear for music. Like all drummers in the army, he would have been proficient on the bugle and fife, as well, but by mid-February 1908, there would have been more important matters to think about besides his responsibilities in the band. The 1st Battalion, West Yorkshire Regiment, had been placed on a war footing.

Ten years earlier, the Zakka Khel Afridis had been among the last of the Pathan tribes to accept British terms forced on them along both sides of the frontier following a mass uprising in 1897. In order to realize the difficulty of controlling that turbulent and lawless region, it is first necessary to understand something of the nature of those who inhabited it.

For centuries along the Northwest Frontier, these tribesmen had lived from birth until death in a sinister environment dominated by reprisals for wrongs, both real and imagined. Their code, the law of *badal*, required them to avenge a multitude of offenses, ranging from petty insults and tribal disputes over land ownership to bad debts and murder.

These issues might have arisen before a Pathan was born and might continue well beyond his death. So complex were his feuds that they existed not only on an intertribal level but could also erupt within his own tribe. They might even involve him in vendettas against his own relatives—a point underscored by the Pashtu language in which the words for cousin and enemy are the same.

To cite a single example of this, a man might have to build a stonewall between his home and his field on lower ground that was below his enemy's line of sight from across a gorge. By walking at a crouch behind this wall, he could avoid being seen. Days and months might go by with no trouble, but one moment of forgetfulness could launch a bullet to his brain from a *jezail*.[85]

The vast majority of these Moslem people were tied by poverty to a stony, mountainous terrain that yielded few blessings to either crops or goats. So it was inevitable they would seek excitement and loot in a dangerous game in which the most coveted prize of all was a British soldier's *bundook*.[86]

Ever adept at stealing British rifles, even from inside army posts, by 1905 the tribesmen were also receiving castoff Martini-Henrys and other weapons from gunrunners on the Persian Gulf and caravans that carried this contraband equipment into their villages. Superb marksmen and masters of dead ground, they were familiar with every rock and shrub on their cruel landscape and were never slow to capitalize on their enemies' mistakes. On more than one occasion, their determination and cunning had resulted in several serious British defeats, and Kipling explained the hazards faced by British soldiers who fought in this unforgiving land:

> 'When you're wounded and left on Afghanistan's plains,
> And the women come out to cut up what remains,
> Just roll to your rifle and blow out your brains,
> And go to your God like a soldier.'

When moving through hostile territory, a column of British and British Indian Army soldiers along with their supplies had to be protected from attack all day and all night while advancing through a mountain pass. This was accomplished

---

[85] A long-barreled native-made rifle.
[86] A native word for 'rifle,' it was adopted by British soldiers serving on the Northwest Frontier. To prevent losing it to late night thievery, every man was expected to sleep with his bundook chained to a wrist.

by sending men high above the column and on both sides of it to form a series of defensive *sangars* built of rocks. As the column below them advanced beyond the first *sangars*, new sections of men would be sent up to take the lead and build new rock protections. At the same time, the rearmost sections were called down to help the rear guard protect the camels, baggage and mountain guns.

During these changes, the men remaining above the column would provide protection for those returning to it by firing on any tribesmen who might attempt to interfere with this process. These manpower rotations would continue between dawn and dusk until the column was beyond tribal territory and no longer in danger.

Every night the tribesmen would carefully observe these *sangars*. Persistent but cautious and remarkably determined, they would silently creep close to a handful of soldiers behind their rock barriers and watch for the least signs of carelessness. If their occupants remained quiet and on guard, these tough hillmen would slip away but would often return on the following night to watch and wait. While pressed close to the ground, a tribesman who needed to urinate would direct his stream down a reed so as not to cause the slightest splashing sound. They were the soul of guile and patience, but if given a chance, they were onto their foe in a flash and would then disappear just as rapidly.

To beat them, it was almost always necessary to fight them on their own terms. They were natural and intuitive warriors but, ironically, their hatred of the infidel never quite overcame their respect and even affection for the British soldier whom they readily recognized as an equal. Not that they wouldn't steal his *bundook* or kill him if they could!

By 1907, well armed and whipped into a frenzy by their fanatical *mullahs*, the Zakka Khel Afridis were making frequent raids from the Bazar Valley. Intransigent and truculent under the best of circumstances, these tough and treacherous men were unquestionably among the most formidable members of the Afridi clan. But they pressed their luck too far with a bold armed robbery right in the heart of Peshawar, an important British Indian Army city.

So in early 1908, a punitive expedition set forth under the command of Major-General Sir James Willcocks, a veteran officer who had served in the Second Afghan War of 1878-80 and had been mentioned in despatches for services rendered along the North West Frontier in 1897-98.

Moving west from Peshawar on February 15th with the 1st Division, he thrust one brigade forward on a little-used track. Marching rapidly for sixteen miles without their slow supply column, these troops reached the Zakka Khel's main village at Walai and burned it. For the next several days, other villages were taken and razed and their surrounding crops destroyed.

Willcocks' mountain guns caused so many casualties that the tribesmen were left with little choice but to submit, which they did on February 27th. The division had lost only three men killed and thirty-seven wounded. To the men of British battalions who had faced these tribesmen before, it all must have seemed too easy. And it was. These events encouraged the Mohmands to rise and try their luck against Shabkadr Fort and a number of villages north of Peshawar that offered plunder. But Willcocks was equal to that challenge, as well.

On April 24th, he confronted a force of 16,000 Mohmands whose banners snapped defiantly in the morning wind on hilltops to his front. Having uncharacteristically accepted a standup fight, perhaps because of their large numbers, the tribesmen were decisively defeated, nonetheless. But still the *mullahs* wailed a *jehad* from the tower of every mosque, and this call for a holy war triggered one final uprising, this time by Ningrahar Afghans, who assaulted the garrison at Landi Kotal in the Khyber Pass.

By May 2nd, this force had also been beaten, and by the end of the month, Willcocks had snuffed out what might well have developed into a full-scale war on the frontier where failure had always been a prelude to disaster.

This time, the 1st Division had sustained 280 casualties, not only in fire fights among the hills but also from night activities in which the tribesmen continued to demonstrate their prowess. Accurate sniping into Willcocks' camps had exacted a steady toll, and three times a terrifying tactic, the *ghazi* charge, had claimed victims among the unwary.

Unlike the usual nighttime attack, this one would be launched in daylight by a handful of suicidal fanatics who rose suddenly from dead ground as if from nowhere and practically on top of their enemy. Their frenzied rush would be made with a curved sword in one hand or, as often, a knife in both hands. Slashing and stabbing in all directions, they could chop up a small group of soldiers in a hillside picket in less than a minute and then vanish with whatever weapons they could carry off with them. And anyone lucky enough to survive such an onslaught was unlikely to ever forget it.

A veteran of the fighting by now, Arthur Horner would soldier on in the East, relieving his boredom by boxing and sitting for his first tattoos. This information was given to me by his niece, Mrs. Margaret Butler, whom Mr. Wigley had located for me in Acomb. When we met in her home, she explained that her father used to speak about these tattoos, which eventually covered Arthur from the neck down. He entered many competitions and frequently won prizes. A Union Jack decorated his chest, and in a hunting scene on his back, the hounds and horses chased a fox retreating toward the space between his buttocks!

While at Rawalpindi in 1911, the 1st West Yorks were notified they were due to return home. In December they arrived at Lichfield, Staffordshire, to become part of the 18th Brigade in the 6th Division, of which Albert Armitage's battalion would also form a part three years later.

During Arthur's absence from England, tragedy had struck his family. His father, a heavy drinker, often became violent when intoxicated. So severely had his rages impacted on his son Robert that he also became an alcoholic, and while in York on the night of April 21st, 1909, he had fallen into a flooded chalk pit and drowned. He was twenty-six when he died, and he was buried in St. Stephen's Churchyard in Acomb, a place to which the Horner family would be drawn again.

With the beginning of the war with Germany in 1914, the 1st West Yorks did not leave for France until September 16th, eight days after Albert Armitage had crossed the Channel. However, Arthur was among those chosen to remain home as replacements when needed, which would soon require much larger numbers than anyone had anticipated or could provide.

On September 19th, the 1st West Yorks relieved the 1st Battalion, Coldstream Guards, taking over trenches east of Troyon along the Chemin de Dames, while Armitage's battalion was in the process of relieving the 2nd Battalion, Royal Sussex Regiment, then in the front line in the same general vicinity.

On the following morning, a party of Germans was observed on the right flank, moving forward toward the West Yorks under a white flag. Assuming they wanted to surrender, men of A and B Companies scrambled out of their positions and advanced to meet them. But suddenly, the front rank of Germans opened out, and an eyewitness to what followed, Sergeant T. Murphy, later wrote in his diary, 'Those behind had machine guns on stretchers and surprised our lads. They opened a heavy fire. . . What they did not kill or wound. . . they took prisoners.'

Within a matter of minutes, this treacherous act had accounted for eight officers and 436 men who were rounded up and hastened away under guard. The enemy then occupied the vacated part of the British line. Order was not restored until the afternoon when C Company dashed forward with battalion headquarters personnel, recaptured the lost trenches and held them until 8 p.m. when they were relieved. In addition to those captured earlier, losses on the 20th amounted to 218 officers and men killed and wounded.

According to Sergeant Murphy's diary, 'At dawn [on] 21st September, we were told to report at HQ for reorganization where we were able to get a good feed and some tea, also a good drop of rum to pull our nerves together as we were done up, [this] being our first time in action.'

Roll call followed, Murphy noted. 'A more pitiful sight you [n]ever saw. Chaps looking for their chums and others breaking down with the strain. . .' Of the twenty-seven officers and 959 other ranks who had landed so confidently at St. Nazaire only five days earlier, only 305 members of the 1st Battalion now remained.

As news of this event reached England, replacements made ready to leave for France, and Ministry of Defence records indicate that Arthur arrived there on September 24th. Undoubtedly, he was among a draft of ninety-six men under an officer who on the 27th reached the battalion on the heights north of the River Aisne. On the next evening, they moved up with the rest of the battalion into support positions northeast of Troyon.

By that time, the battalion's losses were also being made good by members of the 3rd (Reserve) Battalion, then stationed at Whitley Bay in the Tyne Garrison. On October 9th, Major H. T. Cliff and Captain H. B. Spence, both of whom had served on Malta with Arthur in 1901, arrived at St. Sauveur.[87] With them came three other officers, including a twenty-year-old subaltern, Oswald Moncreiff Tennent, younger son of the vicar of Acomb. A graduate of St. Peter's School where he had

---

[87] While recovering from a wound in October 1914, Captain Spence wrote to a friend that Major Cliff was about ten yards away from him when the latter 'was shot clean through the head [on October 13th] and never regained consciousness.' The bullet that killed him was part of German enfilade fire from a farm south of the French village of Bleu.

excelled at sports, this youth was soon to play a brief, tragic role in one of Arthur Horner's wartime experiences.

Within one hour of the arrival of these officers, the battalion entrained for the north as part of the rapid 'Race to the Sea'. During this attempt to outflank the Germans, the 1st West Yorkshires were not seriously threatened until shortly before noon on October 21st when a German counterthrust hit the 18th Brigade around the village of Ennetières where Albert Armitage of the 2nd East Yorks had died.

Hard pressed to prevent encirclement, Arthur's battalion fought back for over four hours against waves of determined attackers, who were finally beaten back. Relieved during the night, the 1st West Yorks passed into Brigade reserve. Not far to the north, sickening events were unfolding at Ypres.

On the 22nd, wildly enthusiastic German schoolboys who had recently been brought into the army with next to no training, attacked the British while linking arms, singing patriotic songs and advancing with flowers in their ornate leather *Pickelhaube* helmets. At day's end, thousands of them had been slain by BEF bullets. Older soldiers on both sides of the line were sickened by the sights and sounds of it, and the Germans would always refer to this as *Der Kindermord bei Yypern.* Roughly, this translates as 'The massacre of the innocents at Ypres.' There both sides would methodically continue to squander the cream of a generation to discordant tunes played by stuttering machine guns and exploding shells.

Not surprisingly, little else is known about Arthur's experiences through more than four years of war. Only fleeting glimpses of him remain visible, largely through the memory of his nephew, Raymond Vipas. For one of these glimpses, we must now move to the vicinity of Ypres in June 1915.

On the 16th of that month, the 1st West Yorks were under orders to protect the left flank of the 9th Infantry Brigade while the latter took part in a 3rd Division attack of Bellewaarde Ridge to the east of Ypres.

Occupying trenches about 1,300 yards northeast of 'Hellfire Corner' and slightly north of the Ypres-Roulers railway line, the Yorkshiremen were able to support the left flank of the attack with concentrated rifle and machine gun fire. Soon enough, however, German observation posts on higher ground along the ridge brought down heavy and accurate artillery fire in which fifty-eight officers and men of the 1st Battalion were killed, wounded and gassed.

As usual, lives had been sacrificed in vain. After an initial advance to part of the enemy's third line on a 1,000-yard front, the attackers were cut off from their reinforcements by a curtain of high explosive shells that churned up huge fountains of sodden soil. Although forced to retire, they managed to hold the German's original front line trenches.

The West Yorkshire's regimental history pays tribute to the 1st Battalion's medical officer as well as Sergeant M. Burke and the stretcher-bearers who, like Arthur, toiled around the clock for two days to help their own wounded and also those of the 9th Brigade.

Among the mortally wounded was the 1st West Yorks' machine gun officer, Second Lieutenant Tennent, whom Captain Spence had earlier referred to as 'a splendid subaltern, quite fearless,' This young officer's name was to ignite another spark in Raymond Vipas' memory and also lead me to the son of a soldier who was with Tennent when he was hit.

When I met Raymond Vipas for the first time in the Micklegate in York, I had already known for some months that he was awaiting an operation for cataracts in both eyes, but to my surprise, he was standing on the street when I arrived.

'I can't see you," he said, "except in outline."

Even so, he managed to lead me up the stairs to his flat where we spoke for about two hours. When I mentioned Tennent, he sat forward in his chair. "Yes," he responded. "I know that name. He was one of Arthur's officers. Arthur brought him in before he died."

Reasoning that there might be more I could learn about Tennent, I wrote to the *Yorkshire Evening Press* upon my return home, outlining my interest in him. This prompted a letter from H. T. Buttress, a resident of Osbaldwick, York, who wrote, 'I don't know any of the surviving relatives of Lt. Tennent, but his death has a very special interest for me.'

He then explained that his father, 1027 Lance-Corporal Samuel Buttress, had served in France with the 1st West Yorks, having been posted to them from the 3rd Battalion, and that he had his father's notebooks which included two pages of instructions on the care of a machine gun.

'As a child, I often reread the letters he sent to my mother,' he added, 'and in particular, I can recall my father writing in 1915 about the death of a young officer in his group, 2nd Lt. O. M. Tennent.

'He was a tall man. And this caused him to stand too erect and expose his body above the trench. He was shot through the head by a German sniper, and my father was part of the burial party.' Mr. Buttress later sent me a copy of Tennent's obituary, which included an especially tragic fact. He had died on his twenty-first birthday.

Throughout the summer of 1915 in Belgium, the front line surged forward and back in relentless tides of human blood. At a point about 1,400 yards southeast of where Lieutenant Tennent had died stood the shattered remains of Hooge Chateau. Captured by the Germans on June 2nd, these ruins sheltered enough enemy troops to pose a serious threat to the British front line, which formed a salient around Hooge village on the Menin Road.

Officers of the British High Command were never slow to claim significant penetrations of the enemy front line, and the press was encouraged to report them as such even though few of them were. And no fighting man liked to defend salients because they goaded the enemy into pinching them off and killing their occupants with heavy enfilade fire. In the case of the Hooge salient, the British launched two assaults on the chateau before the enemy countered with a strong attack on July 30th in which they used flamethrowers for the first time in the war. This enabled them to overrun Hooge, cross the Menin Road and press within 120 yards of the northeast corner of Zouave Wood.

This appalling 'liquid fire' immediately burned through everything it touched and sometimes asphyxiated its victims with heat and smoke. But, somehow, enough Yorkshiremen still stood ready to defend their position and unleashed a storm of rifle fire. Ten days later, the British countered with a carefully planned attack on August 9th, and the shattered village changed hands once more,

Held in reserve throughout most of that day, the 1st West Yorks were finally unleashed at 4:30 p.m. to relieve elements of the first wave. By nightfall, they were in captured German trenches, which they worked long hours to strengthen. Progress was slow because the enemy had placed their own dead in the parados walls, and removing them released thousands of maggots, which added to everyone's misery. All that night and into the next morning, the stretcher-bearers were active under the tireless Sergeant Burke whose citation for the Distinguished Conduct Medal explains the hazards they faced:

'For conspicuous gallantry on the night of August 9-10, 1915, at Hooge when in charge of a party of stretcher-bearers who were out searching for wounded in exposed ground in front of the lines. This situation was quite unknown at the time, and heavy shelling was in progress, but he continued to lead and direct his party until daylight, and through his efforts many wounded were found and brought in. . .'

And what had the wounded and killed really accomplished? To the north and south of Hooge, the front lines had scarcely moved from where they had been on the date of Lieutenant Tennent's death. On balance, then, the British were hardly a step nearer Germany.

By November, Arthur Horner was home on leave. There he wrote his will in which he requested 'that all my personal property, money to my credit in the PO Savings Bank, any debt to me shall, in the case of my decease, become the property of my mother, Maria Horner.' He signed this document on the 3rd, and his signature was witnessed by his brother-in-law, W. H. Vipas, and by Dr. J. H. Sutcliffe, for whom Arthur's sister Lily worked as a housemaid.

According to Raymond Vipas, Arthur always looked his best when on leave. "He was a very smart dresser," he told me, "complete with bowler hat and walking stick. On one occasion, he bought me a book, and I can see him now, coming down the street with it under his arm."

To the newspapers serving York and its vicinity, November 3rd, 1915, was just another day to air a patriotic spirit, but the press was still heavily censored regarding what it could report on the war. Letters to the editor of the *Yorkshire Evening Press* praised the twenty-two unmarried constables of the York Police Force who had enlisted during the preceding week. And Mr. F. D. Stuart of Acomb was accepting contributions of money to provide Christmas gifts for more than 100 soldiers from York who were being held as German war prisoners.

On the preceding day, two men crossing on the boat train to France had attracted attention to their uniforms, which bore curious green sleeve badges with the words 'War Office Kinematograph.' These early filmmakers were the first of their kind since the start of hostilities to be allowed to proceed to the war—no doubt to the consternation of the Army High Command, who almost certainly would have prevented them from going close to the fighting.

Men returning from leave often had misgivings and premonitions. How much longer could their luck hold out? Would they get a 'Blighty one?' Or worse?

Lance-Corporal Samuel Buttress was among those on leave in November of 1915. On the day of his return to France, he boarded the train at York railway station, looked down at his wife and seven-year-old daughter and staggered them with this statement: "I shall not come back. But Jerry will not get me."

At the age of 32, Buttress met death in the manner he had predicted. Due home on another leave in April 1916, he was taken ill on the train and removed to Lahore Hospital in Calais. On the night of the 15th, his wife awoke suddenly in York and saw a vision of her husband lying on a hospital bed. "They're killing me here!" he said. Transfixed with horror, she watched as a spectral nurse covered him up with a white sheet. Four or five days later, a telegram arrived from the War office to state he had died of pneumonia on the same night as his wife's vision.[88] Experiences of this nature were shared by more than a few soldiers' loved ones throughout Great Britain during the war.

As more British soldiers became casualties, the Empire began sending more of its own troops to help hold the lines. On May 8th, 1916, stalwart, flamboyant and iconoclastic Anzacs—already fighting in the Middle East—arrived in France and would soon demonstrate their remarkable toughness, not only in combat but also behind the lines in brawls with practically anyone who got on their nerves, including the Military Police.

During the Christmas season in December, Arthur Horner came home again, and Raymond Vipas recalled "an uproar downstairs, and I made my way down. Arthur was in uniform. He grabbed hold of me and said, 'This is the lad I want to see'!"

Throughout Great Britain, Christmas of that year was a time of continuing resolve tempered with a nagging undercurrent of anxiety. People in Acomb and

---

[88] Samuel Buttress is buried in Plot C, Grave 16 at Calais Southern Cemetery. His widow would spend the rest of her life scrubbing floors to supplement her state pension of twelve shillings per week. When she died, she was buried with her husband's service medals, as she had requested.Ed

elsewhere were beginning to seek answers to questions posed by the prolongation of a war that appeared to have no end. What would its resolution be? What *could* it be?

In the preceding month, Prime Minister Lloyd George had finally rid himself of Sir John French, for whom he had little use, and replaced him as overall commander of the BEF with the taciturn Sir Douglas Haig, who was promoted to the rank of field-marshal.

Stubborn, inarticulate and seemingly devoid of imagination, this aloof aristocrat arranged for the killing to continue with next to nothing to be shown for it except mounting casualties. But in fairness to him, his strategy was based on holding Germany in a death grip on the Western Front where almost no reserves were left for the Kaiser to send elsewhere. And Sir Douglas sensed correctly that, win or lose, the war would be decided in France and Flanders. So he deserves great credit for his determination to win it there, whatever the cost and regardless of the prime minister's nagging disapproval.

In 1917, the Allies desperately needed some good news, and events in the Middle East would bring it from an unlikely source in the form of 28-year-old Thomas Edward Lawrence. One of five illegitimate sons of an Irish baronet, he emerged from obscurity as a junior officer in British Military Intelligence in Cairo to accomplish something no one believed could have been possible. With remarkable leadership abilities and a friendship he had established with Prince Feisal, he rallied to a common cause Arab tribes traditionally antagonistic to each other but eager to throw off their Turkish yoke. This he was able to do by convincing Feisal that even a tiny force of Arabs could capture Aqaba, a coastal town in Jordan of great strategic importance to the Turks who were denied access to the British-controlled Red Sea.

Lawrence's tactical plan called for attacking Aqaba from the desert, a direction considered so unlikely that all of the town's twelve-inch guns were sited out to sea. When the town was taken, the Turks were forced to rely on the Hejaz railway for moving supplies, men and munitions to their garrisons along the Arabian peninsula. Other Arab attacks followed, including numerous severings of the railway line, which eventually forced Turkish forces to crumble and its government to accept an armistice, which would be signed but not until thirteen days before the war ended.

As for Lawrence, he was touched by genius but with an underlayer of self-destruction, as were Gordon of Khartoum before him and Wingate of Burma in World War Two. Resigning his commission, he later enlisted in the Royal Air Force under several different assumed names in an effort to avoid all publicity. In later years, he met his death on a motorcycle while trying to avoid hitting two bicyclists on a country road.[89]

In the war at sea, fourteen German U-boats had gone forth as early as August 6th, 1914, on their first attempt to find and sink enemy surface vessels. Although the Royal Navy would draw first blood when H.M.S. *Birmingham* rammed and sank U-15 on August 9th, the Germans would even the score on September 5th by sinking H.M.S. *Pathfinder* off the east coast of Scotland. She would then take the lead when Otto Weddigen, commanding U-9, sank three Royal Navy cruisers with five torpedoes on September 22nd to win Germany's highest decoration, the Pour le Mérite. Known as 'The Polite Pirate' for the chivalrous treatment he showed his victims, he would meet his match six months later when he was rammed by H.M.S. *Dreadnought*, which sent him and his entire crew to the bottom off Moray Firth.

---

[89] The Arabs' dream of a homeland in surrendered Turkish territories encompassing Iraq, Palestine, Syria and Transjordan would not be realized. As mandated by the League of Nations in 1921, these lands would be divided between the British and French, thereby sowing seeds that grew bitter fruit that exists to this day in these troubled regions.

Ratcheting up the pressure, Germany announced on February 18th, 1915, that all enemy merchant ships sighted around the British Isles would be subject to sinking and not always would it be possible for passengers and crews to be forewarned. Britain countered by declaring a blockade to prevent neutral vessels from entering German ports.

The sinking of the Cunard passenger liner *Lusitania* by U-20 on May 7th and the drowning of 1,198 of those on board, including 124 Americans, created a white hot anger in the U. S., but it would be another seventeen months until action could be taken in a manner it would have liked to adopt at once. Active, aggressive and highly successful in British waters, these German undersea marauders operated out of both Belgian and German ports. Eventually, they would appear to be everywhere else as well—off Crete, Syria, Egypt, Gibraltar and even the east coast of the U. S., sometimes collectively sinking as many as seven ships per day.

In the war's darkest days in 1917, these unrelenting attacks would result in only one British merchant ship returning to port out of every four which had sailed. These losses were impacting seriously on the delivery of essential war materials and food supplies to Great Britain, as they were in Germany from a similar Allied blockade.

Germany shot herself in the foot on February 1st 1917, when it made known the start of unrestricted naval warfare. But this was unavoidable following the huge sea Battle of Jutland in the preceding year because the Kaiser's High Seas Fleet was no longer strong enough to provide adequate protection for his mercantile shipping. So these vessels seemed doomed to lie at anchor in their harbors while Germany ran ever shorter of food and war materials.

Germany's U-53 wasted no time by sinking the American ship *Housatonic* on the same day as the declaration of these unrestricted attacks. The next major outrage came on March 1st when it was learned that British code breakers had intercepted and deciphered a telegram sent to Mexico's president from German Foreign Secretary Arthur Zimmerman, offering him Arizona, New Mexico and Texas to his north in return for joining the Central Powers. Venustiano Carranza would not even be sworn into office until the 11th, and he showed no interest in this proposal anyway, but Woodrow Wilson and the American public were justifiably outraged.

Wilson asked Congress to declare a state of war against Germany, which it did on April 6th. But it would be another seven months before America's army would be sufficiently trained and equipped to take its place in the front lines. By this time, Germany, Austria-Hungary, Turkey and Bulgaria were aligned against sixteen nations and also colonial forces from French Indochina, India, Jamaica, Morocco and Senegal. Greece held back until July 2nd when it became the seventeenth country to join the Allies.

Meanwhile, U-boat sinkings continued at an alarming rate, although the tide would eventually turn against Germany. The last U-boat attack against a merchant vessel occurred on November 7th, 1918, just four days before the end of the war. Ironically, its torpedo missed. Few others had during this deadly confrontation. On the 9th, the last British warship was sent to the bottom off Cape Trafalgar. Equally ironic, its name was H.M.S. *Brittania*.

In the end, the Royal Navy's blockade of German harbors proved to be more successful in denying the Kaiser's people of food and essential war materials than had their enemy's, but at an enormous price. A total of 1,858 British warships, auxiliary vessels, colliers and oilers plus other vessels and even hospital ships with a total of more than 7,759,000 gross tonnage had been sunk, not only by submarines but also by mines, surface vessels and aircraft. So it was 'a close run thing,' as the Duke of Wellington had described the Battle of Waterloo in 1814.[90]

[90] These statistics on ships sunk by U-boats are the result of the author's count of each such sinking as noted in *The Times Diary & Index of the War 1914-1918.*

By the start of 1918, military and political thinking in France and Great Britain had crystallized into a rigid determination to continue the fight, which General Foch—soon to become Allied generalissimo—estimated could be won in a final offensive, but not until 1921. Newspapers would warn about the realities the war was still likely to bring, but few of their readers believed them any longer, having been numbed by four years of disappointing setbacks.

In Germany, time was running out for the Kaiser. Hunger was taking its toll, and food strikes were spreading in Germany and Austria. To stave off disaster, one last, colossal series of offensives seemed to offer the best opportunity to finally win a decisive victory. Though recognized as a risky move, no illusions remained. Regardless of what happened with this gamble, the war would have to end before 1919 or Germany would collapse.

Cloaked in secrecy and organized into five separate attacks extending from late March to mid-July, the initial assault would be code named 'Michael II' and would fall on General Sir Julian Byng's Third Army and General Sir Hubert Gough's Fifth Army along a front of roughly fifty miles extending from a line slightly east of Arras down to Noyon. North of them and stretched out for fifty-six miles were the British First and Second Armies with a combined total of twenty-six divisions, which were not to be as heavily involved as the Third and Fifth Armies below them.

German preparations were made in total secrecy by hordes of men who moved up to villages in which no outdoor movement was allowed until after dark. Guns, wagons and ammunition dumps were cleverly hidden beneath trees to prevent observation from the air.

Allied forces knew an attack was coming, but no one could be sure where it would begin, and the enemy launched several feinting assaults on the French in sectors designed to cause the latter to move troops away from the British right flank.

Facing the British Third and Fifth Armies were seventy-six well-equipped and rested German divisions brought up to full strength by men brought west from Russia plus another four returned from Italy. Standing in their paths were Byng's fourteen divisions and Gough's pitifully small force of twelve infantry and three cavalry divisions. These twenty-nine British divisions consisted of many fine battalions of the old Regular Army and, in general, their morale had been raised from the low point it had reached by all those who had suffered earlier at Passchendaele. However, they were all well below full strength.

Haig had pleaded for reinforcements from England, but Lloyd George insisted on holding back 645,000 officers and men as a brake against what he considered to be a profligate misuse of troops in earlier costly battles. Only he could release them, and he was not about to do so. Granted, his refusal had political motives, but he had the right to retain them because of his influence with both the Army Council and the War Cabinet.

This proved to be only the first missile launched by L-G at Haig who learned that his most loyal supporter, Field-Marshal Sir William Robertson—Chief of the Imperial General Staff since December 1915—had been replaced by Sir Douglas's nemesis, Sir Henry Wilson, whose appointment in mid-February 1918 immediately made him Haig's superior in rank.

A confirmed Francophile, Wilson ordered Haig to send troops to take over twenty-five miles of French trenches, further diminishing his forces facing the expected German assault. Earlier, the dangers facing Haig had been increased when five British divisions were sent to Italy. True to form, Lloyd-George deliberately provided Parliament with incorrect information on the number of troops still available to the BEF.

Denied further reinforcements, Haig at his headquarters in Montreuil, more than sixty-five miles west of the front lines, reasoned that German breakthroughs were to be expected in Gough's weak sector. He also estimated that when they came, the Germans would occupy ground to the west of no strategic significance and would then have to swing north for a considerable distance in a bid to capture the major French North Sea ports of Dunkirk, Calais and Boulogne to block the BEF's escape routes to England. It was a perilous gamble, but no viable options seemed evident. For the time being, Haig would hold well behind the front lines eight divisions in General Headquarters Reserve, which only he could release.

The success of General Erich Ludendorff's huge, five-stage offensive with 3,500,000 soldiers and masses of equipment required movements to be made silently by night, and 1,000,000 Germans were in place on March 21st, ready to launch the offensive's first phase. It is important for readers to understand this disparity in numbers to appreciate the remarkable stand made by the British Army in the forthcoming assault. Haig was now in the finals, pure and simple. There would be no second chance for victory if his men failed to hold out.

At 4:40 a.m., gas and smoke shells from more than 6,400 guns and 3,520 mortars fell on British positions along Byng's and Gough's fronts. This stupendous barrage continued for five uninterrupted hours in a deluge of death and destruction of unparalleled intensity made worse by a heavy fog that obscured visibility for the defenders.

At 10 a.m., the German storm troops holding flamethrowers with a range of thirty-five yards moved forward in the lead and smashed through the Fifth Army line within less than one hour. Close behind them came hordes of regular troops to create a flood tide of humanity in field gray uniforms bent on destroying whatever was left.

The Western Front had never seen such an overwhelming assault as enemy infantrymen surged forth practically unchecked. Overhead, Royal Flying Corps pilots courageously dropped their aircraft down to less than twenty-five feet and went after their prey with guns blazing in the slim chance of slowing them down.

On that first day of this huge German assault, Arthur Horner's former battalion, the 1st, totaled twenty-four officers and 627 other ranks. Within just forty-eight hours, its numbers were reduced to only one officer and forty-six men. Among the wounded was Lieutenant-Colonel A. M. Boyall, who was taken prisoner during this local engagement that became known as the Battle of St. Quentin.

By the end of the 21st, this *Kaiserschlacht* had taken almost 100 square miles of land held earlier by the British Third and Fifth Armies. In 1916 on the Somme, the combined British and French assaults had taken almost the same amount of ground but had needed almost five months to do so at a cost of more than half a million casualties. Within two days, this German avalanche of destruction had punched a forty-mile wedge through the British lines which can best be described as a huge 'tear drop' extending south from Arras for fifty miles to a line running east to west from Montdidier to La Fère.

Here and there, surviving British soldiers in small groups fought back with rifles and Lewis guns with panniers which held sixty rounds of .303 bullets that could be shot off within five seconds. However, nothing could slow the German advance for long as enemy momentum continued to roll over everything in its path.

On March 23rd, a gigantic 210-millemeter Krupp cannon near Laon began lobbing huge shells for seventy-five miles into Paris and kept this up for seven hours at twenty-minute intervals, killing 256 people and causing a near-panic. And Ludendorff had just begun. On April 9th, his 'Georgette' attack hit General Sir Herbert Plumer's Second Army on Belgium's Lys River to the north, attacking on a thirty-five-mile line between the Yser River in Belgium and La Bassée in France, devastating its front and threatening it with annihilation until General Foch threw in his last reserves to prevent a disaster.

During this perilous time, about 500 American 'Doughboys', still green as grass, helped stem the German advance with accurate, rapid rounds from their Enfield rifles.[91] By then, each side had lost about 100,000 men. Haig was sufficiently concerned to issue an Army Order to encourage his troops which ended: 'With our backs to the wall and believing in the justice of our cause, each one of us must fight on to the end.'

At some unknown point before this offensive, Arthur Horner had left the 1st Battalion, but the reason for this is equally unknown. His gravestone identifies him with the 7th Battalion. However, there were two 7th West Yorkshire Territorial Force Battalions—the 1/7th, a so-called first line Territorial unit, and the 2/7th, a second-line battalion of conscripts, both of which had assumed the name of Leeds Rifles. But for reasons that will become obvious later on, Arthur clearly served with the former because the latter had been reduced to cadre strength by June 16th, 1918, and was returned to England.

Understandably, efforts to trace his experiences in the war's last year led me nowhere. He was just one soldier in a vast assemblage of anonymous beings. But the 1/7th West Yorkshire Regiment was known to have been frequently committed to the fighting around Ypres prior to Ludendorff's offensive and during it. In 1916, one of its corporals, George Sanders, had won a Victoria Cross near Thiepval in France.

---

[91] This word dates from the time when American soldiers were involved in Mexico in 1916 while chasing down Pancho Villa's bandits who had crossed into New Mexico and killed residents of the town of Columbus. During these operations, the Americans' uniforms became covered with adobe dust. Hence the nickname 'Doughboys.'

Attacks in Flanders across a depressing morass of mud and desolation were especially trying for the 1/7th Battalion and made worse by German high explosive and poison gas shells that caused many casualties. Exhausted and expecting a well-deserved rest, the men learned on April 10th that they had been loaned to the 62nd Infantry Brigade. Marching off at once, they would not reach their destination until 4 a.m. on the 11th. Within less than one hour, they then moved east under shellfire to fill a gap in their front line near Wytschaete to slow up the relentless German advance. From then until the 16th, the battalion's survivors stood their ground. They would be held in high esteem as shown by this brief report, which the 62nd Brigade's commanding officer sent to the 39th Division:

'I should like to draw attention to the very gallant behaviour of the 1/7th West Yorkshire Regiment of the 146th Infantry Brigade, and of No. 2 Composite Battalion, 39th Division, who were attached to my brigade.'

As can be seen from this report's mention of 'Composite,' miracles of improvisation had been necessary to hold the line, and men of various different battalions were shunted back and forth here and there as necessary to prevent a serious enemy breakthrough.

Heavily shelled on April16th, the 1/7th West Yorks could see a German attack coming toward them. Although their visibility and ability to fire were greatly reduced by a heavy ground mist, they were not broken and finally moved back to rest at a farm which they reached on the 18th after more than one week of nonstop fighting. It had been every bit as bad as Second Ypres and often even worse.

No records exist of losses sustained by Arthur's battalion for this period, but the 146th Brigade's war diary notes that only 180 of all ranks in it turned out on the morning of April 19th. By the next day, the entire brigade had been reduced to about 300 officers and men.

On the 25th, the Germans attacked in force in an effort to take Kemmel Hill by punching a hole through a point separating the French and British line. Their intended objective was the Scherpenberg Ridge from which they hoped to move south of Ypres and then west to the North Sea to cut off the BEF from its lifeline.

With the 146th Infantry Brigade's communications severed by a massive enemy bombardment, confusion reigned as the men of three West Yorks' Territorial battalions formed defensive flanks as best they could. Small counterattacks were made whenever possible, and the line was held against further enemy inroads, but the 1/7th West Yorks were reduced to the equivalent of just one company of 300 officers and men. All ranks were dog-tired after almost non-stop fighting and were in need of rest and reinforcement, as were all other BEF battalions. Few would receive enough of either.

Ludendorff stopped his northern offensive on April 29th but opened his third attack in the south against the French Sixth Army on May 27th and on into the 29th with Cantigny as its goal. It was there the American Army would make a stand and a reputation to go with it. Strong, eager and led from the front by officers and 'noncoms' as tough as a cheap steak, these were the bilingual sons of immigrants from the slums of New York and Chicago, dirt farmers from the fields of Georgia, Pennsylvania coal miners and boys from the sod huts of the Dakotas. Their officers bore names that would stand out in later years—MacArthur, Marshall, Truman and Patton.

Although still full of fight, the Germans were weakening fast. By June 1st, their forces were only forty miles from Paris but could gain no further ground on any significant scale. Having rolled the dice and lost, Ludendorff was left with nothing but a huge chunk of worthless real estate, and the North Sea harbors were still in Allied hands.

Throughout the summer months, the German advance continued to weaken from non-stop fighting over the course of the preceding six months. Exhaustion had become overwhelming, casualties were mounting steadily and gauze bandages had long since been replaced by ones made of paper. Worst of all, goals set for continuing assaults began to seem out of reach as supplies of food and equipment were proving inadequate for further assaults. For example, rifling in German artillery barrels was wearing down, reducing the accuracy of many shells.

On July 1st, United States Marine Corps 'Leathernecks' with their 1903-model Springfield rifles found their war at Lucy-le-Bocage near Belleau Wood. While digging foxholes, they saw a ragtag lot of demoralized French soldiers passing through their position, many of them drunk. One of their officers ordered the Yanks to join their retreat. "Retreat, hell!" snapped Captain Lloyd Williams. "We just got here." They stayed, captured the veritable fortress inside the wood and rolled on into legend. Their spirit had been typified earlier by Sergeant Dan Daly, who shouted out to his men before a bayonet charge, "Come on, you sons o' bitches! Do you wanna live forever?"

During August, Allied forces grew stronger and became increasingly ready to flex their muscles. In the early morning light of the 8th, what began as a low, rumbling cough quickly grew into an angry roar as the British Tank Corps attacked for three days in the opening of the Battle of Amiens. What would later be remembered as 'the black day of the German Army' had begun, and the Allies' forward motion surged steadily onward.

On the 24th along the Somme, La Boisselle, Ovillers, Thiepval and other shattered villages from the 1916 fighting had been taken. By the 27th, the British had moved forward along the entire front as the Germans began pulling back for ten miles on a fifty-five-mile front. September would bring more good news of British advances on the Cambrai front. By the 18th, the British Third and Fourth

Armies had attacked the Siegfried Line's outer defenses, taking almost 12,000 prisoners and 100 guns.

On September 24th, the Kaiser traveled to Kiel and told officers at the U-Boat School he hoped their vessels could still save Germany from defeat, but he was dreaming. By the 27th, the British First and Third Armies had broken through the Hindenburg Line with sixty-five tanks, while the Canadians blasted their way through Bourlon Wood. Allied momentum was quickening, but much deadly work still lay ahead.

On October 8th, the Yanks' aggressiveness was exemplified in the Argonne Forest by the army's Acting Corporal Alvin Cullum York, a rawboned Tennessee mountain man from the Valley of the Three Forks of the Wolf. York found himself facing a strong German position defended by several machine guns with sufficient punch to fire five thousand rounds per minute. The clip on his rifle required replacement after every six shots. As a German officer charged with six men to finish him off, York had only three bullets left. Resorting to an old turkey-hunting trick, he picked off the last man in line and then the two ahead of him. Those in front remained unaware of what was happening as he proceeded to dispose of the rest with his pistol. Still not done, he continued to 'tetch off' the machine gunners. Then he and eight of his men who were still unwounded rounded up 132 prisoners and marched them into captivity, York was awarded the Medal of Honor.

On the 9th in Flanders, Arthur Horner's 146th Brigade was north of Cambrai where orders were received for it to take part in the 49th Division attack on the 10th, which would be known as the battle of Poelcappelle and fought along a front extending six miles east from Zonnebeke. Horner's mob under Lieutenant-Colonel W. R. Pinwill would be on the left, and Zero Hour was set for 9 a.m.

At 5:30 on the morning of the assault, the 1/7th Battalion could see Germans moving into position on higher ground 300 yards in front of them. Enemy machine gun fire indicated the strength of this position and the casualties that might result from trying to take it. But regardless of heavy fire, the first attacking wave overwhelmed the German line, took 300 prisoners and captured numerous machine guns. Soon after, twelve field guns were also taken, but British casualties included Colonel Pinwill who was wounded by a bullet in his thigh.

In typical form as seen so often throughout the war, the German line stiffened, and a hurricane of machine gun fire further back hit the British advance while four enemy light tanks forced the attackers to retreat behind most of the ridge they had just captured, But the Yorkshiremen were not done yet. With support from some Canadians to the left of the 146th Brigade, the East Yorks battalions surged forth in one more bid to take and hold the ridge. In spite of heavy German fire, they managed to do so, and by nightfall what was left of the brigade had not only reached its objective again but also advanced three kilometers beyond it.

Savage fighting continued, but final victory was near. Austria asked for an armistice on the 28th but would not get it at once. Meanwhile, the Germans remained hard nuts to crack and continued to cause their enemy heavy losses. By November 1st, the 1/7th West Yorks had been reduced to fifteen officers and 363 other ranks, and later on that same day the battalion was down by another five officers and fifty-six men. But they and others involved in these last acts of the war on the Western Front could not know that, Hindenburg and Ludendorff, facing the grim prospects of defeat, had decided on the necessity to seek an armistice.

Incorrectly assuming they might obtain more lenient terms from the United States, they agreed this offer should be sent to President Wilson instead of to the British and French whose manpower had suffered such grievous losses. It arrived in Washington on October 4th, but it would require more than one month for all of its details to be finalized.

On the following day, thirty British and two American divisions overwhelmed thirty-nine depleted German divisions, taking 36,000 prisoners, almost 400 guns and widening the Allies' breach of the Hindenburg Line. Cracks in Germany's armor had appeared as early as August 18th of the preceding year when crewmen of the *Kriegsmarine* mutinied on *Prinz Regent Luitpol* and *Friedrich der Grosse*. Although suppressed, this outburst had sown the seeds of resentment that would sprout into violence on November 4th, 1918, when three officers on *König* were shot by their own men at Kiel while protecting their ensign. Throughout the entire anchorage, the red flag was soon being raised in rebellion.

The Belgian coastline would at last be swept clear of Germans as the Allies continued to surge forward, not only in France but in Italy, as well. At 3 p.m. on the 4th, Austria accepted the terms required for its surrender to be accepted.

At 5:05 a.m. on November 11th, the armistice was signed in a railway car at the Rethondes station near Compiègne. At 11 a.m. on that eleventh day of the eleventh month, an eerie quiet descended on the fields of slaughter. At the time, the 1/7th West Yorkshire Regiment was at Evin-Malmaison in Picardy, about six miles southeast of Douai. In the afternoon, Lieutenant-General Sir Arthur Currie, commander of the Canadian Corps, made a symbolic gesture by riding into Mons with an escort of the British 5th Lancers, every one of whom had fought there in August 1914. The war was over, but while it lasted, the German Army had never been required to fight a single battle on its own soil.

Having abdicated on the 9th, Kaiser Wilhelm II crossed over to Eysden in Holland at 8:00 p.m. on the same day. There he would remain safe for life from being turned over as a war criminal, which had been requested earlier at the Paris Peace Conference. In the 1930s as a young child in New York City, I would sometimes see a newspaper photograph of him wearing a long overcoat and felt hat. His face no longer revealed any traces of bombast or arrogance—traits which had led so much of the world so close to its doom. On June 4th, 1941, he died of pneumonia at the age of eighty-one at his estate in Doorn, and Germany's most recent troublemaker would send a memorial wreath. His name was Adolph Hitler.

Nothing more is known about Arthur Horner's experiences during the war's final year until shortly before the armistice when he was stricken in France with meningitis and influenza. Evacuated to England, he was taken to the 4th Northern General Hospital in Lincoln where he would fight his last battle.

Originally set up in 1914 at Christ's Hospital School on the Wragby Road, this long, limestone building in the Jacobean style provided 600 beds and received its first patients when 105 wounded soldiers arrived on September 13th of that year in the aftermath of the Battle of the Aisne. As casualties mounted steadily, wooden huts were built on the playing fields to accommodate them, and two of these buildings were still in use as classrooms when my wife and I visited the school in 1983. By 1917, 1,400 beds were in place, and one year later there were undoubtedly many more, adding to the burden of Major Frederick Lambert, Royal Army Medical Corps, and his staff, who were facing a daunting workload.

A perfect environment for the spread of influenza existed among young men grouped together in damp army training camps, front line positions and on troop transports crossing the Atlantic. Those infected with it might look normal in the morning but become almost helpless by evening with alarmingly high temperatures. Treatment at the hospital in Lincoln was rudimentary and too often ineffective—no food, much liquid and doses of aspirin and quinine at four-hour intervals. Afflicting men, women and children alike, this raging pandemic would kill an estimated 40,000,000 humans worldwide.

One evening in the winter of 1918, Private Fred Lowes of the Lincolnshire Regiment was brought into one of the wards strapped to a stretcher with a German machine gun bullet near the top of his spine. His widow, eighty-three-year-old Mrs. Harriet Lowes, responded to a request for help I had made by mail to *Lincolnshire Life* for information which might be available about the hospital in which Arthur was treated. I later visited her in her home in Potterhanworth, Lincolnshire.

"When Fred was brought in that night," she recalled, "they put him in a bed near the door, and the ward was absolutely full of flu cases. The man next to him said, 'You're lucky'."

"So Fred asked, 'Why'?"

"Well, you've got clean sheets on your bed, and there's been three dying there just lately."

Fred Lowes would live, but in England and Wales alone, well over 4,000 civilians and fighting men in that winter were dying each week because of this virulent and highly infectious disease which no one seemed able to arrest. In Acomb, an envelope written in an unfamiliar hand arrived for Arthur's mother. Sent by a nurse, it held out no hope for her son and was, in fact, his final farewell. To compound his already grave condition, he was suffering from what a doctor recorded as 'thrombosis of cavernous sinus.' Mrs. Horner sat in silence for a few minutes, and then young Raymond Vipas saw his grandmother bend forward and weep for the first time.

Mrs. Lowes described events in the hospital on November 11th. "The head man came and said the war was over, and they just went berserk. The bells were ringing all over. Getting out of their beds in their pajamas, some of the men died of their exertions."

Five days later, Arthur Horner was dead.

"The week of his death I shall never forget," recalled Raymond Vipas. "The arrival of the news, his body being brought home, and the soldiers tramping down the street for his funeral."

Arthur was one of almost 9,500,000 British and Empire men who served in World War One. Of this number, more than 947,000 were killed or died of wounds, accidents or sickness. The number of wounded exceeded 1,121,000.

With full military honors, he was buried in St. Stephen's Churchyard beside his brother, who had drowned in the chalk pit nine years earlier. Among those present was C. H. Wigley, then sixteen years of age. Almost sixty-five years later, I stood beside him in the same spot while we looked at Arthur's grave.[92]

Earlier, he had told me that relatives and friends began to notice that the officiating clergyman, the sixty-six-year-old Reverend R. P. T. Tennent, was becoming increasingly agitated. Stumbling over his words and hesitating, he soon broke down entirely, grieving at the memory of his son and of the man who had tried to save him three years earlier in a muddy trench near Ypres.

I looked around me at the grass and weeds growing high in this section of the churchyard. Arthur's headstone had been toppled from its base. Earlier, it had been explained to me that vandals waited for night to fall to run vicious errands along the paths, desecrating the dignity of those who lay there in silence beneath the earth. But unlike the other seven British soldiers whose medals I cherish, Arthur Horner had come home.

---

[92] These were not Mr. Wigley's only experiences in this cemetery. During World War Two, he attended a funeral there when the pilot of a German Messerschmitt fighter plane spotted the mourners. Banking his aircraft sharply, he straightened out, dropped low and came at them on a strafing run. As his bullets began to kick up clods of earth, several people jumped into the grave and on top of the coffin in an effort to save themselves. Such are the exigencies of war.

BIBLIOGRAPHY:

Barthorp, Michael, *Afghan Wars and the North-west Frontier 1839-1947* (Cassell & Co., London, 2002)

Beatty, Charles, *Our Admiral, A Biography of Admiral of the Fleet Earl Beatty*, (W. H. Allen, London, 1980)

Browne, Captain, D. C., MC, *The Tank in Action* (William Blackwood and Sons, Edinburgh and London, 1920)

Creagh, Sir O'Moore, VC, GCB, GCSI and E. M. Humphris, *The Victoria Cross 1856-1920* (J. B. Hayward & Son, Halstead, Suffolk; facsimile edition originally published in 1920 as Volume I: *The VC and DSO*

Davies, Peter, *The Devil's Flu, The World's Deadliest Influenza Epidemic and the Scientific Hunt for the Virus that Caused It* (Henry Holt and Company, New York, 2000)

Dupuy, R. Ernest and Trevor N., *The Encyclopedia of Military History from 3500 B.C. to the Present* (Harper & Row, New York, 1970)

Elliott, Major-General J. G., *The Frontier 1839-1947* (Cassell & Co., London, 1968)

B. Cory Kilvert Jr.

Farrar, Martin J., *News from the Front, War Correspondents on the Western Front 1914-1918* (Sutton Publishing Limited, Phoenix Mill, Thrupp, Stroud, Gloucestershire, 1998)

Fuller, Brevet-Colonel J. F. C., DSO, *Tanks in the Great War 1914-1918* (John Murray, London, 1920

Hoehling, A. A., *The Great War at Sea, A History of Naval Action 1914-18* (Galahad Books, New York, 1965)

Laffin. John, *On the Western Front, Soldier's Stories from France and Flanders, 1914-1918* (Alan Sutton Publishing Limited, Gloucester, 1985).

Lawson, Henry, *Vignettes of the Western Front, Reflections of an Infantry Subaltern in France and Belgium, 1917-1918* (Positif Press, Oxford, 1979)

Marrin, Albert, *The Yanks Are Coming, The United States in the First World War* (Macmillan Publishing Company, New York, 1986)

Middlebrook, Martin, *The Kaiser's Battle, 21 March 1918: The First Day of the German Spring Offensive* (Allen Lane, Penguin Books, Ltd., London, 1978)

Miller, Charles, *Khyber, British India's Northwest Frontier, the Story of an Imperial Migraine* (Macdonald and Jane's, London, 1977)

Official History, Military Operations, 1915 (Macmillan, London, 1928)

The Times Diary & Index of the War, 1914 to 1918, (Facsimile copy published by J. B. Hayward & Son, Polstead, Suffolk, 1985)

War Diary of the 1st Battalion, The West Yorkshire Regiment, June 6th and September 18th, 1915 Public Record Office, London, Reference WO95/1618

West Yorkshire Regiment Museum, York, folders 253 and 256

Winter, J. M., *The Great War and the British People* (Macmillan Education Ltd., London, 1987)

Willcocks, General Sir James, GCB, GCMG, KCSI, DSO, *The Romance of Soldiering and Sport* (Cassell & Co., London, 1925)

Wyrall, Everard, *The West Yorkshire Regiment in the War 1914-1918, Vols. I and II* (John Lane the Bodley Head, London, no date)

The Yorkshire Evening Press (June 22nd and November 3rd, 1915)

Private Arthur Horner in the uniform of a bandsman with the 1st Battalion, West Yorkshire Regiment. This photograph was taken shortly before the war or during it.

This old postcard shows the army medical staff at Christ's Hospital School in Lincoln, which served as a military hospital in 1914-1918. The photograph dates from January 1917. Private Arthur Horner died here five days after the war ended in 1918.

Epilogue

An estimated 67,000,000 men and women from all of the combatant nations served in World War One. Although an accurate total number of their military casualties will never be known, estimates of their losses have run as high as 11,000,000 killed outright or died of wounds. On the Western Front alone, the death toll probably reached 4,000,000. More than 28,000,000 were believed wounded and close to 2,000,000 were listed as missing. Of these totals, the last figure is generally believed to be substantially incomplete.

For the people of Great Britain, closure of a sort began when it was decided that one of her unidentifiable warriors should symbolize the many thousands of missing sons and brothers, husbands and fathers who had not come home to their families from the war. So on the night of November 7th, 1920, one of these casualties was exhumed from each of the four major battle areas along the Aisne and the Somme and also from the vicinity of Arras and Ypres where so much of the heavy fighting had taken place.

Carried to St. Pol, placed in a tent on stretchers and covered with a Union Jack, these bodies were shown to Brigadier L. J. Wyatt who pointed to one of them at random, and the body was taken to Boulogne where it was lowered into a coffin of English oak to which was fashioned a crusader sword provided by King George V. It was then piped on board the British destroyer H.M.S. *Verdun*, which carried it to Dover.

On the morning of November 11th, the body was drawn on a gun carriage through the streets of London by six black horses, which brought it to the Cenotaph—the shrine designed by Edwin Lutyens to honor the dead in the recent war, which had been installed in Whitehall. Thousands of people watching this procession had been waiting for the entire night to see it and the pallbearers following it, who included Field-Marshal Sir Douglas Haig; Earl Beatty, the First Sea Lord; and Field-Marshal Sir John French.

As 'Big Ben' chimed 11 a.m., King George V unveiled the monument, and for two minutes the Last Post was played to a completely silent crowd. And then the body was carried to Westminster Abbey and down the nave past a guard of honor consisting of 100 holders of the Victoria Cross. This was followed by the burial service, which broke the hearts of all those who had lost their men and boys forever.

That day, at least 40,000 people filed through the abbey, and by the time the tomb was closed on November 18th, approximately 1,250,000 people had paid their respects to the Unknown Warrior who symbolized all of the courage and steadfastness of every British serviceman who had died in the war.

Begun in the 13th century and modified over the next 300 years, Westminster Abbey is known to be full of ghosts, and from time to time, visitors have reported seeing them, including the Unknown Warrior who has appeared in the uniform of a Great War British soldier. If he exists, he must indeed be a tortured soul destined to despair forever at the fading memories and selfish ambitions of mankind.

Other nations made similar symbolic gestures of respect to their dead, and once each year their citizens would gather to remember the sadness and waste which had gone before. But the trouble was that a growing number of them in succeeding generations would begin to overlook what had caused a moment of silence to be observed on Remembrance Day or Memorial Day or whatever else this occasion may have been named. So many people, especially younger ones, in all industrialized countries would glean next to nothing from a national event that would eventually be recognized as little more than a day off from work that might—or might not—be interrupted by one minute of silence.

Most of those who remembered the 1914-1918 war and abhorred the thought of future armed conflicts succumbed to the luxury of assuming they could never break out again. After all, the War to End All Wars had ended. So their collective sigh of relief would blind them to the ambitions of new terrorists bent on aggression and the overthrow of peaceful nations.

America's President Woodrow Wilson, well-meaning but encased in a cocoon of idealism, developed a concept of a league of nations, which was presented to a joint session of Congress on January 8th, 1918, more than ten months before the end of the war. It was based on the premise that wars between nations could be avoided through the medium of peaceful negotiations within this new international body.

By the start of 1919, forty-three countries had joined the League, including Great Britain, France and Belgium. In the same year, Austria came in along with six more countries, and Wilson's dream appeared to be gaining traction. But the U. S. Congress refused to ratify the Treaty of Versailles, which contained the League's covenant. This proved to be only the first stake to be driven through this organization's heart.

Nations came into the League and left it as through a revolving door. Germany joined it in 1926 but, humiliated and enraged by its terms from the start, left it in 1935. Three years later, Hitler occupied Austria, which had been a member since 1920. Japan was in by 1920 and out by 1933. In between, she would stage an 'incident' in Manchuria in 1931, which would lead to her invasion of China six years later and the rape and slaughter of tens of thousands in Nanking and elsewhere. Italy, a League charter member, walked out in 1937. Terrorists were on the move again and were feeding on weakness, as they have always done.

Also in the 1930s, Ethiopia's Emperor Haile Selassi would stand before the League, pleading with its members to stop Benito Mussolini's attack on his frail country. His tiny army of mostly primitive tribesmen, armed largely with spears and sticks but with few modern arms, had been decimated by aerial bombs, machine gun bullets and poison gas, which had also killed large numbers of women and children.

He said, "In 1936, I declared that it was not the Covenant of the League that was at stake but international morality. Undertakings, I said then, are of little worth if the will to keep them is lacking." He was repeatedly shouted down by members of the Italian delegation, and the League did nothing.

In that same year, Nazi Germany reoccupied the Rhineland's demilitarized zone on France's border in violation of the Treaty of Versailles, even though both Britain and France were obligated by its terms to resist this incursion. Three years earlier, Hitler had already thumbed his nose at the Treaty by rearming and introducing a military draft. Again, no one challenged these moves. Instead, Britain would allow Germany to build a powerful navy, including submarines, which the Treaty had proscribed. These silent undersea marauders would play havoc with both ships of the Royal Navy and Britain's merchant fleet in the war still to come.

France, which had promised military assistance to Czechoslovakia, Romania and Yugoslavia in the event of a German invasion, stood aside on the advice of its military leaders who were already trembling with fear. Solacing herself with the knowledge that her people did not want another war, France refrained from acting even though her army substantially outnumbered Germany's and possessed much modern equipment, including excellent tanks. The rot had set in.

Hitler, for his part, would later maintain that, had his Rhineland invasion been resisted, he would have had to withdraw and that Naziism would have been doomed. Consider what happened instead.

In 1938, General Francisco Franco, scenting opportunity, would in time overwhelm Spain's legitimate government by waging a savage war made worse by the use of cruel Moorish mercenaries. Adolf Hitler's Luftwaffe joined Franco, and its airmen would sharpen their bombing skills by destroying an innocent Basque town named Guernica. Not wanting to be left out, Mussolini, the strutting jackal, would also send troops to Franco while there was still time to reap whatever rewards might still remain.

Essentially, these events marked the start of World War Two, but heads of state in countries which had won the previous war were buried too far into the sand to recognize it as such. The League called for an embargo on arms to Spain, but Stalin—an expert in sensing weakness and capitalizing on it—sidestepped it to join the Loyalist cause, but mainly to spread the cancer of Communism. Since then and after the devastation and huge casualties of World War Two plus the human costs of the Korean War, Gulf War and the terror in Afghanistan and Iraq, a new set of troublemakers has always managed to emerge wherever vacillation and weakness have presented themselves.

Cambodia's Pol Pot, Ayatolla Komeni, Manuel Noriego, Syria's Hafez Assad, Osama bin Laden, Saddam Hussein, North Korea's Kim Jong Il. Opportunists all, like Nature they have filled vacuums and left death and misery in their wakes.

Author's Note

Any readers of this book with comments and questions about it may reach me at ckilvert@pobox.com. I will gladly answer all messages.

Printed in the United States
21293LVS00002B/211-237